D0227731

Power and Policy in Education: the Case of Independent Schooling

Brian Salter
and
Ted Tapper

 The Falmer Press

(A member of the Taylor & Francis Group)
London and Philadelphia

UK   The Falmer Press, Falmer House, Barcombe, Lewes, East Sussex, BN8 5DL

USA   The Falmer Press, Taylor & Francis Inc., 242 Cherry Street, Philadelphia, PA 19106-1906

Copyright © B. Salter and T. Tapper 1985

First published in 1985

Library of Congress Cataloging in Publication Data

Salter, Brian.
  Power and Policy in Education.

  Bibliography: p.
  1. Private Schools—Great Britain—History—20th Century. 2. Education and State—Great Britain—History—20th Century. I. Tapper, Ted. II. Title.
  LC53.G7S25 1985 371'.02'0941 85-12941
  ISBN 1-85000-062-X
  ISBN 1-85000-063-8 (pbk.)

Typeset in 11/13 Bembo by
Imago Publishing Ltd, Thame, Oxon

Printed in Great Britain by Taylor & Francis (Printers) Ltd, Basingstoke

Contents

Glossary of Abbreviations Used

ABRC   Advisory Board for the Research Councils
ACARD   Advisory Council for Applied Research and
          Development
APS   Assisted Places Scheme
BTEC   Business and Technician Education Council
CLPD   Campaign for Labour Party Democracy
CNAA   Council for National Academic Awards
CISC   Conservative Independent Schools Committee
CPC   Conservative Political Centre
CPS   Centre for Policy Studies
CRD   Conservative Research Department
DES   Department of Education and Science
DGJC   Direct Grant Joint Committee
GBA   Association of Governing Bodies of Public Schools
GPDST   Girls' Public Day School Trust
HMC   Headmasters' Conference
IAPS   Incorporated Association of Preparatory Schools
IEA   Institute of Economic Affairs
ISBA   Independent Schools Bursars' Association
ISCO   Independent Schools Careers Organization
ISIS   Independent Schools Information Service
ISJAC   Independent Schools Joint Action Committee
ISJC   Independent Schools Joint Council
ISJC (AC) Independent Schools Joint Council (Advisory Committee)
LEA   Local Education Authority
MSC   Manpower Services Commission
NAB   National Advisory Body
NAFE   Non-advanced Further Education

NCES	National Council for Educational Standards
NEC	National Executive Committee (Labour Party)
OMSC	Office of the Manpower Services Commission
PLP	Parliamentary Labour Party
PSC	Public Schools Commission
SCDC	School Curriculum Development Committee
SEC	Secondary Examinations Council
TVEI	Technical and Vocational Education Initiative
UGC	University Grants Committee
YTS	Youth Training Scheme

Preface

It is customary to view the British educational system as in a state of crisis. In recent years schooling has suffered the dual traumas of a severe cutback in resources and repeated attacks upon its established modes of practice. It is the maintained sector that has suffered these indignities; by comparison private schooling has prospered. Since the late 1970s the demand for places in independent schools has increased steadily. In spite of these changes of fortune the private sector has been under political attack for the past two decades, and even now its continued well-being is dependent upon the preservation of Conservative government. For the time being, however, the leading figures in the world of independent schooling can rest comparatively securely upon their political laurels. The central substantive theme of this book is, therefore, to examine the recent political history of private schooling from the insecurity of the days of Circular 10/65 to the relative security engendered by Mrs Thatcher's re-election in 1983. In short, how was this transition in fortunes accomplished? This case study in educational change examines the interaction of a powerful set of organized interests, the political parties and the Department of Education and Science. The underlying political concern is in the class reproduction functions of private schooling. Can the schools be allowed to pursue their traditional purpose of elite reproduction? And, if so, how are they to accomplish this?

In common with our previous work the primary intellectual goal is to understand the process of educational change. We reconsider the claim of our previous book that the process of change is increasingly dominated by the Department of Education and Science (as the main centralized bureaucratic apparatus). This has involved us in an analysis of the concept of the state, and more precisely what constitutes belonging to the state. We maintain our commitment to the diagnosis of the interaction between institutions and the propagation of ideological warfare as the twin keys to understanding the process of change. Our case study — the contemporary politics of independent schooling — offers rich opportunities in both fields. As before, the political goal is to work towards a radical, non-Marxist critique and sociology of contemporary schooling in Britain. It is this that provides the continuing personal drive and satisfaction.

As time passes so our debts increase. We would like to thank the Leverhulme Trust for supporting the research work that formed the basis of Chapter 6 and the Arts Research Support Fund of the University of Sussex for additional resources to cover part of the work for several other chapters. We received widespread institutional support from: the Documents Section of the University of Sussex Library (P. Greenwood, D. Kennelly and S. Schaffer), the Labour party, the Conservative party, the IEA, ISIS, ISJC, HMC, DGJC, ISCO, GPDST and ISBA. Of the numerous individuals who aided us we should especially like to thank: Lady Johnston, Sir James Cobban, Sir George Sinclair, F.G. Robson Fisher, Frank Fisher, John Rae, Michael McCrum, Tim Devlin, D.J. Bird, C.D.A. Baggley, Rodney Exton, H. Evans, Jean Wright, Oliver Letwin, N. Bennett, Professor Kogan, Clive Saville, G. Walford, Joan West, Norman St John-Stevas, Sir William Van Straubenzee, Arthur Seldon, Lord Harris, Christopher Price, Bert Clough, Maurice Cowling, Caroline Benn, Ivor Goodson and Stuart Sexton. With such illustrious help we hope that the factual basis of the book is beyond reproach but we expect that not one of them will agree with all our interpretations. The authors were given access to the minutes of the Direct Grant Joint Committee which are not normally open for inspection. Direct quotations from the minutes have not been given but accounts of Committee discussions and decisions are based on our reading of the actual minutes. A final thanks must go to our secretaries: Jane South of the University of Sussex, Jo Butcher and Betty Fitzgerald of the University of Surrey, and Liz Fraser, and to the Managing Director of Falmer Press, Malcolm Clarkson.

Foreword

Despite the exponential growth in educational research during the 1970s and early 80s the role and functioning of the 'educational state' has received scant attention. Indeed, for many years it actually seemed possible to regard agencies such as the DES as marginal to the real business of education. Secretaries of State came and went without seeming to make much impression on the gradualist, reformist strategies of the civil servants in Elizabeth House. Influence on schools, and the impetus for change it seemed, came from elsewhere: from the Schools Council, the Examination Boards, the LEAs and the teacher unions. Now, in the mid-80s the face of educational politics has undergone a profound change; the control of education has been pervasively restructured. Now 'centralization' is a major galvanizing concept in educational policy and research; the Secretary of State is *the* primary figure in policy-making across a range of issues-examinations, the curriculum, teacher training and teacher quality, school and industry. The dynamics of bureaucracy, policy formation and educational politics are now rooted in an entirely new and powerful ideological framework set by the 'radical intellectuals' of the new right. Educational policy is now oriented to the 'needs' of 'consumers' — parents and employers — and the 'producers' — the teachers — are on the defensive. The 'progressive' forces in educational politics, apparently totally ascendent in the 60s, are in disarray.

At the centre of the ideological shift in policy-making lies Conservative commitment to the cleansing and policing effects of 'the market', irrespective of the morality of that market. In this respect the private school system now acts as a model of prudent practice for the whole education system. From a position of decline and demoralization in the 1960s the private sector has undergone massive revitalization.

More than 13,000 students a year from the state sector are now supported by the Assisted Places Scheme.

This study uses the private school issue to analyze the changing nature of the dynamics of the educational state over the past twenty years. In particular, Salter and Tapper address the long term policies and purposes of the DES. They argue that the DES is involved in a carefully thought out attempt to wrest control of the school curriculum away from LEAs, the teachers, the unions and the examination boards. It is in their terms an 'ambitious bureaucracy'. Here Salter and Tapper are building upon, refining and elaborating previous work. This study can be seen as a culmination of their long term project which aims at the analysis of the process of educational change in post-war Britain. Specifically the examination of private schooling extends work begun in *Education and the Political Order* (1978) and pursued in *Education, Politics and the State* (1981).

S.J. Ball
I.F. Goodson
Series Editors
July 1985

1 The Politics of Educational Change

The first phase of British educational sociology sought to illustrate the relationship between schooling and social stratification. Besides pursuing that intellectual goal this sociology was also an instrument in the process of educational change and top of its agenda was the struggle for comprehensive secondary schooling. It undermined the credibility of intelligence testing as a mechanism for secondary school selection and, although it is still widely believed that social inequality is a consequence of individual differences in personal attributes, it is less acceptable as a means for distributing scarce educational resources, more especially for separating pupils into different kinds of educational institutions at comparatively tender ages. In its second phase British educational sociology turned its attention to the nature of schooling itself: how knowledge was organized and how authority relations were structured. Again the concerns interacted with real political issues as governments of differing persuasions accepted the general drift towards comprehensive secondary education and turned their attention to the process of schooling. What happens in schools and how that relates to the wider needs of society, and more particularly of the economy, continues to be of major political interest.

Although always concerned with educational change it is only in its third and current phase that this has become the dominant theme in British educational sociology. The analysis of educational change has taken two different paths. The first, represented by the work of M.S. Archer, examines the social origins and expansion of educational systems, it has a macro-sociological theoretical base (a combination of general systems theory and exchange theory), and empirically it draws upon the historical development of a number of differing education systems (Archer, 1979). The second strand is less ambitious: its purpose is to explain the contemporary 'crisis' in British education and its historical scope usually extends no further than the 1944 Education Act. Theoretically it is heavily dependent upon Marxism in the sense that no matter how loosely the interconnections may be drawn it sees the changing needs of a capitalist economy as the ultimate determinant of the process of schooling (Centre for Contemporary Cultural Studies, 1981).

This book, like our previous work, attempts to provide an alternative to the above two approaches. We are continuing our examination of the process of educational change in contemporary Britain. In *Education, Politics and the State* we argued that the process of change was increasingly controlled by the Department of Education and Science (Salter and Tapper, 1981). As the central bureaucratic apparatus most responsible for the management of schooling it was initially best placed to respond positively to the new climate in which the British educational system found itself. More than that it had, through skilful orchestration of the Great Debate, actually helped to create the changed environment. But independent of bureaucratic manipulation the objective circumstances were there for all to see. Demographic trends meant that schooling had fewer clients, successive governments in tight economic conditions were intent on controlling state expenditure, and there were vociferous demands from powerful quarters that schooling should be more closely geared to meeting the needs of industry. We took the view, to which we still adhere, that this is not so much a crisis situation as one in which the character of the British educational system is being remoulded. To those on the receiving end it may constitute a crisis, to those attempting the restructuring it may constitute a challenge.

Our contention that the DES was slowly exercising more effective control over the process of educational change received a mixed reception. Some claimed that the Department was way down the Whitehall pecking order partially because its control was so ineffectual. What we documented was the Department's determination to remedy this state of affairs, to make sure it had the power as well as the responsibility. Others claimed that all the traditional partners in the government of education, that is the LEAs, DES and teacher unions, were in fact losing power to other non–educational institutions, most notably the Treasury, the Department of Environment and the Man-power Services Commission (MSC) (Fowler, 1981). In fact, the two processes could occur at the same time, i.e. amongst the traditional partners power is increasingly more centralized within the DES while there is a seepage of power to other state apparatuses. The key question is whether that seepage is so great that it makes the increased centralization of power amongst the traditional partners irrelevant. We must argue to the contrary. The controls exercised by the Department of Environment and the Treasury are essentially financial in nature and, although the DES may have less largesse to distribute, there is no evidence that it is now more constrained by the other state apparatuses as to how it should distribute its resources. In fact the major constraint of innovation — as always — is the commitment to fund ongoing programmes. Although the pretensions of the DES may not be matched by reality, today it has marginally more direct control over how its funds are used and in certain areas — for example the curriculum and the structure of university education — the scope of its indirect controls are steadily widening and their impact intensifying.

It is a fair criticism of *Education, Politics and the State* that it failed to credit the MSC with sufficient importance. We were conscious of the fact that with respect to the education of 16-19 year olds the MSC was acquiring more control. Indeed, as we noted, the DES was itself only too well aware of its limitations:

> Several times the report (the Yellow Book) contrasts its own position regarding financial controls with that of the Training Services Agency (TSA) of the Manpower Services Commission (MSC) in their mutual efforts to help the 16 to 19 age group. 'At present', it says 'there is some risk of distortion because the existing statutory and administrative provisions make it much easier for MSC and TSA than for DES to channel resources quickly and selectively where they are needed'. Consequently, 'if the Department is to play as constructive a role as it could wish, then serious thought needs to be given to some extension of its powers in this direction'. To put it another way, give us the tools and we will finish the job. (pp. 202–3)

But the inexorable rise in youth unemployment has led to an expansion of the activities of the MSC, posed a potent challenge to the new-found ambitions of the DES, and required us to reformulate our argument. This challenge we take up in the next chapter. We will consider why the DES has not been given the tools and why the MSC is better equipped to respond to the supposed needs of many adolescents. The central point is that the MSC expresses the bureaucratic dynamic in a different form from the DES, one that is capable of responding more readily to the pressures that increasing unemployment generates. We place our analysis of the MSC in a more general discussion of the educational state which continues to incorporate the DES as its major component.

What must be stressed, however, is that our previous undervaluing of the MSC does not substantiate the claim that our work is theoretically flawed. The changed environment of approximately the past ten years has afforded greater opportunities to centralized state bureaucracies to control their educational systems. This has occurred throughout much of Western Europe but whether those opportunities have been seized is another matter. Perhaps in comparison to its European counterparts the DES has simply lacked the will to take full advantage of the situation (i.e. it has failed to cast aside the internal inertia generated by its past impotence) or the structural handicaps are so great that it has no choice but to proceed gingerly. Alternatively the Department's ambition may have been blunted by its apparent inability to cope with new crises. For example, the rising tide of youth unemployment is so politically sensitive that governments cannot be thought to be doing nothing and new structures will be created to deal with the problem if the existing ones — perhaps through no fault of their own — are incapable of acting swiftly. Whether the new institutions, like the MSC, are effective in the sense that they are better able to resolve the problem is another matter. Maybe the most that governments can expect is that the state apparatus copes better with crisis thus giving the appearance that solutions are forthcoming.

Although existing institutions may be capable of dealing with new social problems, governments may still prefer to by-pass them because they are not easy to control politically. This points to the necessity of examining the interaction between political and bureaucratic dynamics when analyzing the process of educational change. It is our contention that even if governments create alternative institutions to cope with social problems this does not deny our main thesis that the process of educational change in Britain is increasingly controlled by a centralized bureaucratic dynamic. In the case of Britain that bureaucratic dynamic may be expressed by the MSC as well as by the established Department of State, the DES, but regardless, the power of state apparatuses expands inexorably. To create new institutions gives rise to the probability that they will clash with existing institutions so that there is an internal conflict within the state bureaucratic apparatus. Furthermore, although initially newer creations may be more amenable to external pressure (more specifically to the political demands of government), this will change as they acquire the expertise, confidence, and procedures to resist outsiders. To argue otherwise is to deny the history of a large body of social science research.

Fowler and Kogan come closest to our evaluation of the course of educational change in Britain (Fowler, 1979 and 1981; Kogan, 1978). Fowler has been more impressed by the leakage of power from the traditional controlling partnership, while Kogan is more convinced of the importance of bargaining between the partners and the ability of interest groups to influence them. Their work has both the strength and weakness of the insider's view: a detailed and persuasive account of trends in the machinery of government is allied to an essentially descriptive picture of the changing environment within which decision-making occurs. Moreover, we also concur with the central proposition of the Marxist writers that the most potent influence upon the British educational system is the contemporary crisis of capitalism intensified in the case of Britain by the long-term decline in the comparative fortunes of our economy. Indeed few would disagree, and Fowler's diagnosis of the prevailing environment within which the educational system is located, amounts to making the same point in a different manner. It is our contention, however, that the needs of capitalism can be expressed in only very general terms and most of those needs are identical to what all economies require if they are to function efficiently: that is a workforce that has the necessary technical skills, tolerates the social relations of production, and at least accepts the ideology of the mode of production. Although it is possible, especially with the advantage of reading history backwards, to argue the proposition that schooling in Britain has evolved solely in response to changes in these basic needs of capitalism, we maintain that this is a perversion of the historical truth dependent upon a crunching of the facts and a misinterpretation of individual motivations. The British educational system has evolved in response to differing interpretations of the functions of schooling and furthermore there is no certainty that even the broadly expressed needs of capitalism can be harmonized. To use schooling for the purpose of social control may conflict with the efficient training of a reservoir of skilled labour.

A theory of educational change must therefore incorporate the different philosophical traditions which are embedded in the British experience of schooling and must accommodate itself to the fact that these traditions are not easily reconciled. In this field the Marxist perspective has tended to see order and control where in fact tension and bargaining flourishes. While failing to name particular scholars, Bernbaum (1979) has written:

> Too many take what might be termed a 'Whig historian's' view
> of the recent past. They choose too readily for discussion those
> parts of the educational system which have apparent contem-
> porary significance, and look for explanation of change almost
> exclusively within the framework of the educational system
> itself. To do this, however, is to neglect important social and
> economic elements in the determination of educational policies
> and innovation and hence fail to understand both the dynamic
> of change and its significance. (p. 2)

The problem is that this begs the question of what is really (as opposed
to apparently) of contempoary significance and — more importantly —
draws too sharp a distinction between 'the framework of the educational system itself' and broader social and economic elements. What is
required is a theory of change which accepts that social forces have to
be translated into the theory and practice of schooling and that various
institutions, including those within the framework of the educational
system, are central to this process. Educational change is institutionally
negotiated.

It is only by examining how institutions interact to conduct those
negotiations that one can have a full view of the process of change.
Negotiation leads to the accommodation of the tensions inherent
within the social forces, even if that should mean no more than that
some prevail and others are defeated. We believe that a judicious
historical overview of the British educational system would reveal how
contradictory social forces have manifested themselves within the
British experience of schooling. Like Archer we are general systems
theorists in the sense that the negotiations for change take place within
an interdependent social system whose parties have differential resources and we are resource dependency theorists in the sense that we
believe negotiated outcomes to be the consequence of the distribution
of these scarce resources. What distinguishes us from Archer is our
stress upon the increasing potency of the centralized bureaucratic
dynamic.

Archer's bold attempt to understand comparatively the social
origins and growth of educational systems, in contrast to our more
directed interest in educational change and policy-making in contemporary Britain, partially explains the theoretical differences between us.
Moreover she has purposefully argued against theory which can be
applied widely:

> Again, without exception, time is treated as irrelevant, as a
> theoretical variable. Generally the same theory is held to work

for all periods, with the process responsible for growth simply accelerating over time ... Hence the possibility/probability that different theories (or theoretical modifications) may be needed for different stages of socio-educational development is never even considered. (Archer, 1982, p. 5)

The restricted context of our work, both timewise and politically, makes it possible for us to be more theoretically adventurous than Archer. Moreover it could be argued that Archer's interest in educational change is so all-encompassing that her theories lead to little more than a systematic description of events (by using refined categories to order information) and they certainly do not inform us why matters assumed a particular course, let alone enable us to predict how they will be resolved.

Because the Marxists have proposed a dynamic to the process of educational change we see our work as in dialogue with theirs rather than with Archer's. In concrete terms we have devoted time and energy to demonstrating their limitations, Archer in contrast has been dismissive. Two substantive areas of disagreement distinguish us from the Marxist writers: the role of the state apparatus in the change process and the character of the ensuing ideological struggle. We have accorded the state apparatus a degree of autonomy that few Marxists would be sympathetic to, including its ability to generate ideology to support the broadening of its power base. In the educational field Marxist discussion of ideology has tended to hide behind Gramsci's concept of hegemony and even if resistance or alienation should occasionally intrude it is Althusser's structuralism which ultimately prevails. This book continues the dialogue on educational change through its development of two central concepts: its clarification of our understanding of the state (to the point where we doubt if a concept so riddled with confusion and arbitrariness can be of much use to social science research until some careful reconceptualization has been undertaken) and power. Our view of power is three-dimensional: manipulation of dominant ideology, control of the policy-making agenda, and struggle within the decision-making process (Lukes, 1974). The intention is to show how in practice these various forms of power are closely interrelated, and at a more practical level they assist in the organization of our empirical material. Whereas our first book, *Education and the Political Order*, was a collection of articles within a theme and our second book, *Education, Politics and the State*, illustrated features of the process of educational change through a range of case studies, this present volume concentrates upon the politics of private schooling since 1965. It is, therefore, a precise field of study with a directed theoretical focus.

It is reasonable to ask why a case study that concentrates upon the recent political history of private schooling in Britain is particularly appropriate for trying to understand the process of educational change. As almost every observer of the public schools has noted they do perform exceedingly important social tasks. The dominant sociological view is that they are a vital link in the chain of upper-class reproduction and how the public schools have fulfilled this purpose is a source of never-ending speculation. In similar manner we argue in Chapter 2 that the central goal of educational change is to restructure the class reproduction function of schooling; both how that task is undertaken as well as the end product it is intent on producing.

Perhaps an equally vital issue is why schools that are not ostensibly part of the state apparatus should be trusted to act in such a vital matter. Either — in the manner of Althusser (1972) — the concept of state apparatus can be broadened to incorporate the public schools or the question can be considered through a detailed analysis of the pertinent historical and social contexts. In any book, therefore, which is intent on demonstrating the relationship between state and schooling, the presence of the private sector poses critical problems. Elsewhere we have discussed at some length changes in the traditional public school model, arguing that those were a consequence of the tight institutional links which bound the schools. In order to retain these links the schools had to respond positively to the demands of their increasingly powerful institutional allies or alternatively accept the fact that they would decline as vehicles of upper-class reproduction. Even if these institutional ties do not make them an integral part of the state apparatus are the public schools so inextricably bound to it that it makes no difference?

No case study in educational change is likely to illustrate better the importance of ideological struggle. If the key issue is the class reproduction function of private schooling then inevitably defence and attack is predicated upon assumptions about what is the character of the British class structure, how that is to be accounted for, and what — if anything — should be done about it. Even the debates as to individual rights in this matter will incorporate this dimension for what are the social implications of some individuals exercising a right that others can never hope to possess? If the state should attempt to change this state of affairs can it actually achieve the desired social consequences? As we argued in *Education, Politics and the State*, developed educational ideologies need to relate conceptions of the nature of man to the experience of schooling and both of these to the character of the social order. The political struggle that surrounds private schooling has led some to think carefully at all these levels and others to conjure up no more than emotive slogans. We must, therefore, be very interested in the production and transmission of ideology which in turn has led us to consider in some detail the role of intellectuals in the change process. We define intellectuals in terms of the political functions they perform and attempt to develop a typology of the differing roles they assume within the change process.

The struggle for hearts and minds envelops the institutional struggle — both between and within institutions. In order to strengthen their defences the private schools expanded and reorganized their institutional framework. They are now in much better shape to propagate their message and to coordinate their policy options. In the 1970s part of this newly-created institutional apparatus interacted with elements of the Conservative party with a view to committing a future Conservative government to enacting an Assisted Places Scheme. Of course policy was not forthcoming until the DES had translated the broad strokes into detailed proposals. The ideological struggle, institutional interaction and policy-formation could not occur without generating stresses and strains within all the involved organizations. Were the traditional values of the public school ethos sacrificed in the haste to promote an image of private schooling with contemporary appeal? If so, who objected, and why? What splits occurred within the independent sector as a Labour government gave the direct grant schools the choice of joining the comprehensive system or severing their links to the maintained schools? Did support for an Assisted Places Scheme mean that the Conservative party had been captured by a dedicated but unrepresentative faction? So a rich variety of institutional interaction is matched by equally diverse patterns of internal institutional conflict. High stakes engender conflict: the private sector was fighting for survival, the Labour party was bent on fulfilling long-made promises, and the Conservative party was attempting to reformulate its educational values and policies. All this activity occurred within a shifting socio-political context whose central facets were the decline of the post-1944 educational consensus and intensifying conflict as to both the functions of schooling and how they were to be achieved.

If ideological struggle and institutional interaction clarifies how two of the levels of power, that is the influence of dominant ideology and the control of the policy-making agenda, work in practice then equally it illuminates the decision-making process, that is the third level of power. Two main decisions are looked at in this book. The first is the phasing out of direct grant schools which could be accomplished by administrative action, and the second is the enactment of the Assisted Places Scheme which was placed on a statutory basis in order to prevent a future government that wished to terminate the scheme from doing so by purely adminstrative means! Our main purpose is to show how decision-making cannot be fully understood without examining the exercise of power at all its varying levels. Our thesis is straightforward: the process of educational change is controlled by those who have most power, and although the resources of the varying parties will vary from one situation to the next, increasingly it is centralized state apparatuses that are in a position of dominance.

The fact that the private sector apparently changes in response to market mechanisms makes it attractive to many within the Conservative party. It was widely believed that schooling within private schools had remained more in tune with the wishes of parents because as fee-payers it was comparatively easy for them to withdraw their support by taking their children elsewhere. This was contrasted very favourably with a maintained sector that was allegedly oblivious to parental demands as it remained in the grip of teachers' unions, the DES bureaucrats, or even educational sociologists. We have cast doubts on this view — both as to the influence of parents and their ability to affect changes — but our doubts may not carry much weight and governments may still choose to act as if the contrary were true! The advocates of the Assisted Places Scheme argued that it would increase parental choice and there were expectations that it would be followed by experiments in open enrolment and with vouchers. In fact neither of Mrs Thatcher's governments have — so far — travelled very far down the road of attempting to reshape the character of maintained schooling by extending market mechanisms. In spite of past inaction the government nonetheless remains committed to extending the influence of parents and may well improve on its rather meagre record to date. A study therefore of the politics of private schooling should shed light upon the possibility of pursuing educational change through extending market forces. Our reservations are not based upon opposition in principle to such a move but stem from the sheer scale of the difficulties of implementation. Moreover the temptation to wield the power apparently inherent in state bureaucracies is strong and few governments would readily concede that they are not the controlling force. Invariably the problems are perceived as too pressing to await the emergence of new processes, and to act now means seizing the weapons at hand rather than fashioning new ones. Certainly the government's expansion of the Manpower Services Commission has paled into insignificance all its dabblings in increasing the power of consumer preferences. Who can doubt what will have the greatest long-term impact upon schooling in Britain?

Finally for all the sociological literature on the class reproduction function of private schooling, little has been written about the associated protracted political battles it has generated. The sociological literature has undoubtedly concentrated upon a crucial matter but if the schools should no longer exist, prohibited by legislation, then they can scarcely be expected to perform any functions whatsoever! Our chapter on the Labour party will show much prevarication but there remains a persistent political dynamic within the party that something should be done about the public schools. The fact that an opposing political will exists within the Conservative party makes this an issue area of continuing importance and one which it is difficult for the DES to manage.

It is hard to account for the past lack of serious interest in the political struggle. Fortunately this is now drawing to a close and several volumes have appeared recently or are about to be published (Walford, 1984; Fox, 1985). It is perhaps their continuing survival and the extended political battle associated with the independent schools which accounts for the growing academic interest. It is more fascinating to observe tenacious hunters pursuing the wily fox than to pick over the bones of those who have been led mildly to the slaughter.

This book is organized in two parts. In Part One, *The Established Order*, we provide a framework of analysis for *The Political Struggle* which is the theme of Part Two. Chapter 2 examines our theory of educational change, commencing with a review of the legacy of *Education, Politics and the State* and then proceeding to explore the concepts of state and power and the relationship between them. The purpose is to refine and update the idea that the process of change is increasingly controlled by centralized state apparatuses. Chapters 3 and 4 analyze traditional manifestations of the power of private schooling. Chapter 3 examines the schools' class reproduction function while Chapter 4 reviews the legal basis of private schooling with particular reference to its charitable status. The political attack upon private schools is intimately bound up with perceptions of their class reproductive function and the undermining of the established legal basis is the ultimate purpose of that attack. In Chapters 5, 6 and 7 we examine respectively the evolution of Labour party policy, the private sector's response to that political challenge, and the convergence of the Conservative party's educational policy and the interests of the independent schools. The latter theme is elaborated upon in Chapter 8 through a detailed look at the implementation of one decision, the Assisted Places Scheme. As in our previous book the final chapter reviews the important contemporary developments within the world of schooling, demonstrates their relationship to our theory of educational change, and predicts the future course of events. Because of the varied nature of the empirical foundations of this book, and the more general interest in the research problems associated with both policy analysis and the political sociology of elites, we have decided to add a short methodological appendix. Even those who disagree with our interpretations may be interested in how we acquired our data base. Although theories of change may differ, the search for enlightenment is hopefully shared.

Part One
The Established Order

2   Power and Policy in Education

Introduction

No theory of educational change can afford to rest on its laurels, if laurels it has, and assume that it is immutable and that there is no more work to be done. Given education's key functions in today's society, it is inevitable that the way in which education translates the pressures placed upon it into new policies and practice will shed further light on the dynamic of change. Indeed although the general outlines of the theory should remain constant in the face of new developments, specific theoretical elements may well have to be refined and fresh ones added. This is no bad thing. It means that an approach to theory construction is adopted which builds in a process of review as a necessary part of maintaining the relevance of the theory to contemporary developments.

Such an approach involves admitting past mistakes and former confusion in one's theory rather than clinging religiously to a set of concepts which no longer adequately fit the facts. Some will find it easier to adopt this approach than others. Those who vocally combine theoretical position with political commitment will find it more difficult to amend their theories significantly without evoking accusations of political betrayal from their peers. We discussed in our previous book the distortions this can produce (Salter and Tapper, 1981, pp. 3–67). At the same time, it is important to avoid shifting one's ground too readily, perhaps in response to changes in sociological fashion, so failing to accumulate understanding along a line of consistent theoretical development.

Bearing these points in mind, our intention in this chapter is to provide the context for our study of the independent sector by reviewing the adequacy of our theory of educational change, identifying areas of weakness and developing fresh concepts where necessary. Independent schools play a significant part in the reproduction of class relations and as a case study in educational change can be used to illuminate and explore our theory at all levels. In preparing the theory for this task it is important that we retain the broad perspective and do not focus narrowly on those aspects which appear most immediately relevant to independent schooling. Furthermore, updating the theory in the light of developments since the publication of *Education, Politics and the State* inevitably means including empirical material unrelated to private schools. There should be no apology for this since the purpose of the book is the further development of the theory and the study of independent schooling is a vehicle to that end, not an end in itself.

Our theory of educational change places great stress on the role of the educational state in translating pressures for change into educational practice. Given the centrality of the state to the theory, we begin the review by examining whether there is any common understanding of what the state is and what it does. This is a broad-ranging discussion designed to elucidate the assumptions, hidden or otherwise, on which existing definitions are based. Specifically, how do we decide which institutions form part of the educational state and which do not? Given their functions, can private schools be included in a definition of the educational state? Having identified the problems in defining the educational state and its relationship to educational change we then develop a theoretical answer to these problems in three stages. Firstly, we consider the operation of the bureaucratic dynamic within the institutions of the state and, in particular, the theoretical significance of the rapidly changing role of the Manpower Services Commission (MSC). Secondly, and more directly related to the needs of the case study, we examine the role of intellectuals in supporting and manufac-turing political party ideologies capable of challenging the policies of the dominant institutions of the educational state. Finally, we draw together the previous discussions and place independent schools within an approach where educational power is defined in terms of its relationship to educational policy-making and educational change.

Clearing the Undergrowth

The state is one of those ideas whose frequent use is largely a product of the fact that it is all things to all men. It is a convenience which can be implicitly expanded and contracted to suit different theoretical concerns. To ask that all those who use it should define what they mean by it is inconvenient because the 'state' is such a common-place part of sociological exchange. Its rigorous definition would hinder the fluidity of that exchange by revealing that different concepts are being given the same name. The major difference is between definitions based on functional criteria and those based on organizational criteria. It is our argument in this chapter that a satisfactory definition of the state can only be developed if both types of criteria are employed. In *Education, Politics and the State* we implicitly defined the educational state as that institution which has the function of translating the needs of the economy into educational policy geared to reproducing the technical and social relations of production. We maintained that the organization principally concerned with carrying out that function is the Department of Education and Science (DES) — the central, publicly financed educational bureaucracy. However, although both functional and organizational criteria are used in this definition it is, for a number of reasons, unsatisfactory. In reviewing its adequacy it is important that the assumptions we make are clearly spelt out.

To begin at the beginning, Marxism makes a fundamental distinction between the economic base of capitalist society (the unity of productive forces and the relations of production) and the superstructure which carries out the function of the maintenance and reproduction of the economic base. The state forms part of the superstructure; that much is agreed. The problem is, which part? Althusser (1972), following Gramsci, distinguishes between the position of the state in political society (the police, courts, prison, army) and in civil society (religion, education, the family, politics, trade unions, culture). He calls the former the Repressive State Apparatus (RSA) because it uses violence in carrying out its function and the latter the Ideological State Apparatus (ISA) because it depends on the manipulation of ideology in fulfilling its task. The criterion for Althusser's definition of the state is clearly functional. He states:

> It is unimportant whether the institutions in which they (ISA's) are realized are 'public' or 'private'. What matters is how they function. Private institutions can perfectly well function as Ideological State Apparatuses. (p. 253)

It is a gross definition of the state and the tantalizing question becomes not 'what is part of the state?' but 'what is *not* part of the state?'. One only has to read Miliband's (1969) *The State in Capitalist Society* , with its seemingly endless list of institutions which support capitalist society in one way or another to realize, in a numbed sort of way, the indiscriminate nature of this approach. Apart from anything else, its blanket conviction that all social institutions contribute towards the reproduction of the conditions necessary for the process of capital accumulation is clearly at odds with Marx's belief that the bourgeois state also creates the conditions for the development of working-class revolutionary consciousness.

A slightly more focused view of the state, but one which also fails to theorize about possible contradictions in its operation, is held by those who deal with the 'liberal–democratic' state and the contribution of the democratic system of government to the capitalist mode of production. The boundaries of the state remain hazy. It is not always clear whether the democratic institutions themselves (parties and Parliament) combine with the government bureaucracy to form the state or whether the state is composed of the bureaucracy alone. This ambivalence is particularly acute in the case of theorists such as Poulantzas who view the state as reflecting and responding to the political struggle and as having little autonomy of its own (Poulantzas, 1973 and 1975). Since the political struggle is seen as taking place within the democratic institutions, it has to be assumed that democratic institutions are external to the state. Thus the state merely passively implements policy determined by the democratic government. It does not have a formative influence of its own.

There appears to be a tacit acceptance in the discussions of the liberal–democratic state of the ambiguity of the concept and of its implicit redefinition depending on the nature of the argument. The concept is expanded and contracted as its function is deemed to vary. There is never any doubt that this function is to maintain the conditions for capitalist enterprise and accumulation by providing a forum in which the dominant class can bargain or compromise, by hiving off working-class discontent into emasculating democratic activity and by legitimizing the existing power structure.

In the mid-1970s, increasing government intervention in the economy led to the development of the idea of the 'corporate state' as a substitute for what was seen as the redundant concept of the liberal–democratic state. According to this view, the major power centres of big business, trade unions and government bureaucracy were reaching an understanding on the interventions necessary to ensure the sub-ordination of labour and the preservation of the means of capital accumulation. Democratic institutions were no longer up to the task (see, for example, Cawson, 1982; Mandel, 1975). The result, it is argued, is a more authoritarian and pervasive state apparatus.

All three approaches rely heavily on functional criteria to define the state and fail to develop appropriate organizational criteria which would enable them to include some institutions and exclude others. In large part this failure is the result of an exaggerated confidence in the ability of the state (however defined) to perform its functions successfully and reproduce the conditions of capital accumulation. There has been little attempt to take note of Gramsci's arguments about the tensions between economic base and superstructure and the capacity of institutions to resist economic pressures (Hoare and Smith, 1971; Salter and Tapper, 1981, pp. 55–6). Had note been taken, the state would have had to be defined in more precise institutional terms in order to explain why one part of it was more supportive of the capitalist order than another, why the efficiency of the state as an instrument of the ruling class can vary from one historical period to another, how the nature of the state changes over time, how internal conflicts and rivalries are resolved or perpetuated, and so on. As it is, the failure to perceive any need for the state to be defined in specific institutional terms allows Poulantzas, for example, to advance this kind of ethereal definition: 'The state is not an instrumental entity existing for itself, it is not a thing, but the condensation of a balance of forces' (quoted by Crouch, 1979, p. 39).

In the absence of a general definition of the state which links functional and organizational criteria, it is not surprising that the educational state in particular remains equally ill-defined. In discussing how an adequate definition can be developed, we take as our starting point the Marxist view of the functions of education in the perpetuation of capitalist society. Education has three main functions: it organizes and certificates knowledge thus reproducing the 'technical relations of production'; it inculcates in individuals attitudes and values which will enable them to meet the needs of the production process (the social relations of production); and it generates and maintains the ideology which legitimates the existing distribution of class power. We will examine each of these three functions and discuss what conceptions of the educational state can be derived from them.

The first two functions are interlinked. Education is said to socialize individuals in a way appropriate to the needs of the production process. At the same time, it imposes a hierarchical system of certification which legitimates the transmission of different types of knowledge to different groups of individuals. The most comprehensive version of this thesis is by Bowles and Gintis (1976) who identify a 'correspondence principle' between the world of school and the world of work. Both worlds are hierarchical and differential certification of the schooling population serves to reproduce the class structure by allocating successful graduates to managerial and senior occupations. Below come less successful pupils, reflecting the descent through middle range occupations to the uncertificated products of school, children destined for menial occupations such as unskilled factory work.

The conception of the state incorporated in these two functions includes the formal institutions of education (primary, secondary, further and higher education) where the transmission of knowledge, attitudes and values takes place; the transmission agents, the teaching and academic professions; and the examination system, or systems, which structure and legitimate the process of transmission. This is a descriptive conception of the institutions of the educational state and the boundaries are prescribed by the first two functions 'education' is deemed to perform.

Not all writers on the educational state are convinced that its implicit institutional definition in terms of functional criteria is satisfactory. Dale (1981), for example, argues that the state should be limited to 'publicly financed institutions' though it is unclear as to why he regards this as a useful criterion apart from the need to restrict the concept in some way (p. 10). However, as soon as one introduces into the debate an institutional characteristic as a criterion for definition of the state one then confronts, or should confront, the question: why this characteristic rather than another? If the selection of institutional characteristics is not guided by an overall theory, which in Dale's case it is not, then obviously the resulting definition of the state is purely arbitrary. This is easily illustrated by juxtaposing the definition of the state resulting from the two functional criteria discussed so far to the definition resulting from Dale's 'commonsense' criterion of 'publicly financed'.

The two definitions give rise to differing interpretations of the same sets of institutions: consider for example, the independent schools and the exam boards. According to the criterion derived from the function of the state in reproducing the class relations of capitalist society, the independent schools must be seen as forming part of the educational state. It is after all elementary political sociology that the public schools are a training ground for the dominant social classes. If the independent sector is removed from the equation then the reproduction thesis collapses. Yet according to the 'publicly-financed' criterion the independent schools should be excluded from the definition of the state since the majority of their funds comes from private sources (even allowing for direct and indirect state subsidies via the Assisted Places Scheme, tax relief, teacher training and the like).

Similarly, the secondary examination boards are by definition an essential part of the accreditation process and, therefore, functionally part of the state. However, although their authority is derived from powers vested in the Secretary of State by the 1944 Education Act their finance is self-generated and thus counts them out of the state on the Dale criterion. The picture becomes even murkier if the accreditation agencies of the further and higher education sectors are included in this example (Business and Technician Education Council, City and Guilds, CNAA, individual universities) given the diversity of their historical and financial lineage. What these examples illustrate is the danger of employing a definition of the educational state such as 'publicly-financed institution' which may be in everyday use but which lacks a theoretical context.

Turning now to the third function of education, that of ideology generation, as traditionally conceived it does not extend the educational state beyond the boundaries already established by the other two functions. The maintenance of value and knowledge systems and the creation of new ones is traditionally viewed by theorists as being the function of those institutions at the top (so far) of the educational hierarchy: the universities. In Gramsci's terms, academics are the enduring group of traditional intellectuals who act as the officers of the ruling class and service the existing hegemony.

To summarize, the advantage of using the Marxist view of education to define the educational state is that it is possible to place specific institutions in a theoretical context by looking at the function they perform in the reproduction of class relations. The disadvantage is that the result is hopelessly gross and indiscriminatory and leads writers like Dale to try and introduce refining institutional criteria, with confusing effects. There has been no attempt to discriminate between the different levels of operation of the educational state, no attempt to examine the state as a less than monolithic institution. To a large extent, this failure to theorize the details of the state is an inevitable legacy of writers like Miliband who promoted the idea that the reproduction of the conditions for capitalist production is not problematic. It becomes unnecessary to trace the application of educational power once it is assumed that the exercise of power can have but one result: the service of the capitalist economy. According to this view, it is only necessary to define the state in terms of how it implements its reproductive functions and it is not necessary to identify separately those institutions which decide on how these functions will be performed. Thus the focus is on the implementation of policy, educational practice, and not on the way in which policy is formed. The conviction that the process of reproduction is unproblematic leads to a complete neglect of those institutions of the state which translate the demands of the capitalist economy into one set of policies rather than another and, equally important, decide on what resources should be allocated to the different policies. In other words, the exercise of educational power and its relationship to the reproductive functions of education remains untheorized.

It is difficult to understand why an attempt to develop a more sophisticated conception of the state was not stimulated by events over the past fifteen years. Student unrest, progressive education, right-wing attacks on education (see pp. 162–70) and the alleged education-industry mismatch all suggested a lack of efficiency in education's contribution to capitalist society. The educational state seemed to be failing to identify economic needs correctly, to translate those needs into educational policy, to ensure the implementation of policy into educational practice and to suppress ideological movements which challenged the existing hegemony (O'Keeffe, 1979). Why was no analysis developed of the educational state under siege? The answer must be that the monolithic conception of the state produces an impotent analysis not only of educational power but also, a related issue, of the dynamic of educational change. There is an in-built resistance to regarding the exercise of state power as problematic and any educational change short of the revolution as significant.

In *Education, Politics and the State* we employed a definition of the state which deals with some of the conceptual problems discussed so far but leaves others unresolved. There we argued that the central educational bureaucracy, the DES, is an important part of the state because it is the main arena in which attempts are made to translate pressures from the economic base into educational policy. As such it acts as a focus for the exercise of educational power. However, we also argued that for a number of reasons it is not a particularly efficient part of the state: it does not respond very readily to demands that new types of social relations, certification and ideology should be engineered through fresh educational policy to suit the needs of the economic base. Firstly, because as an established bureaucracy it has goals, needs and ideology of its own which may well run counter in educational policy terms to the demands of the economy. Thus the emergence of policy is conceived as the result of the interplay between the economic and bureaucratic dynamics; an interplay which can take time to draw to a conclusion given both the shifting nature of economic pressures and internal inefficiencies in the Department's policy-making procedures (such as tensions between long-term planning and Public Expenditure Survey Committee (PESC) requirements, and inter-branch policy rivalry). Secondly, the ability of the central state to ensure that policy, once formed, is then realized in the form of educational practice varies depending on the educational sector concerned and the controls required to implement the new policy. In a decentralized educational system many of the administrative lines of control run through the local state, the LEAs, which have clear identities and policy preferences of their own. These may or may not be in tune with DES priorities. There is much debate about how much freedom for policy formation and implementation LEAs have given national statutory requirements and DES financial control.

Our previous work emphasizes the importance of formal bureaucracies to the formation and implementation of educational policy and to the operation of the educational state. It ties the reproductive functions of the educational state to particular institutions (principally the DES and LEAs) and shows how the characteristics of those institutions influence the way the functions are carried out. While this approach succeeds in linking functional and organizational criteria it does so in a way which is too narrow in its institutional focus and too limited in its understanding of the bureaucratic dynamic. It requires considerable development before it can provide a suitable theoretical context for a case study of policy making on independent schools. The following three sections develop that context by updating and refining our concept of the bureaucratic dynamic in a study of the MSC, by examining the role of intellectuals in providing political parties with the ability to mount an ideological and policy challenge to the educational state bureaucracies, and by establishing the position of the educational state in the relationship between power, policy and change in education.

The Bureaucratic Dynamic

Understanding the way in which the educational state works is central to understanding the process of educational change in contemporary

Britain. In *Education, Politics and the State* (1981) we dealt only peripherally with the MSC and focused on the DES in the discussion of the bureaucratic dynamic as a motivating force in the operation of the educational state. In retrospect, it is clear that this focus, though illuminative, does not provide a full understanding of the potential of the bureaucratic dynamic. As a guide to our analysis of the DES we took the classical Weberian approach to bureaucracy with its emphasis on the permanence of the bureaucracy due to the characteristics of

> technical advantages (precision, speed, continuity etc.); the cult
> of the objective and indispensable expert; its hoarding and
> control of specialized knowledge; its use of secrecy to increase
> the superiority of the 'professionally informed'; and its general
> protective cloak of rational organization and operation. (pp.
> 57–8)

These characteristics give rise to an institutional dynamic in the DES which interacts with economic demands for particular forms of educational support. There is no guarantee that the bureaucratic dynamic will work harmoniously with the economic dynamic, no guarantee that it is able to ensure that the appropriate policies concerning the organization of knowledge, certification and the attitudes and values inculcated in school will duly emerge to service the capitalist order. For like all institutions, the Department has over time developed its own momentum, and its own inertia, which mean that its exercise of educational power runs in certain policy grooves. While, on the one hand, the Department has succeeded in expanding its control over policy formation in the interests of greater efficiency in the educational system, on the other, it has shown itself less than adaptable in the face of new pressures for educational change.

Over the past few years the DES has actively sponsored the idea that education should be more in tune with the needs of the economy and that, properly equipped with the right controls, it has the ability to promote this objective. It is unfortunate that while the new economic ideology of education has undoubtedly taken root, as have the policy preferences it embodies, the internal dynamic of the Department has not been able to produce the policies required. In part this is due to the weakness of its external controls over the details of policy implementation and therefore its lack of confidence and experience in what are new policy areas but in part, also, it is due to the conservatism of its bureaucratic dynamic and the inflexibility of its policy-making structures. The internal constraints of the Department's organization have therefore made it a victim of the very ideology it has so conscientiously sponsored. In a period of rapid economic change when demands for new types of knowledge, new ways of organizing knowledge and new forms of certification are emerging almost daily, the DES has been unable to cope. Although it has performed its ideological function correctly by promoting an ideology suited to the needs of the economy, its bureaucratic dynamic and capabilities have not been sufficiently flexible to allow it to similarly adjust its functions of reproducing the technical and social relations of production. While some kind of gap has always been tolerated between the demands made by the economy on the educational system and the quality of the labour supplied by that system, there must come a point where changes have to occur if the mismatch between demand and supply is not to result in unbearable tensions and social fracture.

In this respect, an institution's adaptability is a measure of the quality of its bureaucratic dynamic. The more its bureaucratic dynamic fosters the formation of educational policies sympathetic to economic demands the more powerful is an institution. Conversely, if an institution's bureaucracy prevents it from responding to economic demands then its power is likely to wane. Two assumptions underpin this statement: firstly, that the educational system is not dominated by an ideology overtly hostile to the economy which would render economy-sensitive policies illegitimate; and secondly, that access to policy formation and implementation is not monopolized by entrenched interests and that therefore institutional competition can occur.

A major illustration of the importance of the quality of the bureaucratic dynamic to an institution's success or failure is the Manpower Services Commission (MSC). Markall and Gregory (1982) argue that the rise of the MSC has to be seen in the context of problems in the social relations of production caused by rapidly expanding youth unemployment. Youth unemployment, and the political unrest it might produce, presents a problem of control to the state to which the MSC is the possible answer. In filling this functional gap the Commission is working in the ideological space created by the Great Debate and to that extent is carrying out a task generally seen to be legitimate. However, Markall and Gregory (1982) are not entirely sanguine about its chances of success:

> The MSC may now be likened to a field ambulance struggling to service an ever widening and ever more embattled 'front line' than a sophisticated interventionist agency expertly planning and effecting the transformation of our labour market. (p. 11)

While we would agree that the MSC is responding to a demand placed on the educational system and unmet from elsewhere, we would differ in our interpretation of the nature of that demand and in our estimation of the MSC's institutional capacity to meet that demand and intervene at various points in the policy-making process. Firstly, the functional opportunities facing the MSC are not limited to the social relations of production but include the reproduction of the technical relations of production and ideology as well. To operate efficiently, a rapidly changing economy needs to be serviced by an educational system which can readily restructure its organization and certification of knowledge to meet the demands for new types of trained man-power. It needs efficient flows of information between the labour market and educational institutions to promote such restructuring. Furthermore, it needs an ideology which legitimates this process and convinces individuals that retraining throughout working life is necessary and desirable. High rates of unemployment complicate the task of meeting these needs because, at best, the motivation of the unemployed sections of the labour force has to be maintained in preparation for a possible expansion in the demand for their skills and, at worst, they have to be taught to tolerate unemployment.

In competing with traditional educational institutions for the resources to meet these requirements of the economy, the MSC had the initial advantages that as a new institution on the industry side of the industry–education fence it did not share education's customary distance from the workaday world, it was not bound by time-worn patterns of interaction between institutions and did not have a pre-ordained place in the educational policy-making process. These could all have been disadvantages of course. That they were not is due to the way in which the bureaucratic dynamic of the Commission has been able (so far) to exploit the functional opportunities described above and so reach a consensus with the economic dynamic.

Since its foundation in January 1974 under the Employment and Training Act 1973, the MSC has shown itself both willing and able to change its internal organizational form and its external organizational linkages in order to expand its responsibilities, influence and resources. In 1974 the MSC had a budget of £125 million. By 1983/84 this had risen to £1768 million which, even allowing for inflation, is a fair rate of institutional expansion. (Total expenditure by the DES in 1983/84 was £12,550 million). Its original brief was broad enough: 'to help people train for and obtain jobs ... and to help employers find suitable workers' (MSC, 1977, p.1). Initially its internal organization had three parts: the Employment Services Agency (ESA), the Training Services Agency (TSA), and the Office of the Manpower Services Commission (OMSC). The ESA had a national network of area and district officers and job centres and employment offices, and the TSA a separate network of regions, district offices, skill centres and annexes. To begin with the MSC was little more than a conglomerate of previously existing structures and lacked an organizational identity. How did it evolve into a unified organization capable of commanding ever increasing amounts of government resources?

Unlike the DES it did not have institutional constraints preventing it from presenting itself as the agency with the skills and know-how to link education and the economy. Thus by the time the DES launched the Great Debate to sponsor the new economic ideology of education in late 1976, the Commission had expanded its brief with government consent to include 'developing and operating a comprehensive manpower policy for Great Britain' (*Ibid*). In the same year the MSC published a review entitled *Towards a Comprehensive Manpower Policy* and issued a consultative document jointly with the government called *Training for Vital Skills* concerned with the problem of inadequate levels of training in skills of importance to the economy.

Having staked its claim for an interventionist approach to the education-economy issue, the Commission was able to provide a swift institutional response to the economic stimulus of rising unemployment by creating special programmes for the unemployed. At the start, these programmes were rudimentary and basically just kept people off the streets beginning with the Job Creation Programme (JCP) in October 1975 and the Work Experience Programme (WEP) in September 1976. But they, and the organization supporting them, evolved rapidly through the experience of the Special Temporary Employment Programme (STEP), the Youth Opportunities Programme (YOP), Unified Vocational Preparation (UVP), the Training for Skills Programme, the Community Programme (CP) and the Youth Training Scheme (YTS). In its *Corporate Plan 1982-86* the Commission emphasized the need for flexibility in the development and delivery of its programmes: 'The Commission' it said 'must be prepared to adapt continuously its programmes and their means of delivery to changes in the environment and the requirements of its clients' (p. 7). Thus the programmes for the unemployed, for example, were initially run by the OMSC, then by the specifically created Special Programmes Division (SPD) which in turn was integrated into the Training Division in 1983. Each restructuring of the national organization was paralleled by changes in the regional and district organizations. In its public documents the MSC is at pains to claim that this process of adaptation is not ad hoc but governed by a regular system of management and policy review conducted by its Manpower Intelligence and Planning Division. It publicly promotes an image of an organization dedicated to the effective and efficient delivery of services through flexible and adaptive structures.

However, if the flexibility of the Commission's bureaucratic dynamic is to be successfully exploited as a resource for institutional expansion and intervention in educational policy making, it is important that the MSC gains direct or indirect control over the way in which knowledge is organized, produced and certificated: i.e. the technical relations of production. Otherwise it will simply end up subsidizing the work of existing educational institutions. Until recently, the Commission's programmes for the unemployed were either concerned with the social relations of production (for example, maintaining a positive attitude towards work) or, where they dealt with the technical relations of production, worked through existing training and certificating institutions. But the Youth Training Scheme (YTS) has concerned itself directly with what knowledge should be acquired, how it should be certificated, and how the resulting qualification relates to existing systems of accreditation (the issue of 'credit transfer'). At the same time, the Commission has become more interventionist in the way in which it implements its general responsibility for modernizing occupational training. Prior to 1982-83, much of the support and advice for occupational training was provided by the Industrial Training Boards (ITBs) funded by the MSC. At that point sixteen of the twenty-four boards were wound up leaving the MSC in a direct relationship with the certificating bodies for different occupations (City and Guilds, BTEC etc.). The Commission's policy here is 'encouraging change towards the target that, by 1985, training should be to standards of competence without regard to age and that this should be accepted and implemented in both national agreement and local practice by that date' (MSC, 1984, p. 20). In practice this policy means seeking agreements with industrial sectors and certificating bodies to rationalize standards of achievement and the relationship between different qualifications.

As the Commission moves to gain more control over the certification of knowledge so, inevitably, it comes into conflict with those institutions which already have the control. One burgeoning example of this which we will return to in the final chapter is the assessment of the skills acquired in YTS. Not only does this overlap, and therefore compete, with existing courses such as City and Guilds 365 (Basic Skills Profile), it also overlaps with the potential territory of the Certificate in Pre-Vocational Education (CPVE) initiated by the DES and is the subject of a continuing struggle between MSC and DES for control of what both regard as a valuable knowledge area.

An important indicator of the Commission's expanding ability to intervene in the educational policy-making process was the announcement in the Government White Paper *Training For Jobs* in January 1984 that the MSC was to be given an extended capacity to purchase work-related, non-advanced further education (NAFE) from local education authority maintained colleges and other providers. The resources at the Commission's disposal for this purpose would be increased by £65 million in 1985-86 and £110 million in 1986-87 by means of a transfer from the LEA rate support grant. Commenting on this development the MSC (1984) said:

> The development is intended to make the provision of work-related, non-advanced further education more responsive to labour market needs, both nationally and locally. Given the representative structure of the Commission and its wide contacts in employment, training and education, the Government is asking the Commission to extend its range of operation so as to be able to discharge the function of a national training authority. (p. 26)

— thus emphasizing, as is its wont, that it has the unique ability to forge the links between economic need and educational provision.

The success of the MSC in acquiring the power to intervene at all levels of educational policy formation and implementation is a product of the quality of its bureaucratic dynamic. Its adaptive organization, links with industry and the trade unions, interventionist mechanisms and unashamedly economic ideology of education contrasts at every point with the position of the DES and allows it to argue forcefully that it is better placed to carry out the reproductive functions of education. Because its bureaucratic dynamic enables it to respond so readily to the economic dynamic, the MSC is fast becoming an integral part of the central apparatus of the educational state. As such it helps increasingly to influence what are regarded as acceptable educational policies. As its power base expands, the MSC becomes better able to shape the ideological climate within which policies are framed. It is thus an essential part of the empirical, as well as the theoretical, context for an educational policy-making study.

Political Parties, Intellectuals and Ideology

Turning now to the question of how the political parties relate to the operation of the central educational state and to educational policy-making, in *Education, Politics and the State* we were not over-generous in our estimation of party influence:

> The input of the politicians, whatever their formal power may be, consists essentially of providing general rhetorical support for the inevitable logic of the policy-making process. They simply lack the skills, time, resources and inclination to involve themselves in working out the detailed implications of demographic trends or what it means in specific educational terms to set new goals for schooling. (p. 39)

This view fitted easily into our thesis of the encapsulation of educational policy making by the DES. Though slightly more guarded in our opinion of issues such as independent schooling which are linked to the deep-seated ideological predispositions of parties we nonetheless felt that, even here, party policy may fail to be implemented. Ideological commitments', we wrote, 'may be the life-blood of a political party but when it is a question of translating them into precise policies which governments are prepared to enact they have to compete for resources with what may be more pressing considerations'.

In this book we take the issue of independent schooling and explore the accuracy of this view and the implications of our findings for our theory of educational change. In so doing we deal in particular with the way in which intellectuals help translate ideology into policy. The specifics of party intellectual roles are dealt with in Chapters 5 (Labour Party) and 7 (Conservative Party). Here we concentrate on the general theoretical issues concerning the relationship between intellectuals and ideology.

Unfortunately, there is a legacy of conceit in the writings on intellectuals which does little to illuminate the nature of their political role — that is, their relationship to the power structure. Intellectuals writing about intellectuals tend to dwell on the characteristics of social marginality and alienation which, it is claimed, set particular individuals apart from the rest of society and allow them a degree of objectivity not given to the unfortunate masses. Thus Mannheim (1954) promotes the notion of the 'socially unattached intelligentsia' and Shils (1972) sees them as emerging from a disruption of social solidarity. The separateness of intellectuals from the social round is, from this point of view, seen as bestowing high status because their treatment of knowledge is not tarnished by social pressures. Gouldner (1979) for example, is convinced that intellectuals are committed to 'a culture of critical discourse' and autonomy and 'constitute the most progressive force in modern society' and 'a centre of whatever human emancipation is possible in the foreseeable future' (p. 83). Most un-sociological and, in today's climate, most anachronistic of all is Apter's (1964) observation, that the intellectuals' alienation is 'brought about by "superior wisdom", that is, by the ability to penetrate ideologies of others and thereby to emancipate themselves. In this group it is the social scientist, who is the objective observer'! (p. 37).

Analysis based on self-plaudit of this kind either denies that intellectuals have a political role or completely emasculates it and concentrates instead on the nature of the intellectual activity. In contrast the Marxist tradition views intellectuals as the producers of the ideology required to explain and legitimate the power of the ruling class. As we discussed in *Education, Politics and the State* (Chapter 3) with particular reference to Gramsci, this monolithic view of the political function of intellectuals can be refined in a number of ways. We will now pursue that discussion further and then link it to the specific issue of party intellectuals.

Intellectuals are people who are skilled in the manipulation of ideas. Ideas can exercise power in two ways. On the one hand, they can identify, direct and legitimate particular courses of action or, on the other, they can obscure, confuse and make illegitimate other courses of action. The power of intellectuals lies in what they do with their ideas and how well they do it. It is customary to confine the term 'intellectual' to high status groups such as academics, scientists, writers, political commentators and the like: the assumption being, presum-ably, that they exercise a monopoly over the manipulation of ideas. Clearly this is not so. As Gramsci (1957) observed, all men are intellectuals though, as he also noted, 'all men do not have the function of intellectuals in society' (p. 121). One can add to this the observation that not all intellectuals have the same function.

In order to understand the relationship of intellectuals to the dominant power structure it is necessary to examine their social and institutional context. For it is this context which shapes and determines both their handling of ideas and the impact or non-impact of ideas. The importance of occupation is three-fold: it can provide the skills to organize ideas effectively, the status to lend these ideas authority and weight and the means, both formal and informal, to disseminate ideas to various audiences. What Gramsci terms 'the traditional intellectuals' are high status occupations such as the legal and academic professions which use their skills, status and connections to service and maintain the ruling ideology. This can come as no surprise since no society could survive if its ideological presuppositions, be they capitalist, socialist or feudal, were not continually reinforced. Having said that, it should be recognized that high status intellectuals are merely one link in a chain of ideas dissemination. If the other links are missing then the ideological conversation becomes one of elite intellectual talking to elite intellectual with exclusive sophistication and wider political irrelevance. As we discuss in Chapter 5, in recent years the Left in particular has suffered from this problem.

The different functions of intellectuals can be analyzed in terms of their position in the production and dissemination of ideology. Gramsci notes that 'at the highest level would be the creators of the various sciences, philosophy, art, etc., at the lowest the most humble "administrators" and divulgators of pre-existing, traditional, accumulated intellectual wealth' (Hoare and Nowell Smith, 1971, p. 13). Such is the pervasiveness of the high status definition of intellectuals that little has been done to elaborate on this idea. Unless the creative intellectuals are deliberately aiming their ideas at their fellows in the same social stratum, they will need access to intellectuals who are prepared to translate their ideas into a form which makes sense to the mass of the population — in particular the intellectuals of the newspapers, radio, television and publishing. Within this second level considerable differences obviously exist in the way in which the translation function is carried out: for example between the 'quality' press with its emphasis on a considered style of ideas handling and the 'popular' press where slogans and symbolic ideas are more prevalent. Nonetheless, what is most relevant to the intellectual function is how much ideological influence is wielded by such an agency. The manner in which the influence is exercised is analytically subordinate. This means that the reporter on *The Sun* can be a more significant intellectual if his manipulation of ideas has more ideological influence than that of the political correspondent of *The Guardian* . Carrying this argument to its logical conclusion, the most powerful type of intellectual could be the one who combines high professional status (hence authority) with access to the popular media: for example, a Cambridge professor with a regular column in *The Daily Mail* and a chat show on television. (For the most part, occupational norms prohibit this kind of integrated intellectual role.) However, whether or not ideological influence is translated into political power depends on the audience being influenced. Ideological influence over a large audience with little power is politically less effective than ideological influence over a small audience with a great deal of power. Any evaluation of the political impact of a particular intellectual activity has therefore to examine both the nature of the intellectual role and the political position of the target audience.

Not all intellectual roles are occupationally based. Interest groups, trade unions and political parties all rely on a voluntary labour force of intellectuals to promote and sustain particular sets of ideas. Although the skills and status utilized by these intellectuals may be derived from their occupation, the political purposes to which they put them are determined by their membership of, and/or commitment to, certain organizations. To a large extent, political parties in Britain have not coordinated the activities of their intellectuals with the deliberate intent of achieving set ideological objectives. In part this is because they have accepted the anachronistic conception that dealing with ideas is a prerogative of high status occupations. In today's complex society with its manifold forms of ideas distribution, to rely on a conception of the intellectual role derived empirically from the societies of theorists such as Marx, Lenin and Gramsci is to neglect numerous opportunities for ideological influence. As we discuss in Chapter 7, the Right has proved itself more pragmatic and adaptable in realizing the significance of different types of intellectual activity on behalf of the Conservative Party, particularly in generating populist appeal. By contrast, the intellectuals of the Labour Party, particularly those on the Left of the Party, have retained a self-image characterized by a principled and reasoned commitment and a naive belief in the political power of rational argument.

If the ideologies of political parties are not to become moribund and if parties are to recruit intellectuals capable of performing the different functions involved in translating ideology into policy then ways must be found of linking the parties themselves with appropriate intellectual networks. Furthermore, if the search for new networks is not a continuous one a party risks becoming isolated from the main currents of opinion in society. This may preserve its purity but it will also inhibit its ability to solve particular ideology-policy problems. Intellectual brokers are therefore needed to match a party's needs with available intellectual resources.

In his *Friends of Friends: Networks, Manipulators and Coalitions* Boissevain demonstrates the importance of the broker's role in the operation of social networks. Brokers are skilled social manipulators strategically positioned at the intersection of networks. They perform an entrepreneurial role for profit using basically two types of resources: those they control directly (for example, jobs, specialized knowledge) and those they have access to via strategic contact with other people. Profit can be status, goodwill, information, services, psychological satisfaction; only rarely is it money. For intellectual brokers the main currency in which they are trading is ideas. Over time a broker builds up credit by producing results. Within networks, temporary alliances of distinct parties, which Boissevain calls coalitions, form for a limited purpose. They reflect changing circumstances, may disappear as certain goals are achieved and may evolve into social forms of a different structural order. They may, for example, take on more permanent organizational form and become an institution of some kind. This raises the issue of how social networks may coalesce around particular institutions because those institutions facilitate interactions of interest to the networks. For example, they may act as 'clearing houses' for ideas of one ideological persuasion.

A party which becomes isolated from supportive social networks of intellectuals is bound to find it difficult to advance a serious challenge to the policies emerging from the dominant institutions of the educational state. In such a situation, it can neither promote detailed policy options nor sway the dominant system of ideas, or hegemony, to which the educational state must be responsive. Its capacity to exercise educational power by having an impact on educational policy-making is directly proportional to the intellectual resources at its command. Political parties face two institutions of the educational state, the DES and the MSC, with established policy preferences. If a party wishes to place on the political agenda a policy which does not easily mesh with those preferences then it will require continuing intellectual support: to develop the policy within the party structure, to translate the policy into different forms for different audiences (for example specialized interest groups, general public) and to maintain the momentum of policy implementation when the party is in office (see p. 100–110, 156–62). This in turn means that a party must have three broad types of intellectual roles supporting the production and distribution of a particular set of policy ideas: the producers, the translators and the disseminaators (including brokers). In reality, a single individual may well carry out more than one of these roles but they nonetheless remain analytically distinct.

Power, Change and the Independent Schools

The discussion of the relationship between the central educational state and the political parties has been placed in the context of educational policy-making because this is central to the process of educational change. No institution can have a significant impact on educational change unless it relates its activities to policy formation and implementation since this is where the resources are allocated, change is enabled to take place and power is exercised. In this section we will develop this idea further as a means of identifying those institutions which constitute part of the educational state and thus exercise educational power. At present, we have included the DES and the MSC in this definition on both functional and organizational grounds: functionally they are central the reproduction of class relations and organizationally they can be directly related to educational policy-making. The relationship of an institution to educational policy-making thus provides the means of refining a purely functional definition of the educational state which, as we saw earlier, is on its own too general to be of any use. Like the DES and the MSC the independent schools sector is functionally an important part of the educational state in terms of the contribution it makes to the reproduction of class relations. But within this definition, how can we best theorize its access to educational power and hence its capacity to influence educational change?

In considering the way in which institutions can wield educational power we need to be clear what is meant by 'power'. Following Lukes (1974), power can be viewed in one of three ways. Firstly, a one-dimensional view can be adopted which 'involves a focus on *behaviour* in the making of decisions on *issues* over which there is an observable *conflict* of (subjective) interests, seen as express policy preferences, revealed by political participation' (p. 15). Pluralist theorists in particular adopt this approach. It has been severely criticized by Bachrach and Baratz (1962, 1963 and 1970) who maintain that while some issues are organized into politics, others are organized out. Power has thus to be seen not only in terms of the decisions which are taken but also in terms of the decisions which are *not* taken as a result of issues being taken off, and kept off, the political agenda. Nonetheless, Bachrach and Baratz still assume, as do the pluralists, that there is an observable conflict which shows that power is being exercised to prevent decisions being taken and, conversely, they assume that if there is no conflict then power is not being exercised. Noting this, Lukes (1974) advocates a third view of power which recognizes that 'the most effective and insidious use of power is to prevent such conflict arising in the first place' for example by shaping perceptions, cognitions and preferences so that individuals accept their role in the order of things (p. 23). What Lukes is of course talking about here is the exercise of ideological power and, through this, the perpetuation of a particular hegemony.

Although Lukes presents his analysis as an analysis of power what he is principally concerned with, and he does not make this clear enough, is not power per se but the way in which power is viewed. His three-dimensional categorization is derived from a critique of *methods of observing power* not from the phenomenon itself. He is concerned with the way in which different methods place different empirical boundaries on the concept of power according to the weight these methods attach to observable and non-observable phenomena. Lukes's analysis is important because it warns us against excluding aspects of power through the use of certain methods. It is therefore a prior step to theorizing about power. But it should not itself be taken as an exercise in theorizing about power.

Our own position is that all three views are equally important in the study of power and this is reflected in the range and type of evidence used in this book. Obviously the exclusion of one or more of these views of power would limit our ability to theorize about how power is exercised. In *Education, Politics and the State* we argued that educational policy-making is

> the process whereby the various pressures for educational change are translated into formal governmental expression. In becoming policy, the dynamic for change takes on specific form and is endowed with whatever legitimacy and power the dominant political structure commands. (p. 87)

The pressure for change we saw as being mainly derived from education's function of reproducing the technical and social relations of production and generating ideology.

The contribution made by an institution such as the independent schools sector to educational policy formation and implementation is a characteristic of the exercise of educational power. Institutions can be seen as playing different parts in the chain of events between the pressure for educational change, the development of an appropriate educational ideology, its translation into policy demands, the negotiation of those demands into specific administrative form, the allocation of resources to policies and the implementation of policies into educational practice. No institution will focus exclusively on a single part of that chain but some will specialize in one function rather than another. This is an approach to institutional characteristics in line with Lukes's first view of power since the exercise of power in this process will be capable of being observed. Similarly, a second characteristic can be readily derived from this approach simply by seeing each stage in negative terms. That is to say, what is made *not* to happen at each stage.

For example, examination boards exercise considerable power by resisting attempts to raise new issues about how knowledge should be organized and certificated. Two decades of effort by the Schools Council which, until lately, was charged with the responsibility of introducing change into the primary and secondary curriculum, foundered largely on the clearly observable power of the examination boards to keep things as they are, to keep particular issues off the educational agenda (Salter and Tapper, 1981, Chapter 6). A similar example of agenda-setting, and hence of non-decision making on certain issues, was the structure imposed on the Great Debate in 1976-77 by the DES. The teacher unions found themselves having to accept a debate on terms they did not like but nonetheless had to accept (*Ibid*, Chapter 9). Their discontent was observable, as was their powerlessness to alter the situation.

The third view of power, when applied to the policy-making chain, takes us into the field of ideology construction and policy legitimation. What ideology does an institution promote in order to legitimize some policies and render others illegitimate and how does it do it? Here the process of agenda control is not direct and therefore cannot be directly observed. It has instead to be inferred from ideological shifts which make it 'natural' that one policy rather than another should be pursued. Some institutions will be better placed than others to engage in ideology construction. While the power of an ensconced ideology is difficult to trace when it forms part of the social climate of opinion inhabited by the observer, who, detached though he may be, must still be influenced by it, its earlier development is easier to track because it will have come into conflict with other bodies of opinion as it strove for dominance. Thus in *Education, Politics and the State* we charted how the (then) new 'economic ideology of education' was assiduously promoted by the DES during the Great Debate. The Debate was therefore an example of both direct and indirect agenda-setting. Similarly, in this book we show how the resurgence of right-wing thought and its impact on Conservative Party policy on education worked through specific institutional channels.

Distinguishing between the institutions of the educational state in

terms of the contribution they make to policy-making and implementation means that we are interested in those institutional characteristics
which determine how they make their contributions. Thus we are
interested in the amount of resources (financial, legal, ideological,
intellectual) institutions have to allocate and the controls they exercise
over the means of allocation.

To summarize the implications of this discussion for our study of
the private schools, the independent sector, like other institutions
which functionally form part of the educational state, exercise educational power to the extent that they translate the demand from the
economy for the maintenance of, or change in, the patterns of class
relations into educational policy and practice. In simplified diagramma-
tic form the relationship can be portrayed thus:

Figure 1

DEMAND (Economic dynamic)	Reproduction of the technical and social relations of production and their legitimation

↕

TRANSLATION (Bureaucratic dynamic)	Institutions of the educational state

↓

EXERCISE OF POWER ⎱ EDUCATIONAL CHANGE ⎰	Educational policy making and policy implementation

The different ways in which institutions contribute to this relationship,
either positively or negatively, constitute institutional characteristics
which can be used to identify their position within the web of the
educational state.

In this chapter we have also dealt with the theoretical issue of how
institutions whose purposes are not educational and who therefore lie
beyond the boundaries of the educational state nonetheless intervene in
the above relationship. Specifically, we have examined the kinds of
intellectual resources political parties require in order to make an
impact on educational policy and so exercise educational power. This
extension of our theoretical concern is essential to understanding how
the independent schools sector, functionally a key part of the educational state, has organized itself in order to preserve its position within
the educational state. It provides us with the theoretical base for
examining the formation of an alliance between a political party and

one part of the educational state (private schools), flows of political and ideological influence across the boundaries of the state, the organization of parties' intellectual resources and the relationship of these resources to party ideology and policy-making.

3 Private Schooling and the Reproduction of the Class Structure

Introduction

Much of the literature on public schools is devoted to an analysis of their responsibility for the perpetuation of the British class structure. It was to be expected that the political parties would draw upon the pertinent material for their own ends, and that in particular the Labour party would use the charge of social divisiveness as a rod with which to beat the independent sector:

> Attendance at a private school means something far more than an education. In Britain it is the basic requirement for membership of the hierarchy which still dominates so many positions of power and influence. Private school fees therefore buy far more than examination success. They are the admission charge for a ruling elite whose wealth gives them power and whose power gives them wealth. And the main means of transferring economic status, social position and influence from generation to generation is through a private education system which ensures that merit can be bought. (Labour Party, 1980, p. 10)

The sensitivity of the private sector to such claims only heightens interest. In recent years much of its public relations machinery has been devoted to softening the image portraying the schools as willing to broaden their social base and eager to engage fully in the wider society. The main stumbling block, we are led to believe, is financial; many parents who would like their children to be educated privately cannot afford the fees and the state limits the support it is prepared to offer. This is considered to be an unfortunate state of affairs for not only are many children denied a form of schooling that would probably best suit their needs but also the private sector, contrary to its own wishes, remains more socially exclusive than it would do otherwise. Thus the independent sector views itself is one of the unwitting agents of class reproduction as opposed to being *the* cause of social divisiveness.

The politics of private schooling emerges out of two central issues: what the character of schooling should be in the light of wider social needs, and how best to achieve the relationship between schooling and social needs. To express the same idea in different terms, the political struggle itself is about the nature of class relations in Britain and the part that schooling plays in reproducing the class structure. The purpose of this chapter is to review how the public schools have performed this function. As we discussed in the previous chapter it is the performance of this function that makes the public schools part of the state, although they are not an integral part of the state apparatus. The fact that relatively autonomous institutions are responsible for educating such a broad segment of Britain's future ruling elites is within itself a fascinating state of affairs. Besides the theoretical and political legitimations of this chapter, the prevalence of the class reproduction theme in the existing literature on public schools provides us with an opportunity to review the state of the discipline. Although we have criticized elsewhere the failure to consider wider aspects of social reproduction (for example the lack of attention paid to girls' private schools, the religious differentation of schools, and national variations) this chapter will for the most part reflect the existing bias in favour of class reproduction. Not only is this consistent with the theoretical direction of our work but also it provides some focus to a virtually boundless topic.

Some Traditional Themes

The previous quote, taken from the Labour Party's discussion document on private schools, reiterates what is probably the most common-place sociological observation on independent schooling, i.e. it is integral to the perpetuation of class privilege. How, in the usual parlance of the literature, do the private schools help to reproduce the British ruling class with its accompanying privileges? Three characteristics of the private sector are seen as essential to this process: the pupils are selected academically, and more importantly, socially; they are then exposed to very esoteric socializing experiences within the schools; and on the completion of their schooling there is a good chance that they will continue their education at university (frequently at an Oxbridge college) so enhancing their career prospects. The ties to Oxbridge, and indeed to most factions of the ruling class, have been established over a long period of time by a variety of means, consequentially, so the argument goes, the competition for valued resources and the nation's command posts is heavily biased in favour of the products of independent schooling.

Although these general facets of private schooling are invariably referred to in any analysis of the part it plays in the process of class reproduction, the more precise relationships have been less frequently drawn out. Moreover the concentration on recruitment does assume that class reproduction is non-problematic i.e. upper-middle class children will attend private schools and that they will take up those careers that are usually classified as being part of the upper middle class. Alternatively if private education represents an opportunity for social mobility then the fortunate individuals will readily succumb to a process designed to ensure that round pegs fit snugly into round holes.

However, if recruitment is related to the socializing experiences of the schools then the questions are more interesting and the answers more complex. It is reasonable to assume that the more a school restricts its intake of pupils in social terms then the easier it is to impose a rigid code of values — restrictive pupil recruitment aids the effectiveness of the socialization process. Presumably what applies to an individual school also applies to groups of schools with similar recruitment strategies. The more restricted the recruitment then the greater the probability of a common pattern of social control with the concomitant expectation that it will be successfully applied. Of course there will be maverick individuals and purposefully deviant schools but these are the exceptions that prove the rule. If these propositions are correct then we need to know how the relationship between the socially differentiated segments of the independent sector is to be understood. In what sense is it meaningful to categorize them as even belonging to the same sector? Furthermore, we will want to know what kinds of problems are posed by changes in recruitment patterns. For example, how feasible is it to change them? What form is this likely to take? What are the consequences of differing rates of change for a school's social control mechanisms?

Meisel (1958), in his seminal work on Mosca, has claimed that effective ruling elites must possess three essential qualities: 'To put it into a facile formula, all elites shall be credited here with what we

should call the three C's: group consciousness, coherence, and conspiracy' (p. 4). In a straightforward reformulation of Meisel's concepts
Giddens (1974) has argued that elites require moral integration (consciousness) and social integration (coherence) if they are to persist in the
face of those constant pressures for social change that are to be found in
all societies (p. 5). Although much of the discussion of the experience of
schooling within the private sector (especially within the prestigious
boys boarding schools) is both trivial and purposefully embellished, it
is this experience which sociologists correctly believe lays the foundation for Meisel's three C's. Even if it is difficult to demonstrate the case
for social integration, there are fewer pitfalls in the weaker — but
related — argument that the social distance between children in the
maintained and private sectors is considerable (Tapper and Salter, 1978,
pp. 48-56). Again one would expect the top end of the boarding school
network, regardless of its own internal divisions, to be more isolated.

Until comparatively recently the private schools could devote
themselves to nurturing the consciousness of Britain's future ruling
class safe in the belief that the hegemony which protected their rights
was more or less intact. The schools were concerned to legitimate the
established social order in the minds of their pupils and to reinforce the
prevailing belief in their own privileges and obligations within that
social order. The moral integration of ruling elites was based on the
premise that the pupils of the public schools had an obligation to
assume leadership roles. One would have to search hard to find many
explicit references to the virtues of social inequality, rather it was
believed to be inevitable and as such an unquestioned feature of social
reality. In response to political attack the public schools have refurbished their images and placed considerably less stress upon leadership
training. Ironically the political struggle to preserve their existence has
incorporated an attempt to legitimate social inequality in the minds of a
much wider audience than their traditional clientele.

Conspiracy is a word with unpleasant connotations but the many
critics of the public schools have contended that there is something
conspiratorial about the fact that their pupils dominate so persistently
and so completely the commanding heights of British society. This
may be blatant nepotism at work, with the old boy network operating
in an exceedingly effective, if highly crude, manner. Alternatively,
and perhaps more persuasively, the bias can only be understood by
examining what criteria determine elite membership and what qualities
are possessed by those who have received private schooling. It could be
argued that the independent schools have proved themselves masters at

matching the two, partially because they have been so influential in deciding the terms of elite membership so that schools which would compete with them have to do so on grounds not of their own choosing. The three traditional themes can be interrelated to form a simple model of class reproduction. Selected recruitment makes it easier for the schools to establish effective social control mechanisms so ensuring that their pupils are internalizing the desired messages. The well-socialized private school pupil has several social advantages when competing for scarce places in higher education and/or for prestigious, well-rewarded occupations: his school expects him to do well, it has equipped him with the correct resources, and it may even have furnished him with useful direct contacts. Although it may be difficult to demonstrate conclusively that schooling exercises significant an *independent* influence upon either individual examination results or career success, only a few parents are likely to be familiar with the intricacies of statistical argument, and whether even this would have much bearing upon their decisions is doubtful. When deciding the future of one's own children it is easy to believe that they will escape the fate suggested by the law of probability! Parents of sufficient means persuade themselves that their offspring will gain enough tangible rewards from private education and they see it as a good investment so perpetuating what many believe is a cycle of privilege.

Examining the Traditional Themes: Who are the Private School Pupils?

Survey after survey reveals that most pupils in independent schools have fathers with middle-class occupations whereas, by equally impressive margins the majority of pupils in maintained schools have fathers with working-class occupations (Halsey *et al.*, 1980, pp. 35–8 and 51–5). If the class composition of a school's pupils is therefore a measure of social divisiveness then the independent schools are undoubtedly socially divisive. But such bald description disguises the subtleties and uncertainties in the process of class reproduction. If private schooling is a non-problematic link in the recruitment channel between middle-class family backgrounds and middle-class occupations then one would expect an ingrained loyalty towards the independent sector by an overwhelming majority of middle-class parents.

The most substantial studies of parental attitudes towards private schooling were undertaken by Bridgeman and Fox in 1977 and by Fox in 1979-80 (Bridgeman and Fox, 1978; Fox, 1984). The first survey was composed of 330 parents (167 mothers and 163 fathers) whose children were attending one of three preparatory schools of differing prestige. These parents, the authors concluded, fell into one of two categories which we would term 'traditionals' and 'pragmatists'. The 'traditionals' tended to be well-established members of the upper class who were locked into a very specific educational model in which their children moved from a prestigious preparatory school to a boarding secondary school and from there (and less assuredly) onto an Oxbridge college. They excluded therefore the possibility of their children attending schools in the maintained sector. The 'pragmatists' on the contrary were purposefully opting out of the maintained sector; they percieved certain advantages in educating their children privately which they considered to be worth the cost. If the situation changed, presumably if the maintained schools conformed more closely to the model presented by the independent schools, then the pragmatic parents might alter their minds. On the basis of her 1979-80 survey Fox has stressed the strong belief of most parents who were educating their children privately that the independent schools produced better academic results and developed character by instilling discipline. She has described this as a crisis of confidence in the comprehensive system of education.

Current educational realities, as well as parental values, permit the pragmatic parents to exercise their discretion. In their book *Origins and Destinations* Halsey and his co-researchers show that middle-class parents (i.e. their 'service' and 'intermediate' occupational categories) are more prepared to use the maintained primary than the maintained secondary schools (pp. 51-2). At the sixth-form stage there does appear to be a two-way flow of pupils: whereas some independent school pupils seek the perceived freer atmosphere of the sixth-form colleges (undoubtedly evoking mixed feelings amongst their parents) others move into the sixth-forms of the independent schools in the hope that this will boost their chances of obtaining good 'A' level results. Moreover, parental values may result in their making differing decisions about the schooling of their children for example, girls are educated in the maintained sector and boys privately, or bright daughters attend a local ex-direct grant school as day pupils and dull sons are sent as boarders to a distant and mediocre public school.

The private sector's function of class reproduction is further complicated by the movement into and out of independent schooling across generations. Halsey's survey reveals that in those families in which at least one of the parents had received some private schooling less than 50 per cent of their own children were similarly educated, whereas 11.7 per cent of those families in which one or both parents had attended selective maintained schools (mainly grammar schools) and 3.1 per cent of those families in which both parents had attended non-selective maintained schools (mainly secondary moderns) sent their children to private secondary schools (p. 51). Although the fortunes of families change over time these figures demonstrate that it is impossible to sustain the claim that there is a deep-seated tradition of loyalty to the independent sector on the part of many middle-class parents. Halsey's data point to considerable intergenerational defection from the private camp and a much smaller percentage movement (but of a much larger number of parents) into it. In other words, the pragmatic parents appear to outnumber the traditional parents by a wide margin.

With the phasing out of the grammar schools, both maintained and direct grant, it is possible that the intergenerational movement between the state and private sectors has declined somewhat. Those parents who sought free places at the direct grant schools, their children having obtained the necessary entrance qualifications after attending a state primary school, no longer have this incentive to use them and other parents, as Fox's survey suggests, may not want their children to attend comprehensive schools although they found a grammar school education perfectly acceptable. These speculations must, however, be treated cautiously in light of the fact that just over one-fifth of the parents in Halsey's study who had been educated privately had to be satisfied with non-selective secondary schooling for their children (p. 76).

Since about 1977 the independent sector has experienced a modest revival in its fortunes, but nonetheless it still remains a very small segment of the total education system. As the independent sector comprises only some 6 per cent of the total school population of England and Wales the inevitable consequence is that it is used by only a minority of parents regardless of their class status. For example, by a significant margin a majority of parents in *all eight* of Halsey's occupational groupings send their children to maintained rather than private schools. Of those parents placed in class 1 only 32.7 per cent send their children to private primary schools and 35.7 per cent to private secondary schools (p. 51). The figures drop sharply for class 2 parents, 14.3 per cent sending their children to private primary schools and 15.6 per cent to private secondary schools. Moreover in terms of educational scatter, that is making use of different kinds of schooling, the same survey reveals that '...the class of higher professionals, managers and proprietors is the one with the greatest educational scatter' (p. 71). This evokes from Halsey and his co-researchers the terse conclusion that 'classes, we must always remind ourselves, are not castes'!

More significant than Halsey's rather obvious comment is to consider the implications of these findings for those who see private schooling as a potent vehicle of class reproduction. Our previous discussion on why parents decide that their children should be educated privately revealed a small group of traditional parents who showed unswerving loyalty to the private sector. Assuming that these parents belong mainly to Halsey's class 1 occupational category then they do not appear to be even typical of their class peers. If independent schooling is a link in the recruitment channel between the middle-class family and occupational success then it performs this function for only a comparatively few individuals. We need to know more about the eventual occupations of those children with, in the terms of Halsey's study, class 1 and 2 family backgrounds who did not receive their schooling in the private sector. Are they downwardly mobile? Or could it be that in certain circumstances schooling is unlikely to have much of an independent effect upon the process of class reproduction? It may, for example, make little difference one way or another to highly intelligent children with upper middle-class parents whether they attend maintained or independent schools. Either the quality of their schooling is irrelevant for this purpose (i.e. they succeed in spite of it) or alternatively for them it would be roughly of the same standard in either sector. In several parts of the country selective secondary education still prevails and elsewhere many comprehensive schools go to considerable lengths to ensure that their academically gifted pupils develop their talents to the full. It may make little difference where middle-class children are educated if they are still enveloped by an independent school model of acceptable practice.

The classical literature on ruling elites stresses that if they are to avoid the steady process of degeneration into eventual collapse then it is essential that they recruit into their ranks talented individuals from other classes. Although it is difficult to find reliable trend data on the class composition of the private sector, it does appear to have performed this function. Whether ruling elites in Britain have as a consequence performed their duties more effectively is an entirely different question. There is broad historical agreement that the public schools were revitalized from about the middle of the nineteenth century thanks to the influx of the sons of an expanding, prosperous bourgeoisie. Bamford writes (1967), 'Between the accession of Queen Victoria and 1869 no less than thirty-one classical boarding schools were founded and this figure does not include independent day schools or old endowed schools which had acquired new energy and life' (p. 24). Initially, however, the old and new schools were not competing for the same clientele for, as Bamford claims, many of the existing schools still had empty places. However, what mutual suspicion existed disappeared comparatively quickly and after 1850 the gentry and aristocracy started to patronize the newer establishments, and when the *Public Schools' Year Book* first appeared in 1889 it listed thirty schools, many of them quite recent foundations, that its editors (representatives of Eton, Harrow and Winchester) regarded 'as belonging to the same genus as their own' (*Ibid.*, p. 188).

If the initial influx of the bourgeoisie was met by an expansion of the private sector then it is equally true that the eventual class accommodation that occurred within its confines led to a clearly differentiated internal pecking order (Honey, 1977, pp. 272-95). When the list of schools to be entered into the first *Public Schools' Year Book* was being drawn up the representatives of Eton, Harrow and Winchester were thinking essentially in terms of boarding schools that provided a classical education and were sufficiently expensive to exclude all but the more prosperous sons of the bourgeoisie and their betters (Bamford, 1967, p. 37). Attempts, therefore, to ascribe the independent schools a class reproduction function have to take into account their internal hierarchy.

Although the private schools proved themselves capable of absorbing those members of the bourgeoisie who wanted to be absorbed (to the point where the sector could be labelled a bourgeois institution) they have had much more trouble in responding to the educational demands of the working class. This is in spite of the fact that several of the most prestigious schools were founded with the purpose of providing a schooling for talented but poor children. Such an element still exists in many private schools but it is generally swamped by those children from families that are well–heeled. The reasons for the exclusion of the working-class child are self-evident. Few working-class families possess sufficient resources to pay the fees even assuming they would want their children to receive a private education. Moreover it is not part of working-class culture, even assuming it were financially possible, to send their children to boarding schools.

Power and Policy in Education

In the past, one of the larger wedges of working-class pupils in the independent sector was to be found in the direct grant schools. Kalton, in his survey of schools belonging to the Headmasters' Conference, reported the following class distributions:

Table 1: *Father's Social Class for School Entrants*

	Independent				Direct Grant		
	Day	Mixed		Boarding	Day	Mixed	
		Day	Brd.			Day	Brd
Professional	29	35	37	32	25	27	27
Intermediate	48	50	56	60	45	45	61
Skilled, non-manual	13	9	4	5	14	14	8
Skilled, manual	7	5	2	2	13	11	4
Semi-skilled	2	1	1	1	3	3	0
Unskilled	1	0	0	0	0	0	0
Total %	100	100	100	100	100	100	100
Total nos allocated	873	1841	3789	2964	2731	1746	786

Source: Kalton, G. (1966) *The Public Schools: A Factual Survey*, London, Longmans, p. 35.

These distributions reveal that the critical difference in social class composition between the independent and direct grant schools was a consequence of the respective sizes of the boarding element each provided, the larger the boarding element the lower the percentage of pupils from working-class families. In the mid-1970s one prominent theme in the campaign of those endeavouring to save the direct grant schools was that they had provided high quality schooling to countless thousands of working-class pupils. The inference we were meant to draw was that, although in certain respects they may be close cousins of the independent schools, they could not be labelled as socially divisive. But in class recruitment terms Kalton's data show the distinctiveness of boarding education; once this is taken into account then the class profiles of direct grant and independent schools were not that radically different.

Of course the HMC schools are only one segment of the independent sector and to concentrate on it to the exclusion of other segments does give a skewed picture of independent schooling both in relation to boarding provision and class composition. The 1983 ISIS Survey reveals that whereas 217 schools belonging to HMC were educating 48,047 boarders in comparison to 91,988 day pupils, the other 1115 independent schools participating in the survey were educating 66,651 boarders in comparison to 206,584 day pupils (p. 6). These differing proportions of boarders and day pupils has, as the research of Halsey and his colleagues suggests, its expected impact upon the class composition of the differing segments of private schooling:

Table 2: Class Composition of Different Types of Secondary School in the Private Sector

Class Scale	Non-HMC (%)	Direct Grant (%)	HMC (%)
I, II	47.7	50.4	66.7
III, IV, V	41.1	33.6	27.0
VI, VII, VIII	11.2	16.0	6.3
Total numbers	(197)	(131)	(189)

Source: Kalton, G. (1966) *The Public Schools: A Factual Survey*, London, Longmans, p. 53.

The non-HMC private schools increases the representation of pupils from middle and lower-middle class (Halsey's 'intermediates') as well as working-class families. Whereas class representation in HMC schools is sharply hierarchical, the non-HMC schools are more evenly balanced between the varying subsections of the middle-class, so much so that in comparison the class profile of the direct grant schools could be described as polarized. Although it is difficult to obtain information on the changing class composition of the independent sector, it is highly probable that the balance of middle-class parents has shifted somewhat in recent years from (again in Halsey's terms) 'the service' to 'the intermediate' class. This would be accompanied by an infusion of more working-class parents encouraged in part by the Assisted Places Scheme. This shift would be a reflection of the comparatively greater expansion of the less expensive and prestigious end of private schooling accompanied by the growing predominance of day pupils in recent years.

It is possible to paint a much more refined picture of class recruitment channels within the private sector than we have done so far. Private schooling is not simply a segment of the educational system or an amalgam of somewhat contrasting bits and pieces but also the product of a considerable number of *individual* schools which create their own very special identities. Obviously these are not merely a product of the kind of pupils they tend to attract but undoubtedly it plays its part in forming the image of the school. For example, it is hard to imagine that Eton College would be Eton College if it were not so appealing to the British aristocracy; that Winchester would remain Winchester if it failed to attract so many sons of either those who run the state machine or the universities; or that Dartington Hall could sustain its notoriety without the patronage of disaffected intellectuals and artists. The consequence may well be that many private schools have their own peculiar patterns of socialization and are part of a very confined class reproduction channel. To put it differently, the process of class reproduction may at this level of the class hierarchy consist of a number of overlapping, but nonetheless still clearly differentiated, recruitment channels.

It is important to note that while the fortunes of private schooling have fluctuated, individual schools have likewise both consistently declined and prospered. As Bamford's study of the nineteenth century public schools revealed, after 1850 certain aristocratic families started to patronize the newer foundations. These were presumably the more successful schools that were moving upmarket and their ability to attract the sons of the aristocracy confirmed this. Status change is an ongoing process and one that is likely to be consistently related to the kinds of families that are persuaded to send their children to a parti-cular school. A school increases its status by becoming more socially exclusive.

Schools may wish to retain their traditional recruitment pattern whilst modifying the experience of schooling they have to offer. For example, it is clear that during the years Michael McCrum was Headmaster of Eton College it emphasized more strongly the impor-tance of formal academic success which was reflected in 'A' level examination results and success in the competition for the scholarships and exhibitions of the Oxbridge colleges. Such a policy could be pursued without changing the *formal* academic entrance requirement, that is a simple pass in the Common Entrance examination. Parents can be informally attuned to changing value systems and in any case they are likely to be affected by the publicity that surrounds academic success which is invariably presented in a pecking order of schools. One suspects that Eton started to signal families, no matter how great their eminence or the longevity of their connections with the school, that they should think seriously whether Eton was really the right place for their duller sons.

In spite of all the qualifications it is impossible to deny the conclusion that private schooling, especially its upper reaches the great boarding schools, is virtually a closed world as far as the British working class is concerned. The research on the nineteenth century public schools shows that, partly because of the expansion of the system and partly because of the infusion of the bourgeoisie into the traditional foundations, it was possible to incorporate at least segments of the middle class. Like most successful accommodations of differing social forces the transition took place over a reasonably lengthy period of time. The sheer size of the working class would make it more difficult to absorb; either the private sector would have to expand rapidly or the absorption process would have to be very lengthy indeed. A rapid infusion of working-class pupils would clearly impose an immense strain on the traditional value system. The problem of commencing with a less ambitious programme and extending it over a longer period of time is that its opponents would recognize it for what it was, i.e. as an attempt to preserve the values of the private sector intact and to inculcate at least a part of the working class into that value system. The independent schools' critics would probably find this even more unacceptable than their alleged social divisiveness.

Whereas the entry of the bourgeoisie into public schools was financed privately, the incorporation of the working class could only be accomplished by the provision of state funding. If this is provided on any scale then the private sector has to live with the uncertainties that can follow from a change in government policy. Fluctuations in parental preferences may undermine a school but, if it is too heavily dependent upon state support, a change in government policy could destroy the private sector as a whole. This is not wishful thinking for the direct grant schools were removed from the educational map by a shift in government policy. Admittedly most of them survived the blow and were reconstituted as independent schools but the transition was far from smooth. If state money is accompanied by the possible intrusion of government influence and the Character of the Schools is to be retained, then the input needs either to be highly diluted (as with the present government's Assisted Places Scheme) or carefully confined (as in the case of the direct grant schools). It also has to be remembered that the direct grant schools were always a rather special part of independent schooling. Whereas the public boarding schools were traditionally devoted to educating the whole man (Christian gentlemen some would say) the stress upon academic success was stronger in the direct grant schools. Later we shall argue that the direct grant schools were a political buffer between the independent schools and a Labour government so complementing the cultural barrier they had established between boarding schools and the British working class.

If, following Pareto (1968), schooling is to act as a means of incorporating new class elements into ruling elites then we need to know more about the terms that govern this process. Mangan (1981) has argued that the spread of the cult of athleticism in the Victorian and Edwardian public school was in part a response to an internal problem of social control (pp. 22-8). The pre-Victorian public school was a remarkably unruly institution with the boys being left to their own devices for long stretches at a time. With the influx of the bourgeoisie the situation was likely to get out of hand and a means had to be developed whereby all that restless energy could be controlled and channelled. Presumably, and Mangan has less to say about this, the Victorian bourgeoisie was not prepared to entrust its sons to schools that left them to follow their own whims, they feared the consequences. The cult of athleticism developed within the schools and they sold it to the parents (so successfully that many parents were its most ardent advocates) who provided the essential resources if the cult was to flourish. Honey (1977) has argued that the nineteenth century public school pecking order was based upon mutual recognition, in particular the willingness of groups of schools to play games with one another and to exclude those schools they did not consider to be their equals (pp. 252-62). In other words, the schools controlled both their internal status hierarchy and the framework within which class accommodation was to occur.

Elsewhere we have argued that the class accommodation that occurred within the nineteenth century public schools, an accommodation between, 'gentlemen' and 'players', was achieved on the terms of 'the gentlemen'. On further reflection it seems to have been accomplished on the terms of the schools themselves, although within the framework of the compromise package gentlemenly values predominated. The gentlemen may have been required to become 'Christians' and 'classicists' but 'the players' had to foresake the central bourgeois value of aggressive entrepreneurialism or, in short, they were required to become 'gentlemen'. The outcome may have been a mitigation of class conflict but whether the terms of the compromise made the ruling elites any more effective is another matter. Many have argued that at the apparent height of its industrial supremacy the seeds that led to the steady decay of British capitalism were sown i.e. the public schools were turning a hard-headed bourgeoisie into synthetic gentlemen.

In view of the difficulty of maintaining control of their value system if large numbers of working class children were to be incorporated, it is not surprising that the response of the independent sector to the first report (1968) of the Public Schools Commission was so lukewarm. At the heart of their concerns were the very issues we have been discussing: numbers, the kind of pupils to be admitted, over what period of time the change would occur, and what control the schools would have over the process. Of course the official response was tactical rather than negative. Thus the Chairman of the Headmasters' Conference, D.D. Lindsay, stated in his address to the Annual General Meeting of 1968 that:

> There isn't a hope in hell of a 50 per cent start by a few schools, but there is every hope, even with a modest influx of Government money, that we could all make a start. So my plea is simply this: Don't fix an exact percentage to qualify for integration — all our schools are fully prepared to accept a substantial proportion of assisted pupils. Find out the exact nature of the need and how far it is accompanied by a demand for boarding. (p. 7)

In fact the main practical proposal to be subsequently established, the Assisted Places Scheme, selects a limited number of pupils essentially according to their academic ability. It is as good an example of tokenism as one could wish for.

The preoccupation with the part that private schools play in the reproduction of the class structure may be understandable but unfortunately it has almost swamped any consideration of their other social characteristics. As this chapter is concerned with class reproduction the attention we will pay to these other variables is limited but it is our firm belief that it is an important topic and should be more widely researched. That the major public boarding schools have been closely identified with the Anglican Church is clearly exemplified by the fact that for at least much of the nineteenth century their headmasters were invariably also in holy orders. In fact in the eyes of many the schools seemed to be educating Anglican gentlemen rather than Christian gentlemen. However, there are important Methodist, Roman Catholic and Jewish foundations at all levels of the private school hierarchy. If class accommodation was the main social function of the nineteenth century public school then it made sense that this should embrace as many social groups as possible. Mangan's (1981) account of how Stonyhurst, a Jesuit foundation, interpreted the ideology of athleticism makes the point beautifully (pp. 163-4). In pursuance of the same social ends the public school network stretched to the further shores of the United Kingdom. Although there are distinctive national educational traditions within the United Kingdom, the private sector has at the upper reaches of the class structure helped to create a common national culture. Its influence has extended beyond national boundaries with the creation of replicas in most Commonwealth countries, reinforced by the fact that some families send their children to Britain for the express purpose of obtaining a public school education. The 1983 ISIS Survey reveals that 13,211 pupils had non–British parents who lived overseas which represented 3.3 per cent of the total number of pupils in the schools surveyed. Of these approximately one-third (4173) were in schools belonging to the Headmasters' Conference (p. 11).

A fascinating development in recent years has been the increasing tendency of long-established single-sex schools to become co-educational with most of the traffic travelling in the direction of the boys' schools (*Ibid.*, p. 7). As far as the HMC schools are concerned the trend was started by the Headmaster of Marlborough College, John Dancy, with the admission of girls into the sixth-form. The ISIS annual surveys reveal the following increase in their numbers:

Table 3: Boys/Girls in HMC Schools

	No. of schools	Boarders		Day Pupils	
		Boys	Girls	Boys	Girls
1974	207	46,208	1,195	63,295	2,330
1977	210	45,420	1,973	67,871	4,871
1980	209	44,155	3,806	71,063	7,003
1983	210	42,388	4,177	77,605	11,378

Source: Walford, G. (1983), 'Girls in boys' public schools: A prelude to further research', *British Journal of the Sociology of Education*, 4, p. 42.

Accepting girls as pupils widens the social base of the schools without the financial hassles involved in trying to recruit working-class pupils. Dancy claimed that his motivation, besides an interest in broadening the social diversity of Marlborough, was to buttress a change in values that was already underway before the girls arrived. The girls would help to reinforce the new ethos. Many of those who feared that it would perilously weaken the financial base of the girls' schools if HMC schools in general followed in the same direction have pointed to baser economic considerations, although, we hasten to add, not with particular reference to Dancy. The ISIS data show that in the HMC schools that girls, as a proportion of total pupils, increased from 3.1 per cent to 11.5 per cent between 1974 and 1983. So far this has not affected unduly the well-being of the girls' schools as their numbers have held up remarkably well in spite of what some would consider to be poaching. The worry must be for the future if the trend should intensify as demographic changes start to bite.

The establishment of schools for non-Anglican families, or the setting up of schools outside England, raises the question of whether the public schools were able to retain any semblance of an overall identity. Mangan's research, which amongst other schools placed Stonyhurst (a Jesuit foundation) and Loretto (located at Musselburgh outside Edinburgh) under the microscope, answers the question in the affirmative. However, he does demonstrate that the cult of athleticism was interpreted differently from school to school. So, although the public schools may have created a common class culture out of differing social elements, the insider at least would be aware of the nuances which distinguished its varying elements. The motivation to extend the network of schools by embracing an ever wider range of social groups was obviously complex. The sociological observation that there was a need for class accommodation is probably more a reflection on what occurred rather than what was the driving force. Individuals recognized that an expanding middle class required schools for the education of its children and they acted to fill the gap. In some cases the incentive may have been primarily financial but this could coalesce with educational and wider social considerations. Honey (1977) has claimed that Nathaniel Woddard had a vision of creating a national system of education for the middle classes but his purpose was not simply 'to identify the need and devise educational provision for it' for he also saw it is 'as being an opportunity to re-assert the educational authority of the Established Church' (p. 49).

Regardless of how the extension of independent schooling is to be accounted for, once a particular school is founded many vested interests will want to keep it in business. Without incorporating the bourgeoisie not only would the nineteenth century public school system have failed to expand but also the traditional establishments would have slowly withered on the vine. It was essential therefore for the schools to expand their recruitment base if they were to prosper. Contemporarily the independent sector as a whole has been prepared to widen its recruitment net in order to survive. In each case the problems are the same (once the question of who pays the fees has been resolved): how many can be accepted and on whose terms. Assuming that the schools value their identity and their independence, they will want to control both numbers and terms. The real conundrum arises if survival is so precarious that a school has no choice in the matter, i.e. it has to accept whoever is prepared to pay the fees in order to stay afloat. In such circumstances an individual school is exposed to market forces to a degree that it would probably find intolerable. The market would become too demanding as a change mechanism. Of course, like Dancy at Marlborough, social diversity may be encouraged in order to confirm desired internal changes but unless matters are to get out of hand the changes need to be closely monitored. For example, are the HMC schools prepared to become truly coeducational schools in the sense of educating approximately equal numbers of boys and girls? Or to raise a possibly even more frightening scenario — what price survival for a Christian foundation if over half its pupils are the children of foreign nationals and Muslims to boot?!

Examining the Traditional Themes: What are the Schooling Rituals?

In discussing the experience of schooling within the independent sector our focus is the public schools, i.e. traditionally boys' boarding schools, that belong to the Headmasters' Conference, recruit their pupils nationally and are socially exclusive. The most prevailing interest in this topic has been likewise focused for it is these schools above all that have been accused of creating social divisiveness. It is our contention that they form a model for much of the independent sector, that is, where they go others will be required to follow.

In the past the public schools were isolated both physically and socially. Physically because they were inclined to be rather grand institutions, placed in spacious grounds which were set apart from the local community. Socially because they educated a very particular segment of the class hierarchy and kept their pupils free from all possible contaminating social influences. Contact with parents would occur during the holidays (assuming the parents were at home) or on infrequent highly ritualized school occasions for schools distrusted parents especially the over-weaning mother. They could subject their captive clientele to the most peculiar learning process with its intricate rituals of games, the combined cadet force, chapel and the house system run by prefects and serviced by fags. Of course the boys did receive a formal education but through a curriculum heavily biased towards the classics and against practically everything else, especially the applied sciences, the social sciences and the fine arts. The purpose of such a schooling was to isolate the public school product from all but his very immediate class peers and to solidify their common identity or, as we have expressed it earlier, to ingrain within them the idea that they were a leadership class (Salter and Tapper, 1981, pp. 161–78). In a nutshell the traditional goal was to turn out muscular Christian gentlemen. This was the epitome of the private school model, what the world understood by private schooling and what the schools by and large prided themselves on achieving.

It can still be intelligently argued that the public schools intensify social divisiveness by educating a few selected pupils in a very special manner. However, the nature of that very special manner has changed radically, although there is some debate as to when the changes commenced and how far they have proceeded. The schools are less isolated both physically and socially than in the past. Some of them encourage various contacts with the local community: through welfare programmes in which their pupils participate, the leasing of their facilities, and the sharing of activities and resources with neighbouring schools. Families are more difficult to keep at arms' length for today's parents are less willing to delegate to the school the upbringing of their children. The schools have responded by allowing more exeats for home visits and by encouraging the parents to have closer contacts with the school. The automobile has closed the gap between school and home. In a competitive market situation many schools have been forced to sell their wares to parents which has meant making themselves accessible.

Within the schools boys will find that games, the combined cadet force, chapel and the house system are still important. However, the cult of athleticism is dead. Mangan (1981) claims that the Great War marked a turning point, although 'The pressures for change were inexorable in nature but gradual in effect' (p. 207). Nowadays the pupil will be offered a wide range of activities rather than the staple diet of team games. Whereas membership of the combined cadet force was often compulsory now it is voluntary (usually in practice as well as in theory) with those who decline to serve frequently engaging in community welfare activities. Chapel has made something of a comeback since the heady days of the 1960s but the number of compulsory services are limited and it could scarcely be described, as in the past, as the heart of a school. In some schools the house used to be the focus of a boy's loyalty with housemasters exercising considerable control over the selection of pupils (McConnell, 1967, pp. 178–9). It was such customs which helped to perpetuate family dynasties within houses. The strength of the house system has been eroded by a combination of economic factors (it is much cheaper, for example, to have centralized dining services rather than to allow houses to feed their own boys) and a greater concentration of power in the hands of headmasters. There may still be personal fagging but in many schools this has been replaced by boys undertaking house duties, thus further cutting the costs of running the school! Certainly the authority that senior boys once exercised (the prefects invariably were responsible for the day-to-day running of the houses) has waned considerably. Their right to beat smaller boys, which justly received much notorious publicity, is now all but extinct.

These changes in the way that schools are run have been complemented by equally significant developments in the formal organization of knowledge. In recent years the classics have been on the defensive with Greek especially on the wane. As long ago as the late 1960s, the Headmaster of Charterhouse, Van Oss — more in sorrow than anger — wrote (1969): 'The fourth thing we have lost is Greek. Even as late as the early sixties there was one school left where more boys had done some Greek than had done none. That is no longer even remotely possible ... Greek has, vanished from the curriculum like the spring out of the year' (p. 8). Although with reference to his precise point the Headmaster was undoubtedly correct, it does seem that he was sounding somewhat prematurely the knell for the classics. Kalton's (1966) survey of 166 HMC schools revealed that in the 1963 summer 'A' level examinations 114 had entered candidates for Greek and 148 for Latin, and that in forty-nine of the schools Latin was studied by all boys for more than one year after their thirteenth birthday (pp. 104–5).

The classics may be experiencing a lingering death (with a further erosion since Kalton's survey) but the hold of the sciences and mathematics has held firm for the past twenty years. Kalton's data reveal the following specializations at 'A' level of school leavers with at least one 'A' level pass.

Table 4: 'A' level passes: Kalton Survey

	Independent				Direct Grant		
	All Day (%)	Mixed (%) Day	Brd.	All Board (%)	All Day (%)	Mixed (%) Day	Brd.
Science	56	54	47	40	53	48	53
Arts	42	43	48	54	39	44	41
Science/arts	2	3	5	6	8	8	6
Total nos	576	1152	2348	2029	1734	1045	465

Source: Kalton. G. (1966) *The Public Schools: A Factual Survey*, London, Longmans, p. 93.

By comparison the 1983 ISIS Survey of 217 HMC schools indicates that the proportions of pupils taking GCE 'A' level courses is as follows:

Table 5: Take-up of 'A' level courses: 1983 ISIS Survey

	First year of study (%)	Second/later year of study (%)
Science/mathematics	35	37
Other subjects only	37	36
Mixed	28	27
Total numbers	15,163	15,148

The two sets of data, although by no means strictly comparable, reveal a decided shift towards studying a mixture of arts and science subjects in the sixth-form. We can only surmise a greater sensitivity on the part of the pupils (presumably encouraged by the schools) to the changing demands of the job market, thus arts students need to be numerate and it would not be amiss for those intent on pursuing a career in engineering to have taken business studies or economics. Regardless of how this apparent trend is interpreted, it would be an absurd caricature of the contemporary public school to describe its curriculum as either other worldly or classical.

As important as the changed character of the curriculum is the evident pursuit of examination success that pervades the present day public school. The 1983 ISIS Survey reveals that of leavers aged 15 and over on 1 September 1982 only 403 pupils out of 20,867 had left HMC schools without having say any GCE/CSE exams and that 12,328 (59 per cent) went on to a higher education course either in the United Kingdom or overseas (p. 16). This stress on academic success is neither new nor completely all-encompassing. It is a traditional requirement for membership of the Headmasters' Conference that the headmaster's school has a well-established sixth-form with a certain percentage of its pupils proceeding regularly to university. Furthermore, a public school education usually had some vocational merit and even the classics can be defended in such terms. However, it is our contention that the current intensity of the stress on examination success marks a new and distinctive stage in the history of public school education. It is impossible to escape the impression that academic well-being is equated with a school's 'A' level record and the ability of its pupils to win Oxbridge places. Measured in these terms nearly all the schools have succumbed to the pressure.

The advantages of the new experience of schooling offered by the independent sector, and the public schools in particular, are considerable. Judged by the relatively healthy demand for their places it has been approved by parents — besides being assured that their children are well cared for, they believe they are receiving a schooling which will benefit them later in life especially when it comes to looking for a job. Whereas once it was possible for educationalists to claim that the schools were increasingly out of touch with contemporary trends it is now difficult to substantiate this charge. For example, Marlborough College pioneered the 'A' level business studies course as well as being in on the ground floor in the promotion of new ways of teaching mathematics (Barker, 1978). The new ethos strengthens the political case for the private sector. It is much easier to defend private schooling if it is part of well-established educational practice (note the traditional grammar school stress upon academic standards), if it is appealing to a wide segment of society (working-class as well as middle-class parents, according to opinion polls), and it is seen as serving the needs of contemporary society (as curriculum innovations suggest) rather than simply the interests of its own clientele. In the past it was asserted that the public school hold upon top jobs in this society was a direct result of nepotism but the contemporary ability of the schools to compete effectively in public examinations undermines this charge. In other words, to express the point in sociological terms, the schools may still be crucial to the process of class reproduction, but they perform the task in a more legitimate fashion.

But the new model is not without its critics. There is a certain amount of nostalgia for the past, not only for the values it represented but also because it was an age of stability (Hodgkinson, 1966). Some have been worried by the pace of change for constant flux makes it hard to develop a secure value system. For all its weaknesses the classical public school world had a clear view of the social order, a model of the educated man, and an ardent faith in its ability to relate these to each other through the experience of schooling it offered. What impact have these changes had upon the moral and social integration of ruling elites (that is Meisel's coherence and consciousness)? It is impossible to make definitive statements but one would have thought that the old feelings of social solidarity (nurtured by team games, house spirit and a sense of community) have been eroded by the contemporary emphasis on personal achievement whether it be in terms of examination success, community service or athletic endeavour. Whereas in the past public schools trained a class of leaders (with a tendency to be suspicious of eccentrics, those with specialized, especially intellectual, gifts, and charismatic figures) the present stress is upon producing an elite of merit, that is gifted individuals rather than a class of leaders. The consequence is an inevitable fracturing of social and moral solidarity intensified by the fact that a public school education represents a declining percentage of an individual's formal training. The more institutional diversification that the individual experiences during his educational career then the greater the difficulty in ensuring the continuity of socializing experiences.

Examining the Traditional Themes: Links to the Ruling Class

A large number of surveys have shown that most factions of the British ruling class are dominated by the products of the public schools (Boyd, 1973; Glennerster and Pryke, 1973). As significant as the figures may appear it must be kept firmly in mind that they represent only a small percentage of pupils who have been educated privately or indeed in public schools and most pupils are destined for the more modest ranks of the bourgeoisie. Moreover, even if there is a statistical link between occupational status and schooling, it is difficult to substantiate the claim that schooling exercises an independent influence, i.e. there is a causal relationship (Tapper and Salter, 1984). The public school system that developed in Victorian/Edwardian England showed a marked distaste for entrepreneurial values. Christian gentlemen were supposed to shun trade. If one lacked the personal resources to be a gentleman of leisure then it was considered far preferable to enter government service, one of the professions, the church or the armed services rather than to soil ones hands in industry.

All that we have said about the changing experience of schooling within the public schools suggests that they are highly pragmatic institutions. Their continued well-being is dependent upon their ability to attract a sufficient number of parents who are prepared to pay the fees. Their appeal must wane if expanding segments of the ruling class remain closed to their pupils for the end result would be ossification and decay. The subjects studied by today's sixth-formers in HMC schools suggest an awareness of the realities of the job market. A point which is reinforced by their choice of courses at the degree/HND level. The Independent Schools Careers Organization (ISCO) surveys of HMC school leavers for the past twenty years show that engineering is consistently the most attractive field of study and employment with economics and business studies coming second since 1976, and science dropping from second to third place in that year where it has remained ever since (ISCO, 1983, pp. 22–3).

Table 6: Course of study for HMC school leaves, entering higher education, 1 September 1982

	University courses (%)		Degree courses elsewhere (%)		HND courses (%)	
	Boys	Girls	Boys	Girls	Boys	Girls
Engineering/technology	18	4	17	2	19	1
Medicine	8	9	2	7	1	16
Science	21	17	13	12	19	6
All other subjects	52	70	68	79	61	77
Total numbers	8,276	895	1,852	247	621	61

Source: ISIS (1983) *Annual Census*, p. 16.

One explanation of why independent school pupils do well in the competition for top jobs is that they are expected to do well. The schools have high expectations, and it is assumed that the pupils will realize the schools' and their own ambitions. But self-confidence alone is not enough. The links between school and the process of job selection must be such as to enable that self-confidence to be realized. The existence of an old boy network that pervades the upper echelons of British society has been widely discussed. Thus personal contacts, or perhaps even a simple faith that certain school experiences have an enduring quality, oil the wheels of privilege. The assumed existence of such networks and associated values not only encourages some to apply for high status jobs it also discourages others even though they may possess the minimum formal qualifications. Moreover some job openings may never come to the attention of those who are not members of the network which communicates their availability. Such networks are usually based upon informal contacts and shared values although in some cases they can be institutionalized. Thus special relationships were established between some public schools and individual Oxbridge colleges through the system of closed scholarship. Since these are susceptible to the charge that they are an unacceptable form of privilege then it is possible that the informal links, based on the old boy network, have been refurbished. As formal links are broken so informal ties could be strengthened.

The shared value system that bound the individual members of the network together was usually assumed rather than explicitly stated. The glue was a cultural style in its broadest sense. It must be evident that increasingly the link between schooling and occupational status, at least with reference to the establishing of a career, is the narrow and explicit measure of academic attainment (Gray *et al.*, 1983, pp. 115–30).

This does not mean that the wider benefits of a private education are altogether redundant. As Dancy (1963) notes, '. . . whatever industry is thought to *need* what it in fact *wants* is the public school product', and by way of elaboration he claims that 'many of the qualities of personality that the critics object to in public schools are those which are most sought after in modern industry' (pp. 95–6). In its evidence to the Public Schools Commission, the Confederation of British Industry confirmed Dancy's observation: 'the public school tends to bring out at an early age the qualities of leadership, self-reliance, self-confidence, and self-discipline' (Public Schools Commission, 1968b, p. 228). But as important as these expressive values may be there are few careers for which they would be a sufficient, even if they are a necessary, qualification.

Individuals possess, independently of their schooling, different kinds of resources that help them to establish a career. Furthermore, career success is likely to be the consequence of the ownership of particular resources; that is, different careers impose different demands. The public schools, especially at the Clarendon end of the market, brought together a group of individuals whose families were wealthy, — they had economic capital, and who were well-connected socially, — they had social capital, or in colloquial language they were members of an old boy network before ever setting foot in school. For social outsiders (well-heeled but parvenus) schooling presented an opportunity to obtain social capital, whereas for the insiders it was a means by which an already existing network could be both maintained and extended. If private schooling were abolished it would prove difficult to recreate an institutional framework that cemented social capital as conveniently. The maintained schools would undoubtedly disperse the critical individuals far too widely and the Oxbridge colleges probably exercise their influence too late in the life cycle to perform such a function effectively. Furthermore the Oxbridge experience is available to only a part of the ruling class, and is less all embracing. Moreover there are simply too many outsiders at the universities, although presumably specialized networks can be created within the institutions centred, for example, around some colleges rather than others.

The distinctive contribution of the public schools to the individual's career, other than providing a context for the interchange of social capital, was the imparting of the essential cultural style. At one time this meant turning out well-rounded Christian gentlemen whereas now the emphasis is upon making sure that pupils leave with good formal academic qualifications and have at least started to develop their own particular talents. The ethos of the former direct grant schools has spread throughout the independent sector. This is the price that the schools have to pay if they wish to retain their well-established links to other elite institutions (and Oxbridge is especially critical) and thus to better ensure their continuing domination of the British ruling class.

Accounting for Change

We have been arguing two related points in this chapter: if one examines the world of independent schooling rather than simply the public schools then the gulf, in terms of several variables, between the maintained and private sectors of schooling is not as great as often supposed, and in any case the character of the public school system has changed in several important respects in recent years. Nonetheless it is still realistic to think in terms of a heterogeneous private sector with the public schools at the apex of the system. But the manner in which they perform their function of class reproduction is undoubtedly different. In the past the public schools ensured that ruling elites in Britain had a high degree of moral and social integration, so much so that their domination of the ruling class seemed positively conspiratorial. With a much longer period of formal schooling, with increased significance attached to higher education, then the nature of the social control function has inevitably changed. Of great significance is the growth of an individualistic and competitive ethos within the schools themselves. In view of this it is much more difficult for schooling to ensure either moral or social integration. What we have seen is the move from the reproduction of a ruling class to the reproduction of elite groups which have been selectively recruited and then subjected to specialized socializing experiences (Bottomore, 1965, p. 57). The recruitment and socializing channels of elite education incorporate in a complex hierarchy the best state primary schools, preparatory schools, ex-direct grant schools, some of the remaining grammar schools, perhaps a few very special comprehensive schools and sixth-form colleges, many of the HMC schools, the better minor public schools, the Oxbridge colleges and one or two of the provincial and Scottish university departments.

Assuming that the private sector has evolved along the lines described in this chapter then the next problem is now to account for these changes. Given that the schools are intent on perpetuating themselves then their first concern must be to maintain a viable recruitment base, for without sufficient pupils they will simply fade away. One is forced inevitably to return to the question of why it is that parents are prepared to purchase private schooling on behalf of their children. It is our contention that the limited evidence suggests that most parents are highly pragmatic. They believe private schooling is more likely than the maintained sector to provide their children with those resources that are the best guarantee of successful careers. The parents, therefore, are essentially interested in class reproduction and not forms of schooling. These can be determined by the schools and parents will not intervene as long as they believe that those forms of schooling will give their children the desired resources. Intervention when it occurs will invariably mean parents looking for other schools which they imagine can deliver the goods.

The central premise of the above argument is that private schools are in a marketplace in which parental choice determines their success or failure. Even if this is true not all schools will feel the pressures of the marketplace equally. A few have income independent of fees but more importantly some have been in existence for a very long period of time, thus demonstrating their capacity to garner sufficient parental support to survive. Marketplace pressures may continue to cause anxieties but the proven ability to generate the necessary demand must instill the confidence to do likewise in the future. Halsey argues that some public schools have little incentive to expand in response to increased demand. They wish to remain highly selective as this enables them to perpetuate more easily their cherished educational values (Halsey *et al.*, 1984, pp. 10–17). But it is a fact that even the most prestigious of schools has varied in size over time and more than one ex-HMC headmaster has revealed to us that in the early 1960s their schools struggled to fill the last few places. Presumably if the top schools are in fact turning parents away, which is undoubtedly the case today, then those parents are moving down market. Parental choice is thus a more pressing matter for schools which are less certain of their level of demand and one would expect them to respond to direct parental wishes with some alacrity.

The relatively privileged position of a few top schools (and there are probably no more than a couple of dozen) owes much to their longevity and traditional high status. Assuming (again in comparison to the rest of the private sector) that demand for the schooling they offer has always been buoyant then why should they have changed? Either they have been skilful at anticipating future parental demands and have changed accordingly, fearing that otherwise full numbers would soon evaporate, or they have been responding to other pressures. It is our contention that if these schools wish to retain their position in the marketplace then it is vital for them to maintain the links they have established with other elite institutions. What makes them top schools are their ties to the Oxbridge colleges, Sandhurst, Dartmouth, the Inns of Court, the medical schools, the civil service and their ilk. It is the belief of parents that purchasing private schooling will enable their children to gain access to these institutions that accounts for the ability of the schools to survive. The most prestigious schools have to respond to the requirements of these institutions if they wish to ensure that the links remain in good working order.

Whereas most independent schools experience parental demands in a direct fashion the traditionally high status schools are more cushioned from such pressure. They know that as long as they hold on to their position in the class reproduction process their places will be filled. The two constraints are not, however, mutually exclusive, for parents like schools are conscious of the resources children must possess if they are to have successful careers. The general emphasis upon examination success is therefore a consequence of similar demands being made by both parents (and many HMC schools will be very aware of their expectations) and the elite institutional network. Mutually reinforcing messages are coming from both the schools' clients and those institutions whose exclusiveness persuades parents to become clients in the first place.

If top schools are part of an institutional network then they are well-placed to make their influence widely felt as well as having to respond to the pressures of that network. Likewise, parents will not simply dictate to schools but rather will interact with them which means give and take on both sides. Mangan (1981) argued that the cult of athleticism was highly appropriate in the Victorian and Edwardian eras because a significant percentage of public school pupils would end up serving in the colonies (pp. 135–9). It hardly follows, however, that athleticism was promoted because the Colonial Office or Sandhurst believed that this was the best means of ensuring that colonial officials or army officers would be able to cope with the job. Indeed it could be argued that the lines of influence were in fact reversed, i.e. the public schools determined the style in which the Colonial Office and the army would conduct its business. Mangan's own study reveals that athleticism was encouraged within the public schools to resolve an internal problem of social control and, according to Honey, the structure of inter-school competitions — that is who would play with whom —

was the critical means by which the system determined its internal status hierarchy.

Obviously the lines of influence between parents, schools and the institutional network have always been complex but it is our contention that the schools have become increasingly the dependent partners. Although the more secure schools may still be able to dictate to parents (for example, are the lavish facilities which now prevail — with the concomitant fee increases — more a consequence of parental demand or of the schools selling the parents an image of what their child's school should look like?) they are now minor partners in the network of elite institutions. This is because those elite institutions have been steadily restructured by a bureaucratic state apparatus (in fact some of them are part of the state apparatus) and governments which are politically and culturally unsympathetic to the traditional public school ethos. They have either been forced to change as a result of government intervention or have mended their ways in order to forestall it. Either the public schools responded in similar terms by basing their experience of schooling on a cultural style centred upon certification or they simply faded away for want of parental support.

As the independent sector in general has become more socially heterogeneous so it has grown culturally and politically more united. The cultural convergence is a result of the spread of the academic ethos and the fact that, as the schools are no longer socially isolated, they are less able to resist wider cultural trends. In cultural terms they respond to trends rather than create a distinctive upper-class cultural style. Their political cooperation is necessitated by the threat to their existence that the Labour party poses. It is manifested in both institutional amalgamation and the espousal of the over-arching themes of independence and selection. Whatever else may divide the independent sector the latter have proven potent rallying cries. But class reproduction — *as always* — goes on.

4   *The Charitable Status of Private Schooling**

Introduction

The comparatively small body of literature on the charitable status of private schooling concentrates almost exclusively upon the accruing financial benefits. The protagonists reach differing estimates with the intention of demonstrating either how substantial a subsidy this is to independent schools or how the relatively small input is more than offset by the amount of money the private sector saves the taxpayer. Although this is undoubtedly an important issue, it is yet another example of how a potentially rich field of analysis has been confined to rather narrow territory. Our interest in why the private schools are legally deemed to pursue charitable purposes opens up the nature of the debate. It is our contention that charitable status has never been simply a means of cushioning the independent schools from the effects of taxation, as critical as this may be to their well-being. Charitable status is an integral part of a broad support system for the private sector, in Marxist terms it is a concrete manifestation of its hegemonic supremacy. It is especially important because Parliament has never legislated on the meaning of charity and neither has it defined what constitutes a charitable purpose; it has left the courts to resolve these issues. Given the powerful tradition in Britain that the judicial process should not be subject to political pressure, and the fact that the administration of charitable status is undertaken by the Charity Commissioners within the guidelines set by established case law, it is virtually impossible to influence which institutions should or should not be accorded charitable status by direct political means. What is required is legislation. It has

* Court cases cited in this chapter are listed in the bibliography under court cases.

been widely argued that this is a reasonable — even necessary — state of affairs but what must be equally obvious is that it constitutes a powerful defence of established practice.

Private schooling works within a framework of legal and administrative boundaries that are subject to varying degrees and forms of state pressure. The more favourable those boundaries are to the interests of private schooling, and the more difficult it is to alter them, then the more secure the independent sector must feel in facing the future. Charitable status has up to now formed one such secure boundary and to breach it would mean not simply the loss of the tangible benefits that accrue from it but would also signify that the enemy was perhaps capable of winning the war as well as a battle. The opposition to private schooling probably realizes that the ending of charitable status may cause the schools little more than irritating financial problems but it may not realize how important a symbolic victory it would be. If charitable status goes does anything sacred remain? Or expressed differently the state will have demonstrated its capacity to regulate the independent sector so tightly that it may be no longer necessary to prohibit the charging of fees — slow strangulation rather than abolition by stealth could be the order of the day.

It is necessary to say at the outset that although the legal basis of educational charities makes for fascinating analysis both the political attack and defence are disappointing. The attack has concentrated heavily on one point, that is because independent schooling has an essentially middle-class clientele it has forfeited its right to charitable status. In other words, the concern is with who benefits from the charitable status rather than why certain activities are considered to be charitable. The reason for this is obvious for most of those who want the charitable status of the private sector to be rescinded believe that education *is* a charitable purpose if a school has 'the right kind of pupils'. This may make political sense but it rather limits the opportunities for analysis. Moreover, it is not without its political drawbacks for it suggests some equivocation in the attack on charitable status (what is the precise target and why has it been singled out for special treatment?). On the other hand the defence of charitable status has hidden behind the legal status quo and has been inclined to reiterate what is known rather than to explore the subtleties and uncertainties behind the established order. Again this is political common sense for why provide the enemy with ammunition, but again it limits the scope for analysis.

Besides being a special part of the private sector's defence system charitable status can also be used to counter the charge that independent schooling has negative social effects. The major complaint is that private schools are socially divisive institutions and yet charities have a positive image for they are generally believed to perform socially useful tasks. Although the opponents of private schooling dispute this, it is more difficult for them to propagate their charge in view of the official position. Even if they succeed in persuading many that the official ideology is in fact wrong, without a concomitant change in the legal view it remains comparatively easy for the interests that support private schooling to legitimate their behaviour. This is not to say that if charitable status were rescinded those interests would suddenly be converted. Obviously not, but what would change would be their ability to seek comfort from the law, and furthermore it would be a clear manifestation that they were losing the ideological, as well as the political struggle. Powerful interests need to legitimate their behaviour to themselves as well as their fellow citizens and the law can make this task easier. As is to be expected, the proponents of private schooling do not, and in fact could not, accept that the independent sector is socially divisive.

Although the above argument may sound logical, even trite, it is difficult to track down actual examples to substantiate it. This is mainly because it is so much a part of accepted practice for individuals to act as if the established legal framework were reasonable rather than think constantly in terms of the principles that form the basis of the law. Naturally this is especially true when the law is conducive to the furtherance of one's own interests! In relation to the specific goals of this chapter the point can best be illustrated by some of the cross-examination of representatives of the Independent Schools Joint Committee (ISJC) by members of the Expenditure Committee (Education, Arts and Home Office Sub-Committee) in preparation for the report entitled *Charity Commissioners and their Accountability* (Expenditure Committee, 1975). The representatives of ISJC were asked various questions as to why the private schools should have charitable status. Sir Desmond Lee (ex-Headmaster of Winchester College and very experienced in educational politics) replied: 'If we are asked why we should have charitable status, the answer surely is that education is a charitable purpose, therefore institutions which are providing education are fulfilling a charitable purpose; if the definition of "charitable purpose" were to change then clearly that might change as well (*Ibid.*, p. 259). Later in reply to a question by Christopher Price, MP, (who waged long-term guerilla warfare within Parliament against private schools and their charitable status in particular) Sir Desmond reiterated the very same point: 'I think what you are saying is it (i.e. the provision of education) ought not to be a charitable purpose unless the relief of need is included also. With respect, I think the lawyers would probably be on my side' (*Ibid.*, p. 262). An observation with which Christopher Price concurred.

Sir Desmond's comments represent a classical use of the prevailing legal position as a defence mechanism, and — revealing a personality which suggested a taste for clarity and certainty — he concluded: 'If you want to alter the law, after all, you are the law-giving authority of the country, it is up to you' (*Ibid.*, p. 262). Not surprisingly Christopher Price terminated such an unrewarding line of enquiry and chose to open up the issue, which fortunately proved more fruitful. He drew the conclusion that: 'What I gauge from you is that you seem to value your charitable status not so much from the point of view of the financial advantage which you get out of it, but for other reasons — almost, I may say, status reasons. Is that true?' (*Ibid.*, p. 266). In reply Lord Belstead, the Chairman of ISJC, said that he feared that to remove charitable status from private schooling would have the effect that other institutions, pursuing goals which he valued, would also lose it (*Ibid.*, p. 266). Lord Belstead was conscious of the fact that it would be difficult to remove charitable status from private schooling without redefining the established legal understanding of charitable purposes and that the problem simply could not be approached from the perspective of 'who benefits' alone. In the process, however, he divulged — albeit in a roundabout fashion — why charitable status is so important to the private sector. Charitable status is accorded to institutions that many consider pursue valuable goals and there is an obvious spillover effect whereby the good deeds of one charity embalm the general image which embraces them all. It is an accolade which is desired not so much for status reasons as for ideological and ultimately political reasons.

If the central purpose of the chapter is to analyze the legal basis of charitable status (i.e. why the private schools have it as opposed to why they desire it) then the subsidiary goals follow as a matter of course. The legal expression of hegemony is only as secure as its concomitant administrative base and the chapter will examine the ability of the administrative apparatus to defend the legal understanding of charitable status. The legal and administrative framework within which charitable status has been enveloped affects the political attempts to redefine its scope and the chapter will need to consider the interaction between the political pressures for change and the legal/administrative forces that perpetuate established interpretations of the law of charity. Finally, the chapter will conclude with a brief analysis of the traditional interest in the financial advantages that charitable status bestows upon private schooling. Our concern is not with those financial benefits per se but rather we want to assess the likely socio-political consequences were charitable status to be withdrawn. Should the political attack upon charitable status succeed in the narrow sense that charitable status is rescinded would this then achieve the wider goal of destabilizing the private sector?

Private Schooling: The Legal Basis of Charitable Status

Central to the case that private schools should be denied charitable status is the belief that this represents a subsidy to families that are comparatively affluent. In its customary highminded tone the First Report of the Public Schools Commission argued that: 'It is difficult to see a truly charitable purpose in relieving parents who can pay school fees of £500 a year or more of part of the economic cost of their children's education. It is right that parents should be free to pay school fees if they wish, but not right that they should, without good reason, be relieved by the Exchequer or local authorities of part of the true cost of what they are buying' (Public Schools Commission, 1968a, p. 160). Often the language of the attack is more colourful and the targets more precise and emotive. Thus in a parliamentary debate William Hamilton (MP for Fife, Central), pursuing one of his customary scents, exclaimed that

> It is nonsense that private fee-paying schools — including Eton and Winchester, and Gordonstoun in Scotland — should be regarded as charities and be able to reap enormous tax and rate benefits from the taxpayers and the ratepayer. Children at those schools are almost invariably from wealthy families. They are certainly not from families in the bottom quarter of the incomes groupings. For those children to be subsidized by the taxpayer and the ratepayer is an indefensible obscenity. (Hansard, 16 April 1981, Columns 454–5)

Although it is reasonable to object to Hamilton's notion that taxes not imposed as a consequence of charitable status represent a subsidy to the fee-paying schools (as if the state has a right to extract taxation), it nonetheless must seem an anomaly to many that private schools have charitable status. In the words of the Public Schools Commission is there 'good reason' why this should be so? At present it is sufficient good reason that the law sanctions it, which to the objectors is an argument for changing the law. The attack upon the charitable status of private schools should be based upon a case for restricting the scope of charitable purposes so that either schooling per se is not included or only included if the beneficiaries of that schooling comprise a special category of persons. For example, if charitable status is removed from private schools except those that, let us say, provide an education for children from either poor families (that is by means of scholarships) or are handicapped then their claim would not rest on the grounds that schooling is a charitable purpose but that to relieve need or handicap is. But that is not the present law and the private schools' case for charitable status is disarmingly simple — to requote Sir Desmond Lee, '... education is a charitable purpose, therefore, institutions which are providing education are fulfilling a charitable purpose...' (Expenditure Committee, 1975, p. 259). As we shall see the legal position is not quite that straightforward but it is not very far from it.

The fact that charitable purpose has such a long-established legal basis gives its recipients considerable security. It is a well tried and tested manifestation of hegemony which is controlled by a very special group of intellectuals — judges and law lords. Although others may venture opinions these members of the legal profession have exercised exclusive control over this knowledge area. Whereas they usually interpret or translate the wishes of Parliament, in this field they are the ultimate masters for they define what constitutes a charitable purpose. Most commentators trace back the legal definition of charitable purposes to at least the Statute of Elizabeth, 1601. In the preamble to the Statute various charitable activities are listed including the provision of goods and money for '... schools of learning, free schools and scholars in universities...' (Nightingale, 1973, p. 38). In 1805 Sir Samuel Romilly formulated a four-fold classification of charitable purposes that was clearly derived from the list laid down in the 1601 preamble:

> There are four objects, within one of which all charity, to be administered in this Court, must fall: 1st relief of the indigent; in various ways: money: provisions: education: medical assist-ance; etc.: 2dly, the advancement of learning: 3dly, the advance-ment of religion; and 4thly, which is the most difficult, the advancement of objects of general public utility. (Morice v. Bishop of Durham (1805) 10 Ves 532)

In 1891 Lord Macnaghten reaffirmed Romilly's four categories in what appears to be the last serious attempt, that is within the context of a court case, to establish an overall definition of charity: '"Charity" in its legal sense comprises four principal divisions: trusts for the relief of poverty; trusts for the advancement of education; trusts for the advancement of religion; and trusts for other purposes beneficial to the community, not falling under any of the preceding heads' (Income Tax Special Purposes Courts v. Pemsel (1891) A.C. 583).

And there the matter seems to rest although in 1952 the Nathan Committee (whose task was to examine 'the law and practice relating to charitable trusts') urged that the meaning of charity should be redefined while 'preserving the case law as it stands' (Committee on the Law and Practice Relating to Charitable Trusts 1952, p. 36). In fact the 1960 Charities Act, which was a consequence of the Nathan Committee's report and which provides the main legal guidelines for contemporary charities, refrained from so doing and instead reiterated the established formula: '. . . "charity" means any institution, corporate or not, which is established for charitable purposes and is subject to the control of the High Court in the exercise of the court's jurisdiction with respect to charities' (Gladstone, 1982, p. 46). Therefore, for literally centuries the influence of the Statute of Elizabeth has been paramount and even today many authorities would see its preamble as the basic classification of charitable purposes.

The apparently clear-cut legal position is complicated somewhat by two additional considerations. For an educational trust to be granted charitable status it 'must be for the benefit of a sufficient section of the community'. (Halsbury's *Laws of England*, 1974, p. 322) which begs the questions of what constitutes a section of the community and how substantial it must be to be deemed sufficient. The question of what constitutes a section of the community has been decided on an ad hoc empirical basis. So that 'gifts for the education of named persons, or for the education of employees or of children of employees or former employees of a limited company' are not charitable whereas 'gifts for the education of special classes of persons forming a section of the community, such as women and girls who are not self-supporting, or the daughters of missionaries, or persons professing particular religious doctrines, or the employees in the whole of a particular industry' are charitable (*ibid.*). The dividing line appears to depend upon how private in nature is the relationship between the beneficiaries of a trust; the less private it is the more likely that charitable status will be granted. Where the precise line is to be drawn no one can be sure for as Lord Simonds remarked in the case of Oppenheim v. Tobacco Securities Trust Co.

Ltd., '. . . this time a question is asked to which no wholly satisfactory answer can be given' (Oppenheim v. Tobacco Securities Trust Co. Ltd. (1951) A.C. 305). If charitable status were to be withdrawn from private schooling this could become a more pressing question for it is possible that institutions that retained charitable status would wish to endow independent schools. Would the beneficiaries form a sufficient section of the community so that the funding body could retain its charitable status?

More central to the charitable status of private schooling is the size of the section of the community that benefits from it. Given the fees that are charged, especially for boarding places in the public schools, it is hardly surprising that most of their pupils are the children of middle-class parents. The layman may feel that if the clients are so restricted this cannot qualify as benefitting a sufficient section of the community. Again no wholly satisfactory answer can be given but the courts have for the best part of two centuries ruled in favour of the schools. The trend was established in 1827 in the case of the Attorney General v. The Earl of Lonsdale in which Sir John Leach argued that 'The institution of a school for the sons of gentlemen is not, in popular language, a charity; but in the view of the Statute of Elizabeth, all schools for learning are so to be considered . . .' (Attorney General v. Lonsdale (1827) 1. Sim. 109). Although this is a disputable interpretation of the 1601 Statute, the courts have since then consistently upheld the charitable status of schools that charge economic fees to cover their costs. It is now so much a part of legal convention that in 1951 one presiding judge was moved to comment:

> The other attack which is made by the counsel for the Minister on the charitable nature of the trust deed is of a more general nature, and, as it seems to me, *it is rather a startling proposition* . He contends that an educational trust or an educational purpose is not charitable unless it be for the promotion of education for persons who pay less than the full value of the services which they receive. That seems to me a proposition that might at one time have been acceptable to the courts, *but it is several centuries out of date* '. (The Abbey, Malvern Wells, Ltd. v. Ministry of Local Government and Planning (1951) 2 All E.R. 160, stress added)

Such sentiments must seem outrageous to those who consider the charitable status of private schools to be a moral affront.

To some the charitable status of private schooling seems to be dependent upon a long-established possible misinterpretation of the Statute of Elizabeth. However the case could be reinforced by the advocacy of a broad understanding of the concept of benefit, and occasionally the courts have hinted that they would be prepared to adopt this line of argument. Only a comparatively small section of the community benefits directly from private schooling but the *indirect* benefits, depending upon your point of view, are universal. If private schools save the Exchequer revenue then it is a boon to taxpayers and the quality of the schooling may raise the general level of culture and knowledge. To reason thus is to imply that charities must always benefit a sufficient section of the community; a point made explicitly by Lord Macnaghten in his famous 1891 judgment. Immediately following his reformulation of the four main divisions of charity he added that, 'The trusts last referred to are not the less charitable in the eye of the law, because incidentally they benefit the rich as well as the poor, as indeed every charity that deserves the name must do either directly or indirectly' (Income Tax Special Purposes Court v. Pemsel (1591) A.C. 583). The law of charity can therefore be interpreted in a manner which challenges those who view private schooling negatively. It is a 'startling proposition' to claim that schools charging economic fees should be denied charitable status for (to use Macnaghten's addendum) the public at large benefits from their presence. This is as clear an illustration that legal interpretations are part of a wider ideological struggle and that they give comfort to particular parties within the accompanying political struggle.

If the legal position concerning the charitable status of educational trusts is complicated first by the need to answer the question as to whether they benefit a sufficient section of the community then the second qualifying condition is that they must be non-profit making institutions. There are many independent schools that are the private property of their headteachers who, like most entrepreneurs, are interested in making profits. It is somewhat ironic that the prestige end of the private school market, the public schools that belong to the Headmasters' Conference, are covered by charitable status whereas many less socially exclusive establishments do not qualify. It is possible for schools with charitable status to make profits (i.e. their income exceeds their costs) but as long as the income is 'applied for charitable purposes only' then they are exempt from taxation and the full payment of rates. Presumably if the income was not used for charitable purposes then it could be taxed. If this were to continue the charitable status of the school would be threatened because it would be pursuing objectives inconsistent with what the courts have deemed to be a charity. One strategy for changing the law would be to allow the schools to retain their charitable status (some charters in fact require them to be charities, and this strategy would have the advantage of retaining schooling per se as a charitable purpose) but not exempting them from tax and rate payments. Two categories of charitable purpose would be created, one carrying exemption from taxation the other not (Gladstone, 1982, pp. 67-71). Of course the end result might be simply an accountant's paradise as the schools juggled their books to lessen their tax liability.

Regardless of what the future may hold the present position on the charitable status of educational trusts is relatively concise and straight-forward: non-profit making institutions that provide schooling to the benefit of a sufficient section of the community are entitled to charitable status. Understandably the courts have not attempted to impose a narrow definition of schooling which further restricts the grounds for attacking the charitable status of private schools. Until the law is changed it seems immune to danger.

Although our overall conclusion is that the law as it stands is clear and firm, this is not to deny that beneath this tough exterior some important equivocations have occurred. As the House of Commons Select Sub-committee noted, 'A problem confronting the layman who endeavours to understand the law relating to charity is that there is no statutory definition of the word'. This dilemma is compounded by the widespread belief (in which many eminent legal minds concur) that there is a distinction between the legal and commonsense understandings of charity. The legal understanding is defined by the case history of the concept of charitable purposes which allows for change as witnessed by Sir John Leach's possible misinterpretation in 1827 of the Statute of Elizabeth. The commonsense understanding is likewise flexible but, according to Lord Halsbury (1974) in the Pemsel case, charity 'always does involve the relief of poverty' (p. 552). But the commonsense understanding of other equally worthy citizens can encompass a definition of charity in which the relief of poverty is not a paramount consideration. This is why there have been no statutory pronouncements and Parliament has permitted us to be guided by the legal or technical definition.

In such a jungle it is to be expected that legal minds would clash. Lord Halsbury was prepared for the legal understanding of charitable purpose to follow closely his own interpretation of the commonsense definition, and yet it was in the very same case that Lord Macnaghten formulated his four-fold classification of charitable purposes which eventually carried the day. But Lord Halsbury was by no means a lone voice for in a supporting judgment Lord Bramwell argued that: 'I think a charitable purpose is where assistance is given to the bringing up, feeding, clothing, lodging, and education of those who from poverty, or comparative poverty, stand in need of such assistance... This definition is probably insufficient. It very likely would not include some charitable purposes, though I cannot think what, and include some not charitable, though also I cannot think what; but I think it substantially correct, ...' (*Ibid.*, 564–5). Lord Bramwell maintained that the preamble to the Statute of Elizabeth went beyond the title of the Statute itself and it should not therefore carry the significance previously ascribed to it. Indeed much that was described as charitable behaviour could more realistically be seen as acts of benevolence.

In the very case therefore that justly comprises one of the great landmarks of charity law two of the law Lords are prepared to redefine the legal definition of charitable purposes and Lord Macnaghten's judgment prevails by a four to two margin. To examine the history of charity law is to witness conflicts within courts and between courts and although this may be integral to the process of lawmaking, it is at odds with the air of finality that pervades the eventual outcome. Those who would rest their case on what the law says (like Sir Desmond Lee) would do well to ponder the fragility of their position. In the case of Oppenheim v. Tobacco Securities Trust Co. Ltd. (in which incidentally the law Lords were also split over the question of what comprises a sufficient section of the community) the unease of the lawmakers is manifested clearly in the words of Lord Simonds. In the course of his judgment he remarked, 'No one who has been versed for many years in this difficult and very artificial branch of the law can be unaware of its illogicalities...' (p. 307). Such sentiments must encourage those who believe the law of charity is a suitable case for reform.

In fairness to Sir Desmond Lee he is very aware of the potency of the political threat to the charitable status of private schooling. The private sector's defence of its charitable status has not rested on a simple-minded reiteration of the formal legal position. Besides conducting a sophisticated political campaign it has also presented its case in terms of the legal debate which is all the more effective in view of its sensitivity to potential weaknesses. The key issue is whether independent schools benefit a sufficient section of the community. For example, although the highly regarded Goodman Committee (formed by the National Council of Social Services to examine *Charity Law and*

Voluntary Organisations) reported (1976) that 'It would be remarkable if at this time when education is so widely regarded as one of the main foundations on which civilized life depends — let alone economic life in a technological age — advancement of education were to be withdrawn from the ambit of charity', (p. 25) it was subsequently prepared to make the recommedation that, 'In regard to education the new test of "purposes beneficial to the community" should only admit to charitable status those institutions whose educational systems cater for a range of clear educational needs throughout the whole community' (*Ibid.*, pp. 128–9). It would indeed be foolish for those interests supporting private schooling to ignore such equivocation from those essentially sympathetic to their cause. In fact it has been recognized by some that educational practices within the private sector need to be changed if legal hegemony is to be maintained. The response has been varied: the schools cater for many children who have special educational needs, they offer specialist subjects that are increasingly unavailable in the maintained sector, they have been in the forefront of curriculum innovation, and they have extended the scholarships and bursaries they offer (ISIS, 1983b).

The problem with trying to demonstrate that the schools are indeed satisfying a range of community needs is that it is an open-ended commitment. What may be considered as sufficiently benevolent by some may be evaluated as mere diversionary tactics by others. The granting of charitable status could become a mere bargaining chip in a wider political struggle. Tim Devlin, former National Director of the Independent Schools Information Service (ISIS), has written (1983): 'Within the next 10 years independent schools would be wise to devise some machinery by which each school individually can earn and justify any funds it receives from the public purse. It would be a small price to pay for a place in the mainstream of education and for immunity from party political attack' (p. 4). Rather than buying immunity it may in fact simply intensify the political pressure. For example, would Devlin approve of Maurice Kogan's (1984) suggestion that the present government should '. . . make a majority of parent governors a condition of registration and charitable status for the independent schools'? (p. 4). Charity law may be confusing but to move in this proposed direction could create a madhouse. Either schooling is a charitable purpose or it is not; if it is then the conditions attached to maintaining that status should be clear and simple. To do otherwise is to admit tacitly that schooling is not a charitable purpose and that the law should be changed accordingly. Furthermore, to argue that schools need to earn their charitable status by conducting their business in a prescribed manner (for example, by establishing closer links with maintained schools, or opening their facilities to the community) is to mistake the basis of the present legal position. Schools are charities essentially because of the goal they pursue, i.e. transmitting knowledge, and not because of the way they function — with the sole exception that they must be non-profit making bodies.

A fascinating aspect of the refurbishing of the private schools' legal hegemony is the appeal to international law. Article 2 of Protocol No. 1 of the European Convention on Human Rights (to which Britain became a signatory in 1952) states that: 'No person shall be denied the right of education. In the exercise of any function which it assumes in relation to education and to teaching, the State shall respect the right of all parents to ensure such education and training in conformity with their own religious and philosophical convictions' (Lester and Pannick, 1982, Introduction). This article, which was framed partially in reponse to the experience of state monopolies of schooling in several European countries, would seem to run counter to the long-term goal of the Labour party to prohibit schools from charging fees. More than that it is felt by some lawyers that established interpretations of the article by the judges of the European Court on Human Rights could be used to challenge 'abolition by stealth' including the removal of charitable status.

Although there may be much equivocation behind the tough exterior of the legal position, it has proved to be a very resilient framework. Even the fundamental reappraisal of the concept of charitable purposes suggested by Lords Halsbury and Bramwell in the 1891 Pemsel case is not without its difficulties. To restrict charitable status to institutions dedicated to the relief of need would open up a debate about the concept of need. Is it to be interpreted strictly in economic terms or are there not more pressing needs in todays's materialistic world? To confine our understanding to past interpretations (perhaps going back as far as the Statute of Elizabeth) is to advocate a very static view of social needs. If the law were tied rigidly to past interpretations it would indeed become a dead hand. If schooling is to be removed from the ambit of charity the case must be made in terms of the needs of contemporary society and not of past legal arguments.

Controlling Educational Trusts

Between 1900 and 1974 the administration of trusts for schooling was undertaken by a small branch within the central state apparatus for education, now the DES. Since 1974 that responsibility has been exercised by the Charity Commissioners who now oversee all charitable trusts. The politics of this seemingly innocuous transfer of authority are revealing. In 1952 the Nathan Committee reported that '... we are satisfied that the educational endowments which would be affected ... are so essential a part of a single system of national education that their removal from the jurisdiction of the Ministry of Education would create chaos' (p. 94). But the Committee conspicuously failed to provide evidence to support its bold prophecy. In fact Norman St John-Stevas, in moving the second reading of the bill that sanctioned the transfer, justified it partly in terms of administrative rationality:

> The bulk of charitable trusts — about two-thirds — are subject to the jurisdiction of the Charity Commissioners, who do not constitute a Department of the central Government in the same way as do the Department of Education and Science and the Welsh Office. The question whether a trust falls under the jurisdiction of the Department or the Commissioners will, however, depend on factors which have nothing to do with the fact that the Departments are in charge of Ministers and the Commissioners are not. Therefore, in principle there can be no question but that these functions are more appropriately exercised by a body such as the Commissioners'. (Hansard, 12 February 1973, Column 1053)

Although the chief Opposition spokesman, Mr Moyle, was sceptical, he was prepared to demur to the Government's recommendation and he also explicitly referred to the move as an attempt to increase educational efficiency. In fact the Opposition did not oppose the bill's second reading.

However, much more than efficiency was involved. Whether a charitable trust fell under the auspices of ministers or commissioners depended upon its purpose, i.e. were those educational or otherwise. But the principle which persuaded Norman St John-Stevas that they should all be placed under the jurisdiction of the Charity Commissioners was his contention that the function of controlling charitable trusts, regardless of their purpose, was essentially judicial in nature. In his opinion that function has to be exercised '... without regard to the kind of policy considerations with which ministers are concerned' (Hansard, 12 February 1973, Column 1053). The implication is that as long as responsibility for educational trusts remained in the hands of the DES policy considerations might more easily intrude in any decisions concerning their future. Mr St John-Stevas contended that as a consequence ministers could from time to time be 'placed in an embarrassing position'. But equally a Minister, bent on using his control of educational trusts to squeeze the private sector, might resent the foreclosing of this avenue. No wonder that at a much later date Christopher Price, with reference to the Commons debate on the second reading of the bill that effected the transfer, was to see it as 'a reminder of how our educational powers slipped away' (Labour party, internal memorandum, undated).

While cross-examining the Charity Commissioners on the transfer of authority for educational trusts Christopher Price noted that: 'This is rather important because since the election a Conservative spokesman [Van Straubenzee] said that the purpose of transferring these funds was to make the public schools immune from political interference ...' (p. 40). Mr Keith for the Charity Commissioners replied, 'I was completely mystified by this statement as reported in the newspapers because it was the first I had heard about it. Nobody had told me that this was the purpose of transferring them to the Charity Commission' (p. 40). At a later point in the cross-examination the Chief Commissioner, Mr Green, forwarded yet again the stock legitimation of administrative rationalization — '... so that they (i.e. the educational trusts) could be dealt with on just the same basis as other charities for which we are responsible' (p. 43). To reinforce the claim that this was simply a reorganization of the bureaucratic apparatus the Charity Commission revealed to the Select Sub-committee that the appropriate DES staff had been transferred to it. The administrative pack had merely been shuffled somewhat.

William Van Straubenzee's claim about the true motives for the transfer of authority was perhaps no more than a convenient political afterthought. The incoming Labour government was committed to weakening the private sector, including the termination of its charitable status. Van Straubenzee was warning that the task would be more difficult than imagined. Whether it was wise to almost boast that the administrative apparatus had been manipulated for political ends is another matter. Norman St John-Stevas disclaimed any knowledge that this was the purpose of the transfer, although those with conspiratorial minds were probably not so easily placated.

Although Norman St John-Stevas justified the transfer of authority on the basis of a clear principle, that the function of administering charitable trusts — educational or otherwise — is essentially judicial in nature, there is some doubt as to whether this would be supported by the historical evidence. The Endowed Schools Act of 1869 set up special commissioners to reorganize educational trusts and it was the powers of these commissioners which were transferred first to the Charity Commissioners and then to the Board of Education. As the Nathan Committee noted, 'Thus this jurisdiction, in contradistinction to the Charitable Trusts Acts powers, has been administered not by an independent tribunal but from the start has been subjected to a policy-making body (p. 24). Moreover, Gladstone has claimed that the 1869 Endowed Schools Act (which was repealed by the 1973 legislation) contained substantial policy-making powers for: 'The Labour Party seems never to have realized that the Endowed Schools Act 1869 enabled Secretaries of State for Education to impose their will on virtually all public schools' (p. 62). In reality, these powers were exercised by education officers in much the same way as officials at the Charity Commission conducted their business. Furthermore, if those functions had been subjected to greater political control presumably this would have been contested in the courts. Did the Endowed Schools Act create two classes of charity? Certainly none of the court rulings support this claim but political and bureaucratic discretion averted a ruling on the precise point and for the time being the matter is dead and buried.

Assuming that there was political motivation in securing the transfer of authority for the administration of educational trusts, why was it believed that such trusts would rest more safely in the hands of the Charity Commissioners? The Charity Commissioners are firmly of the opinion that they have to work within the framework established by court decisions and until those change, or Parliament makes new laws, their hands are tied. As we have already shown the legal basis for the charitable status of private schooling is comparatively solid (Charity Commission, 1966, pp. 10–13). Secondly, in carrying out their tasks the Charity Commissioners are virtually immune from political pressure, and the external administrative checks are divided between the Home Office, the Attorney-General and the Inland Revenue.

The Home Secretary appoints the Charity Commissioners and presents their annual reports to Parliament but distances himself as far as possible from their daily business. This is more the concern of the Attorney-General, currently Sir Michael Havers, but in a written answer to a parliamentary question he claimed, 'I have no powers to direct the Charity Commission to conduct investigations and enquiries into organizations registered with it' (Hansard, 22 July 1982, Column 278). By way of elaboration in an oral answer to a more recent question, Sir Michael replied that he had *made representations* to the Charity Commissioners about the possibility of withdrawing charitable status from two trusts associated with the Unification Church (more popularly known as the Moonies). In response to a subsequent suggestion from Christopher Price that charity law should be changed Sir Michael rebutted that such recommendations were more appropriately addressed to the Home Secretary (Hansard, 18 April 1983, Columns 16-18). The decisions of the Charity Commissioners can be appealed but redress has to be sought in the High Court, a costly and time consuming process. The Inland Revenue's involvement is very much of a technical nature for it must be sure that tax exemption has indeed been claimed by a charity and that it is either a non-profit making body or its profit has been channelled into charitable purposes. As long as there is one class of charity, all entitled to the benefits of charitable status, then relations between the Inland Revenue and the Charity Commissioners are likely to remain amicable.

Another reason why defenders of the status quo might be comforted is that the decisions of the Charity Commissioners appear to be final, both in the sense that it is unlikely they will be challenged in the courts and also because the Commissioners rarely reverse their initial rulings. In other words once the Commissioners are convinced that charitable status should be granted they invariably leave the organization to conduct its business as it sees fit. Abuses may occur but these do not necessarily entail the loss of charitable status for the organization but may mean that individuals will be prosecuted via the normal legal process.

Several opponents of private schools have suggested that they have forfeited their right to charitable status because over the centuries their purpose has changed. The First Report of the Public Schools Commission contains several extracts from the charters of some of the more famous public schools which was meant to prove that the schools were founded for the purpose of educating poor, albeit talented, children. Should charitable status be withdrawn because the schools now cater for mainly the children of well-to-do parents? In a House of Commons interchange with the Secretary of State, Christopher Price asked the same question and Mr Edward Short replied: 'I was very interested in this question and took great trouble to look into it. I find that under the Endowed Schools Act, I have certain powers as Charity Commissioner for Educational Charities, but my powers are limited to taking action which is conducive to the advancement of learning. If I accepted my Honourable Friend's proposal, I would insist that only Latin and grammar were taught at these schools, but I do not think that this would be regarded as being conducive to learning' (Hansard, 24 October 1968, Column 1568). In other words, as the Fleming Committee suggested some decades ago, reasons for reform should be based 'on the present needs of the country' and not on 'the inevitably uncertain interpretation of phrases in use five or six hundred years ago' (Board of Education, 1944, p. 9). But the question of how far and in what ways charities can stray from their original charters and still retain their status remains open. Mr Short's flippancy, although apt, failed to answer Price's central point. Furthermore, given his alleged power to take action 'conducive to the advancement of learning' perhaps he could have been pressed to update the public schools.

Except therefore in very exceptional circumstances educational charities have been left to their own devices, secure in the knowledge that schooling is within itself a charitable purpose. The Charity Commissioners have scarcely concerned themselves with the daily affairs of the private sector; as long as everying appears to be running smoothly, and invariably it has, then the guiding rule is 'leave well alone'. In fact there is considerable doubt whether the Charity Commissioners could take effective action even if a charitable trust was running into trouble. Some charities — including Eton and Winchester colleges — are classified as exempt charities and as the Chief Charity Commissioner, Mr T. Green, remarked to the Select Parliamentary Sub-Committee: 'It means we cannot ask them for their accounts or require them to be registered, so we have no control over them as charities' (p. 319). Eton and Winchester come under the auspices of the Universities and Colleges Estate Act of 1925 which gives them a much freer hand in the use of their financial resources. Furthermore, because of undertakings given to the Commons during the passage of the 1960 Charity Act, it seems that charities registered before 1959 cannot be deregistered, although presumably this would not preclude other forms of action by the Charity Commissioners should they deem it necessary. Again the position is far from certain as indicated by another of Mr T. Green's comments to the Select Sub-Committee: 'We were in 1960 prevented from doing that to the pre-1959 charities (i.e. deregistration). Whether we could do it now or not is a matter of opinion. Nobody has asked us in recent years' (p. 317). In the absence of external pressure it is inevitable that the Charity Commission will formulate its own guide-lines and the golden rule has been not to disturb the peace.

With transfer in 1974 of responsibility for educational trusts from the DES to the Charity Commission a potential achilles heel in the charitable status of private schooling was removed. Charitable status can be rescinded by legislation but it cannot be expedited by the more speedy and less costly means of exerting political pressure upon an administrative apparatus. The Charity Commission remains in splen-did isolation recognizing no master other than the Chancery Division of the High Court. It is this situation which has led us to conclude that if a future Labour government were to terminate the charitable status of private schooling it would represent more than a turning of the financial screw. It would be a victory that symbolized the power of the state, that it could dictate more closely the terms on which society functioned. If centuries of charity law can be overturned is there anything sacred left?

The Political Obstacles

Although Lord Butler once described politics as 'the art of the possible' governments with strong political wills and large parliamentary ma-jorities can be denied very little. Having said that it has nonetheless taken the Labour party quite some time to tackle the question of the public schools seriously and for some years the party's position on charities and voluntary organizations could best be described as 'wait-ing for Goodman'. But the party is now committed to ending the charitable status of the private schools and relocating the responsibility for charitable educational trusts in the DES. Furthermore the party can legitimately claim that it has demonstrated the seriousness of its intentions by the fact that a Labour government was prepared to phase out the direct grant schools. Whereas the direct grant schools were phased out by administrative action the party's proposal to withdraw charitable status will require legislation. The political costs (and, of course, potential gains) of legislation are considerable: it takes up valuable parliamentary time, it can easily expose internal party differ-ences, it provides opportunities for the opposition to embarrass the government, and it gives extra-parliamentary forces a rallying focus. Since the move to end direct grant status was implemented the broader educational climate has changed, the Conservative party is more committed to the independent schools, and the private sector has become more politically influential. None of these factors would be sufficient to deter a determined government but they would make its task that more difficult.

Having decided to accept the possible political consequences of ending the charitable status of private schooling, the actual drafting of the necessary legislation will be difficult. The government would have to decide on what particular direction it wanted its legislation to take: it can restrict what is to count as a charitable purpose and exclude those trusts that endow fee-paying schools, it can create two classes of charity and simply deny tax and other financial advantages to one particular class, or it can provide the courts with closer statutory guidance on points of law that would make it more difficult for them to conclude that private schooling is a charitable purpose. For example, the courts, as we have discussed, have to ascertain whether an organization benefits a sufficient section of the community before it can be granted charitable status. To date the courts have drawn the guidelines in ways that incorporate fee-paying schools but Parliament could simply remap the boundaries so that they were excluded.

None of the above courses of action is without its difficulties. To restrict what counts as a charitable purpose presumably requires a definition of charity, a task that has so far eluded the courts, several enquiries and indeed Parliament. Creating classes of charity must tempt political opponents to think in terms of reformulating the categories so that charity law is turned into a political football, which cannot be to anyone's benefit. If the courts are given closer statutory guidance there is no guarantee that they will interpret the law in a way that was intended by Parliament and in any case a different government may tamper with the guidelines. All policies must be subject to similar problems unless they are supported by a broad political consensus but in this case there is the additional difficulty of judging whether the likely minor payoffs are really worth the very considerable hassle.

In recent years there has been pressure upon the Charity Commissioners to show more flexibility when considering requests for charitable status. The general trend has been towards a broadening of the understanding of charitable purposes so any move by a future Labour government to restrict its definition could appear socially regressive. This would be especially so if those independent schools that cater for many children with special educational needs were to lose their charitable status. The Labour party has pledged that it will safeguard the interests of those schools but this can only complicate the drafting of the bill. For example the parents of some children who have special educational needs are fee-payers in the normal manner and few schools cater for children with only special requirements. Where is the dividing line between types of schools to be drawn? Furthermore, the definition of special educational needs could encompass children who are either very gifted or whose social circumstances necessitate a boarding education. If the definition were that wide it would incorporate many of today's prestigious independent schools.

Assuming that legislation is enacted, and it is drafted in a manner that hits its intended targets, and no others, could it be effectively implemented? This would depend partly upon what further role was allocated to the courts, and if that were substantial (for example, the need to interpret within statutory guidelines what constitutes a public benefit to a sufficient section of the community) whether the legal interpretations matched the wishes of Parliament. The private sector has also signalled quite clearly its intention of challenging any such legislation under the terms of the European Convention on Human Rights, and possibly the United Nations Covenant on Economic, Social and Cultural Rights. Whether the fact that the United Kingdom is a signatory to these agreements would prevent a British government from pursuing legislation in the first place or whether subsequent challenges in either the European or international courts would make legislation inoperative is a matter for conjecture.

It is possible that the private sector would not challenge directly any legislation that removed its charitable status but rather would seek to subvert the government's intentions by acting within the letter if not the spirit of the law. We have already mentioned the possibility of charitable institutions directing funds to fee-paying schools if legislation allowed certain kinds of private schools to retain their charitable status. All present independent schools might seek to be classified as such either by changing their pupil enrolment (admitting more pupils with special educational needs) or seeking a broad interpretation in the courts of the clauses that allowed a school to be classified as a charity (so that, for example, special educational needs is defined generously).

The Labour party's attack upon the charitable status of private schooling is intended in the first place to end what many would consider to be a morally reprehensible state of affairs and secondly to weaken the independent sector in order to hasten its demise. If the strategy works there may be no need for the proposed coup de grace, the prohibition on charging fees. The final purpose of this chapter is to evaluate the reality of the strategy by examining the financial advantages that are a consequence of charitable status. The ultimate test of legislation is how effective it is likely to be in changing the character of our society and personally we would pay scant attention to the moral uplift it may give to some individuals.

The Financial Dimension

The contemporary political esteem in which private schooling is held is partially dependent upon the assumption that it is responsive to market-place pressures. It is believed that the schools could not stay in business unless they remained sensitive to customer demands, i.e. the parents who pay the fees. In an earlier chapter we were sceptical about the extent of parental influence and there is no doubt that private schooling does not operate in an unfettered market-place. In various ways the state augments the financial resources of the independent sector: places are either paid for or subsidized, insurance policies can be designed to mitigate somewhat the full cost of fees, and charitable status entitles schools to tax and rate concessions. The purchase of places reflects a willingness on the part of either national government or the local education authorities to use the private sector's facilities. It is payment, therefore, for a service that has been rendered. It is possible to object to such transactions on many grounds but it is by no means a foregone conclusion that all of these services could be provided by the state at a cheaper cost. Insurance policies that provide some relief from the full cost of fees are a product of the taxation system. They do not exist because the Inland Revenue wishes to assist private schooling but they are a means of enabling individuals to lessen their tax burden and it is the taxpayer who decides what ends the policy will serve. Again many will find this objectionable but it should be seen for what it is, as an alleged tax loophole which may help to pay school fees and not as an intended subsidy to private schooling.

If the state subsidizes the independent sector it does so by granting the non-profit making schools charitable status. The main financial benefits of charitable status are as follows: exemption from income and corporation taxes, exemption — up to generous limits — from estate duty and capital transfer tax, exemption from capital gains tax, recovery of tax on deeds of covenant (note the donor can deduct either income or corporation tax on the amount convenanted and the charity recovers the tax from the Inland Revenue), relief from value added tax, and relief — of at least 50 per cent — from local authority rates. The estimates of how much charitable status is worth in financial terms varies considerably, with the higher figures favoured by the opponents of private schooling and vice versa. The memorandum submitted by the ISJC to the Select House of Commons Sub-Committee stated that if charitable status were withdrawn: 'The extra cost to parents at most schools would also be relatively small' (p. 252). In cross-examination by the Sub-committee Lord Belstead offered a more exact calculation: '. . . I must say this: one of our constituent members, the bursars, did some calculations some time ago, and they felt that charitable status was worth to a school somewhere between 5 and 10 per cent of the fees' (p. 255). But there must be some uncertainty as to what the tax position of the schools would be were they to lose charitable status; that is how they would be classified for the purposes of taxation. Given the ISJC's penchant for seeking professional advice it is certain that a large body of expertise would be directed at the task of minimizing tax liabilities!

Regardless of what the final figure may be, the consequences of rescinding the financial benefits of charitable status appear self-evident. Fees would undoubtedly rise probably accompanied by an intensifica-- tion of current fund-raising efforts. The latter, however, would be hampered somewhat by the loss of charitable status. There are tax advantages in contributing to charities and the label is one that attracts donations. Furthermore, there are some organizations that under the terms of their charters can support only charities. Besides raising more income the schools would also try to save costs, something they have been rather good at in recent years. One likely development is that the schools would offer fewer scholarships and bursaries. If they were no longer charities they would, one imagines, feel less inclined to act charitably.

The social and political impact of these changes are harder to predict. The independent sector has been remarkably buoyant in recent years in spite of fee increases that have been above the average rate of inflation. Many parents are prepared to make sacrifices to pay school fees and they would have to weigh this commitment against the additional costs. A somewhat more socially exclusive private sector is the most likely outcome with fewer lower-middle class parents pre- pared to pay the fees and perhaps a decline in the number of scholarships. The cynics would surely see a smaller, more socially refined sector as a self-fulfilling prophecy: a Labour government creates the world that it already believes is a reality.

The political strength of the private sector is dependent upon the unity it has been able to create out of its disparate parts. If the ending of charitable status had a substantial impact so that only the prestigious schools survived then they would be politically more vulnerable. However, if the repercussions could be confined to an increase in fees of somewhere between 5 and 10 per cent then it would prove to be an irritant rather than a bodyblow. In the circumstances the various elements within the private sector would probably be drawn closer together as they sought ways to mitigate their dilemma and as they girded themselves for the final assault. So, politically, the abolition of charitable status could prove self-defeating by forcing the private schools into a stronger defensive alliance without having a substantive impact upon the size and character of the sector. Although the ending of charitable status may not assist a Labour government in its intention to prohibit private schooling, it could help the cause of party unity by demonstrating the seriousness of the government's will. At the same time it delays the tackling of a much more controversial issue — a prohibition of the charging of fees. That, as present party policy dictates, is conveniently a matter for the long term.

The Law, Ideology and Political Struggle

The case law upon which the charitable status of private schooling is dependent constitutes a pragmatically conservative framework for the defence of class interests. Historically that case law has evolved in response to what some would term the changing needs of society and others the altered circumstances of the ruling class. We have demonstrated how case law defends the charitable status of the schools on the grounds that they are of benefit to the community (or at least a sufficient section of it) at large. The legal system in theory remains immune to political pressure, and in the case of charity law the administrative apparatus — the Charity Commission — is cocooned in a seemingly impenetrable shell, responsible to no one but the High Court. The bogus neutrality of present arrangements is illustrated perfectly by the constraints on the political activities of charities. Charitable status will not be granted to organizations which have as their *primary* purpose either a desire to defend or to change the law. As if the opposing parties were equally handicapped by the prohibition!

But as we have shown, to attack the charitable status of private schooling is fraught with danger. It means limiting the legal understanding of charitable purposes by withdrawing it from schooling, something which many of the opponents of private schools scarcely relish. This would be so even if the rescinding legislation tried to preserve the charitable status of some independent schools. Moreover, the latter course of action would complicate the change process and perhaps make its chances of success more remote. And all this for a bill which may prove little more than a financial annoyance and which could gel more firmly the political front of the private sector. It is thus a short run measure which scratches rather than wounds and could succeed in raising the defensive capabilities of the offended party.

But this is to concentrate too much upon the direct financial consequences of charitable status. If educational change is accompanied by ideological struggle then to end charitable status would represent a formal defeat for those interests that support the private sector. Their values may not change but no longer could they find comfort in the law. More broadly it would symbolize a significant intrusion of the state into society. The next logical step is a prohibition on the charging of fees for no further barriers remain, which could be as much an embarrassment to a government committed to ending private school-ing as it would be a threat to the independent schools themselves. When it comes to grasping the thistle it may prove to be more painful than anticipated. What we have hopefully demonstrated in this chapter is that the struggle surrounding charitable status is something more than a question of the financial well-being of the private sector of schooling. To change the law would signify a shift in the balance between state and society, would weaken that system of ideas that nurtures private schooling, and would leave the way open for a significant change in the institutional character of the British educational system through the termination of the private sector. But, as we have also shown, the pitfalls along the way are deep and numerous.

Part II
The Political Struggle

5 *Ideological Power and Political Challenge*

Introduction

The Labour party's political challenge to private schooling has been a long time in the making. Its halting development is not accidental. It can be shown to be the consequence of the continuing interplay of ideological and political forces within the party which shape and guide policy formation and, equally importantly, policy implementation. In this chapter we examine the application of these forces to the issue of private schooling and the unavoidable tensions thus produced. The analysis which we employ in this chapter and in Chapter 7 is based on the ideas concerning the relationship between intellectual roles and party policy making developed in Chapter 2. The first task is to refine these ideas by placing them in the context of the Labour party's formal policy making machinery. Particular attention is paid to the long-established tensions between the annual conference, the National Executive Committee (NEC) and the Parliamentary Labour Party (PLP) and the implications of these tensions for opposing groups of intellectuals within the party. Different political groupings within the party have concentrated on developing different intellectual roles with regard to the production, translation and dissemination of party ideology. The second part of the chapter then applies this analysis to the party's handling of the private schools issue and explains why the political challenge to the independent schools took so long to emerge. It shows the importance to the issue of the deep-seated ideological divisions within the party, and the effect on policy formation and implementation due to the focus on some intellectual roles rather than others.

The Intellectuals and the Labour Party

Wielding ideological influence within the Labour party is a less than straightforward pursuit. Even if an idea can be safely negotiated through the structural rapids that constitute the party's policy-making process, it still faces the obstacle course of policy implementation once the party is in power. Any intellectual who underestimates the difficulties of ideas promotion within the party is wasting his time.

In policy making terms, the major tensions are between the annual conference, the National Executive Committee (NEC) and the Parliamentary Labour Party (PLP). These tensions usually become more acute when the party is in government because the problems of policy implementation then become more tangible and visible; out of government they can be ignored or disguised (though this is slowly changing). An intellectual, or more commonly a group of intellectuals, can promote his ideas in any of these three arenas or in a combination of arenas. Alternatively, or in addition, he can adopt an indirect strategy and view his target audience as the wider public and seek to influence the climate of opinion to which the Labour party, as an electoral party, must remain sensitive. The difficulty with aiming at more than one target audience is that different audiences have different expectations regarding the content and style of ideas presentation. While the annual conference may support a motion attacking private schooling because of persuasive speeches couched in the broad ideological terms of 'an end to class privilege', the Education and Science Sub-Committee of the Home Policy Committee of the NEC will require more empirical and legalistic arguments as well. This implies a recognized division of intellectual labour and the organization of such labour over time. Like many other issue areas, private schooling has not received from intellectuals coordinated attention of this kind.

The relationship between conference, the NEC and the PLP is ambiguous because in formal constitutional terms it is not clear who has the power to do what. Richard Rose (1974) points out that

> A resolution by annual conference can only set terms for negotiation between the NEC and PLP. This is explicitly recognized in Clause V of the Labour Party constitution. A resolution approved by a two-thirds vote of confidence is assured of becoming part of the party programme, but this is not the election manifesto. The manifesto is a separate document .... approved by the NEC and the Parliamentary Committee of the PLP meeting jointly. (p. 162)

When is a Labour party policy not a Labour party policy? On this interpretation, the fact that conference has made policy by passing a motion on an issue is no guarantee that it will then be taken up and developed by an NEC Sub-committee, accepted by the NEC, included in the party programme, included in the party manifesto, included in the party's legislative programme when in power and translated intact into legislative form by the civil service. At each stage a policy can be halted, stalled, amended, expanded, diluted or simply forgotten. And each stage requires an intellectual input to develop or refine the policy ideas further. If this input is missing the chances of a policy's survival are reduced.

The fluidity of Labour's policy making is increased by the amount of discretion accorded the NEC. As Kavanagh (1982) notes, apart from the annual election at conference there are few mechanisms for establishing the accountability of NEC members. No formal provision exists in the conference timetable for members of the NEC to report back (p. 210). It is thus relatively easy for the NEC to blur any lack of progress on policies passed by conference the previous year and, given this large discretion, unwise for party intellectuals to be too reliant on assertions of conference sovereignty such as Attlee's in 1937: 'The conference lays down the policy of the party and issues instructions which must be carried out by the Executive, the affiliated organizations and its representatives in Parliament and on local authorities ... the Labour party conference is in fact a Parliament of the movement' (McKenzie, 1982, p. 192).

Coming from Attlee, this is an interesting interpretation given his reliance on the large trade unions as what McKenzie calls the 'praetorian guard' maintaining the dominance of the PLP (McKenzie, 1976, p. 14). This was a traditional function of the trade unions within the Labour party up to the Wilson government of 1964-70. It formed part of the formula whereby the unions preserved the ascendancy of the PLP and, in exchange, the PLP maintained the conditions of free collective bargaining for the unions through its parliamentary presence. Indeed, McKenzie argues that the Labour party only exists because 'the trade unions entered politics in order to ensure that the state did not intervene in their affairs in a way which they found unacceptable' following the Taff Vale decision in the House of Lords. In Ernest Bevin's phrase the party 'grew out of the bowels of the trade union movement' (*Ibid.*, p. 14).

There is no doubt that both financially and constitutionally the trade unions dominate the Labour party. Over 80 per cent of party funds come from the unions. The unions directly elect twelve of the twenty-eight members of the NEC and control the choice of six more through the strength of their conference vote. Between 1955 and 1977 the unions' share of conference votes grew from 82 to 89 per cent (Crouch, 1982, p. 176). So if they choose, there is no problem in the unions carrying out their part of the bargain and insulating the PLP from policy pressures from conference while paying lip-service to the notion of conference's constitutional supremacy. A corollary of the trade union's pact with the PLP was the unions' control of the Left in the party. In his study of the trade unions and the Labour party Harrison (1960) observed that in any attempt to move the party in the direction of 'red blooded socialism . . . the balance of union power has undoubtedly been a brake' (p. 39). Beatrice Webb explained the difficulty as she saw it in rather graphic terms in 1930:

> The constituency parties were frequently unrepresentative groups of nonentities dominated by fanatics and cranks, and extremists, and that if the block vote of the trade unions were eliminated it would be impracticable to continue to vest the control of policy in the Labour party conference. (McKenzie, 1982, p. 192)

The effect of this aspect of trade union influence was to render conference more sympathetic ideologically to intellectuals of the centre and right than of the left. Constituency activists on the left of the party could always be outvoted if the need arose.

Several things happened to change the situation and thus the policy making context. Firstly, the 1964-70 Wilson government broke the PLP-trade union concordat by trying to introduce *In Place of Strife* and intervene or, as the unions saw it, intefere in the sphere of free collective bargaining by legislating a new framework for industrial relations. Secondly, in the late 1960s and early 1970s, the leadership of several of the largest trade unions moved to the Left with the appointment of men such as Hugh Scanlon (AUEW), Jack Jones (TGWU), Mick McGahey (Scottish miners), Arthur Scargill (Yorshire miners) and Clive Jenkins (ASTMS). At the same time as events were splitting the PLP-trade union nexus, growing calls were being made for the PLP to become more accountable to the party organization. Significantly, when the 1970 party conference discussed the role of conference in influencing the Parliamentary party Wilson took the following constitutional position:

> A Prime Minister is responsible to the House of Commons and acts on the basis of cabinet judgment as to what is necessary in

the public interest insofar and as long as he commands the confidence of the House of Commons, and he cannot be instructed by any authority from day to day other than Parliament's and, (Hatfield, 1978, p. 72) without the praetorian guard, he lost his vote.

When Labour was in office between 1964 and 1970 the party organization's policy-making machinery became virtually moribund as the political action centred on Westminster. Frustrations developed among the party officials in Transport House, particularly among the 'in-house intellectuals' of the Research Department who prepare the background papers and many of the draft policies for party's commit-tees, and who felt their role had become purely one of servicing the parliamentary party. Thus a paper circulated to the Home Policy Committee in July 1970 after the election commented that 'too much time has been wasted in close consultation with ministers often to the detriment of our concentration on future policy matters'. It continued, 'this time can now be spent on the serious consideration of issues. Similarly for the Research Department there is the release from the time-consuming activities of monitoring tiny areas of government policies, often with no political content whatsoever' (*Ibid.*, p. 34). In common with the Left, the in-house intellectuals had seen their ideas and their policies too often ignored by the Labour government. Both felt the need for stronger institutional links to ensure the parliamentary party's accountability to the party organization. With the sundering of the PLP-trade union alliance in 1970, the opportunity arrived.

The way in which this opportunity was grasped resulted in a much greater emphasis being placed on a particular kind of party intellectual role and a new linkage being forged between ideology and policy. Both the Left and the trade unions shared the pressing need to pin down a future Labour government to a specific party programme and the in-house intellectuals had many of the skills, as well as the motivation, to help realize this ambition. The immediate consequence of this coincidence of interest was the up-grading in 1970 of the National Executive Sub-committees which since 1964 had been designated 'advisory' committees and allowed to run down to prevent possible embarassment to the Labour government (*Ibid.*, p. 41). By the end of 1970 these committees (Financial and Economic Affairs, Industrial Policy, Science and Education etc.) had had their status increased. The intention was that the membership should be drawn from external intellectuals, the trade unions and the parliamentary party. As their status increased so did the influence of the in-house intellectuals: the research officers who serviced them, provided outline proposals of a programme of work and in some instances first drafts of the new policy documents.

The function of the intellectual role embodied in the work of the NEC sub-committees was, and is, the translation of the general ideological statements contained in conference resolutions into specific policy statements. From 1970 onwards, this role was expanded and became a vehicle for the attempt by the Left and the trade unions to bring the errant parliamentary party to heel. At the same time, the setting up of the TUC-Labour Party Liaison Committee in 1972 provided the means for the trade unions to discuss and endorse the policies developed in the NEC Sub-committees. This Committee undoubtedly played a major role in the formulation of the party programme for the 1974 election and in formal terms was the forum in which the Social Contract between Labour and the TUC was worked out.

The publication in June 1973 of *The Programme 1973* is a tribute to the new approach to policy making and the faith placed by the Left in a detailed and sophisticated intellectual style of argument. After revisions by the NEC and the Shadow Cabinet the Programme ran to 56,000 words and was followed by a background paper which for the first time in the Labour party costed out the different policy options. Again the intention was clearly to structure policy formation to such an extent that the subsequent process of policy implementation by a Labour government could not easily subvert or dilute party policy. Not surprisingly, the PLP took a jaundiced view of this attempt, Callaghan at one point telling the Home Policy Committee in November 1973 that 'Transport House was making too many policies and not devoting energies to getting across the ones already agreed' (*Ibid.*, p. 225). There was no change in the PLP's general belief that MPs should be responsive to electoral as well as party opinion and that an exclusively programmatic approach would be electorally disastrous no matter how rigorously analytical this programme might be.

At that time the Left's strategy for making the Parliamentary party toe the policy line determined by Conference and the NEC was dependent upon trade union support. So once Wilson's 1974 Labour government repealed the Conservatives' industrial legislation and re-established the PLP-TUC concordat the Left was outflanked and easily outvoted at meetings of the NEC when moves were made critical of the government's policies. (It had in any case been clear before this that Wilson was not prepared to accept the 1973 Programme.) A change in the rules of the game of policy formation was needed if the Left was to make the PLP more accountable to the Party organization without having to rely on fluctuating trade union support in order to do so. This was where the Campaign for Labour Party Democracy (CLPD) came in and a further type of party intellectual role emerged.

Founded in 1973 after Wilson's rejection of the 1973 Programme, the CLPD was concerned soley with constitutional change and not with policy issues. It was therefore able to attract people of different ideological persuasions on the Left (Kogan and Kogan, 1982, p. 41). Its intellectuals had the technical political skills necessary for campaigning for constitutional change: a combination of the skills required for drafting complex conference motions and the political acumen to organize voting support. Beyond this they had to know how to campaign over time for a change in the traditional deference accorded by the Party to its leaders. That they have been successful some do not doubt. In *The Battle for the Labour Party* David and Maurice Kogan, referring to the CLPD, wrote that 'The last eight years of Labour party history has been dominated less by the evolution of new radical policies than by the activities of a small group of able tacticians' (*Ibid.*, p. 14). Two major constitutional victories have been recorded: first, the mandatory reselection of MPs by their constituency parties achieved at the 1979 annual conference; and second, the electoral college for the selection of the Labour leader won at the special Wembley conference in 1981. Both measures render the PLP more accountable to the Party organization. On the other hand, control of the manifesto still rests with the Labour leadership in consultation with the NEC despite vigorous efforts by the CLPD to place that control firmly with the NEC.

Behind the view of policy making held by the Left and conference on the one hand, and the parliamentary party, on the other, lie different conceptions of how to resolve the tensions between the demands of ideology and the demands of the electoral process. For the Left, the issue has always been one of how, in the context of an electoral party, to translate ideology into policy and make it stick. In the 1930s the output of Left intellectuals such as Strachey, Orwell, Wilkinson and Harrington was prodigious as were the activities of groups such as the Fabians, the Far Left Book Club and the International Brigade. Yet their impact was minimal because little thought was given to how these ideas could be translated into a form which would appeal to the bulk of the Labour party and to the electorate as a whole (Pimlott, 1977). They construed their intellectual role in elitist terms and were disappointed when neither the Labour party nor the masses heard or cared what they were saying. The tradition continues today. Hobsbawm (1978) warns that there is the danger on the Left 'of establishing a ghetto in which intellectuals, while claiming to operate within the working class movement, really address each other, often in terms which are incomprehensible to anyone outside' (p. 444). He remarks on the 'enormous growth of marxist metaphysics by philosphers, sociologists and economists whose writings neither interpret the world nor help to change it, but chiefly produce discussion in seminars of other marxist philosophers, sociologists and economists' (*Ibid.*, p. 445). Many Left intellectuals reside in comfortable occupational and status groups which, by virtue of their cultural exclusiveness, auto-castrate their political efficacy.

Not all Left intellectuals suffer this uncomfortable fate. Our discussion has shown that within the Labour party at least, a more pragmatic attitude has developed on the Left as to how intellectuals can translate ideology into party policy through sophisticated manoeuvrings at conference and the assiduous use of NEC sub-committees and working groups. But there remain two further translation functions of party intellectuals which need to be carried out before policy can have its desired effect. These concern the electoral appeal of policy and the implementation of policy when in office. Thus the overall translation function of Labour party intellectuals is necessary at the following points in the continuum between ideology and policy impact (Figure 2).

Figure 2: The Translation Functions of Intellectuals

Ideology	→	Conference Policy	→	NEC/Party Programme	→	Electoral Appeal	→	Policy Implementation

Although Figure 2 presents a neat ordering of intellectual functions one of the problems faced by the Labour party is that its intellectuals do not perform these functions along a consistent ideological path. Instead, different ideological positions within the party focus on different intellectual functions. This gives rise to entrenched conflicts reinforced by mutual scepticism concerning the validity of opponents' intellectual functions.

The decision over which intellectual function, or combination of functions, to pursue is based on the individual's conception of the Labour party. For the Left the party is socialist, anti-capitalist, ultimately revolutionary in its ambition and has a core of principles which can be used to guide the construction of policy. Electoral politics are a vehicle for the enactment of these principles but should not be allowed to subvert them. Some of those who hold this conception of the party tend to lay exclusive claim to its ideology and indulge in 'the failure of the socialist promise' game. It is a good game because their analysis of the power of capitalism to undermine the will of the Labour party means that they cannot lose (see, for example, Anderson, 1964; Coates, 1975 and 1980; Miliband, 1961; Nairn, 1964; Panitch, 1971 and 1976). The intellectual functions which best fit the Left's conception of the party are those which translate ideology into conference policy and conference policy into a detailed party programme.

The Right and Centre of the party, which for convenience we will call the Social Democrats, have a different view of the party's origins and purpose which, though it is a more practical view is no less ideological in terms of the power of the ideas flowing from it. Thus Barker (1972) argues that 'The Labour party derived its ambitions not from political principles, not from broad visions of a different society, but from the social and economic opportunities of which its working class members had experience' (p. 136). Born 'out of the bowels of the trade unions', the Labour party has never been a mass movement or a revolutionary vanguard but was, and is, an electoral machine founded to protect specific social and economic rights of the working class (Pimlott, 1977, p. 196). Given this conception of the party, it follows that Social Democrat intellectuals are more likely to be preoccupied with the translation function between ideology and electoral appeal and to have a weaker interest in the ideology — conference-party programme translation functions.

This preoccupation is clearly apparent in the Revisionist movement of the 1950s and 1960s. Intellectuals such as Crosland, Gaitskell, Jay and Jenkins sought to convince the party of the evidence of a changing electorate concerned not with the control of the means of production but with the distribution of the things produced (Drucker 1979, pp. 48ff; Coates 1975, pp. 80ff). Furthermore they believed that greater equality could be achieved within the framework of a mixed economy. Revisionists pointed to the electoral defeats of 1950, 1951 and 1955 and linked them to Abrams's argument in *Must Labour Lose* that the party was bound to go into irreversible decline unless it adjusted to fundamental changes in voter preferences. Having won the argument, established a clearer relationship between Labour's ideology and its electoral appeal and won the 1964 and 1966 elections, they then sought to protect this relationship by defending the independence of the parliamentary party against the demands for more accountability made by the party organization. For them, the intellectual function of translating party ideology into detailed manifesto commitments was a decided handicap in the pursuit of electoral power rather than a natural part of Labour's policy making. Even after the defeat of 1970, Crosland was convinced that what was needed was a clear affirmation of agreed ideals rather than a mass of new policies (Hatfield, 1978, p. 51). Not only could it be embarrassing for an incoming government to have raised the electorate's aspirations with a wealth of pledges difficult to fulfil, there was also the minor problem of translating complex policies into saleable electoral packages. As Nixon used to say when reviewing a policy initiative: 'That's OK, but will it play in Peoria'? Social Democrats were sensitive to similar considerations.

Although the Left and Social Democrats were divided in their assessment of the importance of the different party intellectual functions, what they had in common was their neglect of the intellectual input to policy implementation when in government. It could be argued that there is no need for such an input; that the impartiality of the Civil Service ensures an unbiased interpretation of party policy. Opinions of Labour ex-ministers differ on this with Crosland, Gordon Walker, Jenkins and Wilson supporting the impartiality thesis (see respectively Kogan, 1971, p. 176; Gordon Walker, 1972, p. 66; Jenkins, 1971, pp. 25–6; Wilson, 1976, p. 42) and Crossman and Castle opposing it (Crossman, 1975, p. 21; Castle, 1973, p. 17). Our own view, based on an analysis of the Department of Education (DES) in *Education, Politics and the State* is that departments have developed policy preferences, established over time and frequently embedded in bureaucratic procedures. In the case of DES policy making there is a heavy reliance on identifying the existing trends in the 'natural' educational demand from schoolchildren, students, teachers etc. (Crowther Hunt, 1976a and 1976b). This form of 'projectionist' planning occurs within the context of departmental moves for more effective managerial control over a traditionally decentralized education system. Moves which the Department seeks to legitimize through the sponsorship of its own ideology of education (Tapper and Salter, 1978, Chapter 7; Salter and Tapper, 1981, Chapters 5 and 9).

The translation of party policy into administrative and legislative form is an intellectual function of which the Civil Service has a virtual monopoly and of which the Left in the Labour party is highly suspicious. One of the main reasons for the trend towards greater detail in party policy documents has been the feeling that policies need to be protected not only from a lukewarm PLP but also from a Civil Service resistant to radical change. For example, Bert Clough, who services the NEC's Education Sub-committee, recently commented on the policies developed over the past few years: 'It will be very difficult for civil servants to change the manifesto commitments backed up by detailed discussion documents' (Lister, 1983, p. 6). This may be over-confidence since the negotiation of the form of policy implementation between minister and civil servants is dependent upon a number of factors other than the detail of the party policy. Firstly, this detail may, in any case, require further translation to render it compatible with the financial and administrative mechanisms of the department concerned since civil servants do not at present have an input into party policy making. This allows for authoritative pronouncements to be made on the administrative viability of the policy, the unforeseen longer term problems to which it may give rise, its cost vis-a-vis alternative policy options, and its relationship to the Public Expenditure Survey Committee cycle which governs the timing and availability of the necessary finance: all of which may give rise to amendments or delay. Secondly, civil servants' reaction to the policy will be influenced by the match, or mismatch, between it and the established policy preferences of their department. Certain of Labour's policies will be more compatible with these preferences, will receive more support because they are easier to implement and administratively less disruptive than others. So an unobtrusive hierarchy of policy priorities will emerge as a result of discussions between minister and civil servants. Finally, the personality of the Minister and his own sympathy for the policy will naturally influence the extent to which he is prepared to push it.

The ability of intellectuals on the Left of the Labour party to predict and, if necessary, counter the Civil Service response to their policies is limited by a lack of knowledge and experience of the intellectual function involved in policy implementation. How can they exercise control in an area where Ministers and the Parliamentary party are likely to be uncertain allies? One possibility is the appointment of political advisers to ministers to monitor the development of policy. But even if the loyalty of such advisers to the party organization can be guaranteed, their ability to insist on the detailed implementation of policy in the face of sophisticated manoeuvrings by civil servants is not going to be very great. Commenting on the use of political advisers initiated by the 1964-70 Labour government, Hudson (1976) observes that the political secretary must become part of the machine in the sense that he is not considered an outsider by civil servants: 'He must be seen as necessary and helpful element in the machinery: otherwise he will be by-passed' (p. 303). This rather sounds as if the political adviser will only be accepted by the civil servants on their terms; which is not surprising but also not likely to assist the adviser in making an independent contribution to policy implementation.

In *Political Parties: A Genuine Case for Discontent*, Blondel (1975) examines the limitations of modern party organizations as revealed in poor division of party labour, inadequate national staffing and research facilities, and the failure to mobilize or develop proper programmes. The major problem, he believes, is at the level of the linkage between ideology and policy (p. 134). In this chapter we have explored the nature of that linkage in the Labour party in order to provide an analytical framework for understanding how and why the challenge to the private sector finally staggered into being in the way that it did. There are three components to the analysis. Firstly, the formal policy-making machinery of conference, the NEC and the PLP has in-built tensions. The party organization wants the PLP to be directly account-able to party policy whilst the PLP prefers to retain sufficient independ-ence to allow it to respond to changing electoral opinion. The arbiters in the conflict are the trade unions. Secondly, these tensions are reinforced by the ideological differences between the Left and the Social Democrats. Thirdly, the linkage between ideology and policy in the Labour party can only be fully established with the aid of a division of intellectual labour. The party has yet to recognize explicitly that different intellectual skills are required at different points in the formation and implementation of policy.

The Labour Party and the Private Schools

In 1980 the Labour party published *Private Schools,* its first comprehen-sive policy document on the independent sector. Yet the party had been debating the issue prior to that for at least thirty years. Annual conference had ritualistically demanded an end to private schooling, year in and year out. Constitutionally speaking therefore, the pressure for a policy to be developed on private schooling had always been present. So why did Labour take so long to challenge what some might regard as the natural educational home of its class enemy? Why was the link between ideology and policy so difficult to forge and why did it take so long for the intellectual roles necessary to forge this link to emerge?

Ideological Ambiguity

The divisions in Labour's general ideology are reflected in the different arguments against the private schools. How to bring an end to the class-based nature of British society, or at least to diminish the effects of those divisions, is a continuing theme in party rhetoric, particularly at conference time. In 1957, when pressing for the independent school issue to be included in Labour party policy on education, Michael Stewart and Margaret Cole wrote in an internal memorandum: 'The heart of this problem is that the public schools form collectively a powerful instrument for preventing the creation of a classless society, by ensuring that the children of the wealthy shall enjoy substantial advantages both in income and power' (RE 161, May 1957, p. 7). At about the same time, Crossman produced an internal paper called 'Elite Education' where he detailed the connection between prep school, public school and Oxbridge in the manfacture of the elite and this argument was reproduced in *Private Education* by the party's Study Group on Education in November 1957 supported by numerous tables of statistics (RE 223, November 1957). The arguments were thorough and the data convincing. Establishing the nature of the chain between class, educational opportunity and social and political power was never going to be a problem. The burgeoning work of educational sociologists such as Douglas, Floud and Halsey building on that of Tawney provided a pool of academically respectable ideas and information to support and legitimize this line of analysis. While comprehensivization of the schools in the state secondary sector was to be the first and major policy response to the class and educational opportunity analysis, the logic of the argument suggested that further policies would be required to sever the links between private schools and the elite.

At the simplistic ideological level of 'attack the elite because it exists and because we are socialists' the arguments and evidence were straightforward. Conflicts arose, however, as soon as the question of what should replace the existing elite was broached. Social Democrats such as Gaitskell argued strongly in favour of a meritocratic elite and therefore supported educational policies which would serve this end. Public schools, Gaitskell argued, should be the prerogative of intellectually gifted children (Parkinson, 1970, p. 107). In effect, he was seeking to establish a new type of link between class, private schooling and the elite.

His assumption, and that of most other Labour party commentators on private schools, was that although the schools' political status as supporters of a particular type of society deserved to be attacked, their educational status seen purely as educational institutions deserved to be respected. This created ideological ambiguity when it was not clear which of these two types of status should be given priority in an argument. High educational value, if given priority, could mean that the private schools should be preserved intact. Thus the 1957 document 'Private Schools' states,

> Present evidence however appears to show that in the best private and Direct Grant Schools the IQ distribution is higher than in LEA grammar schools. Should this concentrated talent forcibly be spread among all schools, thus probably lowering the standards of such schools as, for example, Manchester Grammar School? (RE 223, November 1957, p. 18)

We have discussed in *Education, Politics and the State* (chapter 7) how powerful the ideological marriage of a meritocracy based on the 'scientific' measurement of IQ can be and it undoubtedly produces cross-cutting themes in Labour party thinking. However, when the educational value of private schools is not given an absolute status but is subordinated to the political analysis of the schools' class position the ideological difficulty is resolved. For example, a draft policy statement on education in 1961 said of the public schools:

> In their sixth forms are to be found high standards of teaching, first rate equipment and premises, excellent academic traditions. It is wholly wrong that during a period of intense shortage of educational resources so much of the best is available only to those whose parents can pay for it. (RD 124, May 1961, p. 12)

A class analysis of independent schooling does not necessarily lead to a policy for the abolition of private schools. It depends on one's understanding of the direction of the cause-effect relationship. Aneurin Bevan, writing in *Tribune* in 1955 was pessimistic: 'I do not favour private education, but I would not prohibit it, provided the welfare of the children is safeguarded by State inspection. In a class society, I am afraid it is impossible wholly to prevent class education ... The permanent solution is greater equality in the distribution of wealth'

(Barker, 1972, p. 100). (The economics underpinning the class structure have to be tackled first.) Contrast this statement with the rampant
optimism of Grahame Lane during the debate on private education at
the 1980 annual conference. Citing figures on the public school
background of admirals, generals and so on he continued, 'We are
really altering the structure of society if we make it illegal for school to
charge fees for education. . . Let us vote today to move Britain towards
a classless society' (Labour Party Annual Conference, 1980, p. 36).
Have faith in the power of schooling!

But the ideological ambiguities within Labour's class analysis of
private schools are minor compared to the direct conflict between that
analysis and the principle of parental choice. This conflict was the initial
stumbling block to the development of any policy on the independent
sector. In 1957, for example, under the tentative sub-heading 'Is it
possible to abolish private education?' a Working Party on Education
commented,

> The desire of parents to obtain the best in life for their children
> is not a wrong or immoral one. Can it really be said that it is
> immoral to buy a better house and more room for one's family
> if financial circumstances permit? (RE 166, June 1957, p. 36)

In education, as in other areas of social policy such as medicine and
health, individuals should be allowed to retain the basic freedom of
choice it was argued. 'All post-war social legislation enacted by the
Labour governments,' proclaimed the internal document *Private Education* in 1957, 'allowed individuals some elements of choice either by
using the national service or making some provision for themselves'
(RE 223, November 1957, p. 9). Why should this element of choice be
removed in education?

Simultaneous adherence to the principles of, on the one hand,
ending class privilege and, on the other maintaining parental choice
created an ideological paradox characterized in public statements by
doublethink and inaction. Thus *Learning to Live* (1958) begins by
stating that public school fees buy advantage and that such a 'system
distorts the choice of people for responsible positions; it damages
national efficiency and offends the sense of justice'; it then considers the
possibility of prohibition but rejects this because

> Such a prohibition would mean that a citizen who had paid his
> share of the cost of public education would not be allowed to
> spend any of his own money on sending his own children to the

> kind of school he wished. Labour believes that this would be an
> unjustifiable invasion of liberty.

and concludes that no action should be taken (*Ibid.*, pp. 58–9).
Similarly in *The Future of Socialism,* Crosland (1956) both attacks 'the
glaring injustice of the independent schools' and comes out against
proscribing private education because this would be 'an interference
with private liberty' (p. 191).

A further dimension was added to the ideological conflict by
electoral considerations: abolition of the private schools was never
going to be a vote catcher. A party opinion poll in 1957 showed that
only 8 per cent of respondents wanted the private schools abolished and
80 per cent were prepared to pay for educational privilege (Parkinson,
1970, p. 113). As part of a list of reasons for not taking action on
private schools the 1957 Working Party on Education included:

> The public schools are more or less entirely middle class
> problems, and from an electoral point of view any action taken
> against them could raise a hornet's nest without considerably
> benefiting any large proportion of the child population. (RE
> 166, June 1957, p. 38)

The best interests of the working class would not be served by a direct
assault on the bastions of class privilege, particularly at a time when the
battle on comprehensivization of the state sector had yet to be fought.
The same argument was taken up by Tawney in an internal memorandum in 1957. Is the game worth the candle he asked, given the bitter
opposition likely to be encountered and the importance of the rest of
Labour's educational programme? 'It is a problem whether a Labour
Government would be justified in jeopardizing the remainder of that
programme for the sake of only part of it, however important in itself,
concerned with the future of the independent schools' (RE 238,
November 1957, p. 3). Furthermore, the financial cost of a policy on
independent schools was likely to be high, particularly if some version
of Fleming's proposals (buying places) was used.

Conflict of principle plus the pragmatic constraints of electoral
politics made the evolution of policy on private schooling a tortuous
process. The internal documents of the party's Study Group on
Education in the late 1950s reveal a complete stalemate. No policy
compromise seemed possible. Much to-ing and fro-ing occurred as the
different groups struggled for ascendancy. Thus on 11 December 1957
the Study Group decided that 'no payments, either direct or indirect,

should be made out of public funds (either national or local) to any school which charges fees and is therefore not freely open to all classes of the community, except in respect of payments made in the case of certain special categories of pupil (for example, handicapped children) to be specified' and went into considerable detail about how this would be achieved (RE 301, January 1958). Yet three months later the same Study Group rejected this class analysis of private schools and in a draft policy statement argued that if a parent 'in addition to paying his rates and taxes, ... wishes to buy private education, he cannot in a free country be prohibited from so doing' and concluded 'that at present no scheme for "taking over" or "democratizing" the public schools shows sufficient merit to justify the large diversion of public money that could be involved' (RE 347, March 1958, p. 24). The way forward seemed murky indeed.

While the ideological ambiguity continued the only viable policy was no policy — if possible expressed in positive terms. In *70 Questions Asked and Answered on Labour's Education Policy* (1959) the question 'How will a Labour Government challenge the advantages of private education?' received the answer: 'By improving the nation's own schools in the following ways: (a) by reducing the size of classes; (b) by pressing ahead with better training and qualifications for teachers; (c) by raising the standards in all LEA schools'. A further question on direct grant schools is given the reply that the direct grant list will not be extended (RE 484, January 1959, p. 15). The assumption was that as the state sector improved the private sector would wither away. Different versions of Fleming were also advanced though never endorsed. A policy of state sponsored places in independent schools could be presented both as attacking the class basis of the schools and as respecting the right of parents to buy education for their children if they so wished. The difficulties with it were that it would of necessity retain some form of selection when Labour's policy was to end selection in the State sector, that on a small scale the middle class would make disproportionate use of it and that if on a large scale the cost would be prohibitive. At one point Tawney suggested establishing a large percentage of free places at a small number of schools in order to get round these problems but even he was lukewarm about the strategem (RE 238, November 1957, p. 2).

The unease within the party's policy-making committee structure about the private schools issue is reflected in the absence of any mention of it in the six election manifestos between 1945 and 1964; with the exception of 1955 where, ironically, there is the statement 'We shall insist on the inspection of private schools'. As always, conference was less reticent. *Learning to Live's* conclusion in 1958 that 'at present no scheme for 'taking over' or 'democratizing' the public schools shows sufficient merit to justify the large diversion of public money that would be involved' (p. 60) provoked an outcry at the annual conference that year. The subtleties of principled and pragmatic arguments so prevalent in the committee working papers of the party rarely reappear in conference debates of this period where ideological certitude is more evident. Whether this eventually had its effect or whether it was the recognition, as a Home Policy Sub-committee observed in 1961, that the state schools would not improve to the point where they reduced the appeal of independent schools and that industry had in any case found new ways of assisting private education through scholarships and grants (RD 134, April 1961, p. 2) it is difficult to say. But in the 1961 policy document *Signposts for the Sixties* it was argued that once 'Brought within the state system and purged of their privileged position, the public schools could perform a much more useful educational purpose than at present' (p. 31). To do this, it was proposed that an educational trust be set up under the Minister of Education to recommend the form of integration with the state sector to be adopted by each private school. The class analysis thesis had apparently won, at least at the policy level of public statement of intent. Having thus salved its conscience the NEC and its sub-committees thankfully dropped the issue for decade. No further working papers appeared on the subject until 1971.

There are a number of reasons for this interregnum in addition to the fact that the issue was ideologically divisive and an electoral liability. Firstly, it was not obvious how the policy would be implemented. Of itself this was not a difficulty since normally the expertise of relevant intellectuals could be recruited to help out. However, here was an educational policy which required financial, fiscal, legal and administrative skills to breathe life into it. While the normal pool of educational intellectuals associated with the party could supply the expertise necessary for the justification of the policy (for example, data on the relationship between class background, private schools and occupational destination) quite different skills and knowledge were required to develop ideas on how the policy could be implemented. And it was not clear where the intellectuals with these skills were to come from. Secondly, the rules of the ball-game changed markedly once Labour assumed power in 1964. Much of the Research Department's energies were diverted to servicing MPs rather than constructing policy. Within this, the significance of education as a policy area took a nosedive after 1961 when the Study Group on Education was disbanded. This was probably just as well given Crosland's well-known dislike of being tied down in advance by detailed party policy. (Crosland was Secretary of State for Education and Science 1965-67.) Thirdly, as the Labour party's 1966 manifesto reported in its only mention of private schools 'We have appointed the Public Schools Commission to recommend the best ways of integrating the public schools into the state sector'. The existence of the Newsom Commission from 1965 onwards provided Labour education ministers with a convenient let-out when questioned about their intentions on the independent sector.

This was fortunate since conference, for one, diligently continued to call for the integration of the private and state sectors. With one exception all of the six conferences from 1965 to 1969 passed a resolution to that effect. A problem arose in 1976 because the resolution was 'to bring all public, direct grant and other fee-paying schools within the state system *in the life-time of the present Government'* (Labour Party Annual Conference, 1967, p. 124, our emphasis). Putting a time limit on it obviously worried the NEC and Alice Bacon, MP, argued that they should wait for the results of the Commission. The sponsors of the resolution were not persuaded, pressed their point and were defeated.

Reactions from conference to the report of the Public Schools Commission (Part I) the following year were uniformly hostile. Mr Ackhurst, observing that the public schools 'are fortresses of privilege', saw the principal objective of the Newsom Report as being to 'see how we could integrate our education system, our comprehensive system, into the public schools'. It was 'asking us to subsidize the public schools out of public money' (Labour Party Annual Conference, 1968, p. 234). Everyone agreed, the findings of Newsom were duly formally rejected and the Labour party was back to square one.

Forward Shuffle

In terms of our understanding of the possible functions of Labour party intellectuals, by 1970 it is clear that problems were present at nearly every stage of the translation of ideology into policy practice (Figure 2). Admittedly the ideological conflicts on private schooling appeared to have been resolved in favour of the class analysis and against the parental choice position; or at least, the latter was quiescent. But beyond that, the larger issues of the relationship and gap between policy ideas formulated by the party and policy action taken by the PLP was as true of the private schools policy area as anywhere else. And the same question of what could be done about it inevitably arose. Analytically speaking, there were three types of translation functions to be considered if intellectuals opposed to the private schools were to have an impact on policy practice: the translation of (a) ideology into conference policy (greater specificity of resolutions in order to limit avoidance tactics by the PLP); (b) conference policy into NEC policy (greater detail and sophistication in order to convince and constrain both the PLP and the DES civil servants); and (c) NEC policy into, at best, electoral appeal or, at the minimum, a non–liability with public opinion. This last tended to have a very close relationship to the amount of political will ministers and MPs applied to the subject.

Between 1970 and 1977 conference continued to make its ritualistic calls for the complete integration of the private sector into the state system of education in exactly the same manner as it always had done. Tolerance was not necessarily present though powerlessness always was. At the 1972 Conference, for instance, Mr. Dudley White noted that 'Impassioned speeches has been made over the years on the subject of the integration of the private sector, but both in the years 1945 to 1950 and in 1966 to 1970 nothing was done on the matter'. In the future, he announced, 'I do not propose to pay lip service any longer to this ideal. I do not think the movement will be satisfied with those who do' (Labour Party Annual Conference, 1972, p. 247). It may have been this threat, or the accumulated weight of twenty years of conference resolutions attacking private schools, which in October 1974 led to Labour's first categorical commitment in an election manifesto to integrating the independent schools. The manifesto said that a Labour Government will

> Stop the present system of direct grant schools and withdraw tax relief and charitable status from public schools as a first step towards our long-term aim of phasing out fee paying in schools.

The visibility of the issue had been raised another notch.

Implementation of the first part of this policy commitment was carried out without difficulty, mainly because it used existing administrative mechanisms with which the DES officials were familiar. The phasing out of the direct grant grammar schools was announced in the

House of Commons in March 1975 and was given effect by the Direct Grant Grammar Schools (Cessation of Grant) Regulations 1975. The next step was to overhaul the systems of place buying by LEAs in direct grant schools and other private schools. Section 5 of the 1976 Act gave the Secretary of State powers to require LEAs to pay for private places only in accordance with regulations approved by the Secretary of State and to revoke previous arrangements. Circular 12/76 revoked the general approval given following the 1953 Education Act and Circular 6/77 explained that the approval of 'supplementary' place buying under the 1953 Act would only be given in future where an Authority could show that a particular place was necessary to supplement its own provision. Further pressure against place buying was specifically written into the 1977 Rate Support Grant Circular to Local Authorities: LEAs were called upon to make savings in the place buying expenditure category. All of this policy implementation took place within an existing legislative and administrative framework and was scarely guaranteed to raise much of a bureaucratic sweat.

On the rest of the private school sector it was a different matter. The only action which could be readily taken within the normal range of DES activities was the ending in 1977 of the previous system of DES recognition and approval as efficient of private schools. Measures on, for example, ending tax relief on insurance policies that assist in the payment of private school fees to parents of private school children or the charitable status of independent schools were more complex and involved other government departments. The more complicated are the administrative procedures involved in adopting a particular policy path, the more likely it is that bureaucratic inertia and passive resistance will be encountered. This naturally has to be said with the caveat of ceteris paribus since political will can make a considerable impact on policy implementation — as the Conservatives demonstrated in the case of the Assisted Places Scheme (APS).

The failure of the party apparatus to construct a detailed policy on private schooling left the Labour Education Ministers of the 1974–79 government completely exposed to the 'natural' administrative preferences of the DES. Why was no policy developed in order to translate the strident calls of conference and the 1974 manifesto into specific courses of action? At the very least this would have forced the DES into explaining why these courses of action were administratively untenable. Some attempt was made. In February 1973 Caroline Benn wrote a twenty-four page paper entitled 'Direct Grant, Independent and Voluntary Schools' for the Science and Education Sub-Committee. (Many of the ideas in this document later found their way into the 1980 *Private Schools* policy). Then in September 1973 a Working Group on Independent Schools was formed but did not produce any ideas for the Science and Education Sub-Committee until February 1976 when a discussion paper entitled 'Integration of Independent Schools' was circulated. Frustration was evident:

> ... if Labour doesn't start working on a genuine integration policy soon its credibility on this issue will vanish. The case for doing it now is that known activity on this issue could have a stimulating effect on all kinds of negotiations and various government departments; and a morale-raising one on hundreds of camps. It will also give us back our initiative in educational policy-making. We've allowed ourselves to be thoroughly brow-beaten by the 'freedom of parental choice' lobby and seem to have stopped arguing altogether that freedom of the rich to use their money to buy privilege is not the only criterion to guide national education policy. (RE 485, February 1976, p. 2)

But precisely who should do what was not clear. A sense of outraged justice is no substitute for a clear delineation of intellectual labour. If, as the document claimed when referring to charitable status, 'The usual reflex action of the DES will be to protect independent education but the real barrier is known to be the Treasury' (RE 485, February 1976, p. 2) then presumably it was up to Labour party intellectuals to take on the translation role of making the DES an administrative offer they would find it hard to refuse, in a language the Department would understand.

No such offer emerged in the life of the 1974-79 Labour government and, by default, the initiative remained in the hands of minister and DES. As we have seen, administrative sense and convenience consequently prevailed and policy actions were routed along established bureaucratic channels. Referring to the action taken on the Direct Grant schools, LEA place buying and the ending of the recognition as efficient system for private schools, Stella Greenhall (political adviser to Shirley Williams at the time) reported 'considerable progress' to the Science and Education Sub-Committee in January 1978 and that 'Since 1974 the Government has acted with speed and determination to control and reduce the flow of public money to the private sector of education' (RE 1476, January 1978, p. 1). She, or the DES official from whom she got her advice, was not very encouraging about the further measures that 'might' be taken. For example, the withdrawal of charitable status tax concessions would need elaborate compensation measures and 'would take much legislative time' (RE 1476, January 1978, p. 3). Not everyone was convinced. Two months later, the NEC-Cabinet Working Group on Education and Social Policy commented that 'the Government could overcome any legal obstacles if it had the *political will* to end these indirect subsidies' (RE 1596, March 1978, p. 2 our emphasis). Unfortunately political will is usually related to the availability of political means. Political will may have been weak but so were the proposed political means.

Using lack of political will as the scapegoat merely disguised the Party's inability to translate general policy on private schooling into specific administrative form in order to facilitate its implementation. The failure of this intellectual function was reinforced by the gulf between party and minister. Bert Clough, Secretary to the Science and Education Sub-Committee, estimated that the Secretary of State for Education, Shirley Williams, met the Sub-Committee for roughly half-an-hour once every six months (Clough, 1984). Given this absence of communication and the uncertainty about the role of the party organization when in office the result, inevitably, was a policy stalemate.

The power of conference to break the stalemate was slight given the absence of explicit systems of accountability between the PLP, NEC and conference and the general way in which conference resolutions were usually worded. It is significant that the wording of resolutions on independent schools became much more directive and administratively specific from 1978 to 1980, when *Private Schools* was published, reflecting the increasing technical sophistication of Left intellectuals in the conference arena. For example, in 1978, Resolution 252's list of recommendations included:

> This conference draws the attention of the government to the use of public money to subsidize so-called independent schools. It urges that urgent legislative action is taken to amend section 137 of the Local Government Act of 1972 to prevent 'non-educational' local authorities from using the rate precept to provide and subsidize places in these schools, and that their special status, which is in effect a public subsidy, be ended. (Labour Party Annual Conference, 1978, p. 286)

It would have been interesting to see how the Labour Government would have handled the specificity of this resolution but the 1979 election intervened.

The Big Push

In August 1980 the Labour party published a fifty-three page discussion document *Private Schools* which was subsequently endorsed by conference and included in the Labour party *Programme 1982*. A much shorter version *A Plan for Private Schools* was drawn up by the TUC-Labour Party Liaison Committee, approved by the TUC General Council and the NEC and published in July 1981. *Private Schools* is soundly researched, data-based, administratively sophisticated and has precise policy options. As such it is a direct parallel in party policy terms to the Conservative's Assisted Places Scheme document. How, after twenty-five years of prevarication, did the Labour Party succeed in mounting this challenge to the private schools?

Organizational and ideological pressures undoubtedly there were. Conference and the NEC wanted to develop more effective means of making the PLP accountable to party policy, five years of Labour government had done little more than chip away at the margins of the issue and, to some, party credibility seemed to be at stake, and the Left was thinking much more deliberately about the different roles of intellectuals in the party. However, pressures need to be directed. Two factors combined to direct them on to the private schools issue. One was the Assisted Places Scheme (APS) and the other was Neil Kinnock who, in 1979, became the new Shadow Cabinet Spokeman on education.

If the APS provided the ideological ignition for the issue, Kinnock supplied the fuel. The implementation of the Scheme by the Conservatives on their return to office in 1979 hit the Labour party on a very raw ideological nerve. Up to that point it may have been the case, as Caroline Benn argued, that the 'whole independent school issue was one the party appeared to be dropping quietly'. 'Now, of course,' she continued 'Conservative government policy has put the independent school issue squarely back on the agenda again. No Labour government in future can avoid dealing with it' (RD 166, December 1979, p. 2). By directly subsidizing the independent schools, the APS cuts right across Labour's class and educational sensitivities and at the 1979 annual conference provided a rallying-call for the faithful on an issue over which they could readily unite. Kinnock took the opportunity: 'We cannot tolerate ... the system which will expend seventy million pounds from the public purse on the already affluent while pirating scholastic talent from the state sector', he said. A letter would be sent to every school where a headmaster was likely to recommend undertaking such a scheme making it clear that a Labour government would 'tear out' the scheme with a 'short sharp Bill' (Labour Party Annual Conference, 1979, p. 357).

With the ideological momentum once again established courtesy of the APS, in November 1979 the Independent School Working Group of the NEC was set up with Neil Kinnock as its Chairman. Kinnock thus provided an all important link between conference, the NEC and the PLP. Whereas the independent schools issue had previously been fought out by different people in the different arenas, now the Shadow Spokesman on education brought these three arenas together. The other members of the Working Group were Caroline Benn, Stella Greenhall, Chris Price and Jack Straw with Bert Clough of the Research Department acting as Secretary to the Group. Clough estimates that the Group met for a total of about 100 hours (Clough, 1984).

Prior to setting up the Working Group, the Science and Education Sub-Committee had highlighted the need to translate existing policy 'into a definite and feasible plan which a Labour government could implement' (RD 56, September 1979, p. 3). In taking on this task, the Working Group had, in effect, to develop the means to challenge the fiscal and legal embodiment of the private schools' hegemony which is, of course, class-based (see Chapter 4). Small wonder also that it took the Group outside the confines of educational policy-making and into such areas as tax and charity law. In this situation the normal skills of intellectuals specialising in education had to be supplemented by those of experts in quite separate fields. For example Peter Archer Q.C., the Party's Legal Spokesman, was consulted on the charitable status of private schooling. It must soon have become clear why the DES on its own also lacked the skills to implement the policy.

At the outset the task seemed daunting but the importance of producing the administrative details of the policy was clearly recognized. Commenting on the work to be done, Caroline Benn (1980) wrote: 'So little has really been thought through, and so many issues were avoided by the last governments. It means that many comments are necessary — to be sure we don't set out a policy that is shot to pieces and puts us even further back'. And on the limitations of Labour's previous record on LEA place buying she observed: 'The reason is that Labour's policy here was not able to be implemented, and also that it was never really successfully worked out. We never really sat down and said, as a Labour government, now what principles should guide all place-buying. That's what we are doing now'. While the Working Group itself undoubtedly put in a lot of work, the pivotal role was played by its Secretary and full-time party intellectual, Bert Clough. He wrote the initial and subsequent drafts of the document, organized the Working Group meetings, steered the document through the Science and Education Sub-Committee (where it was changed) and the Home Policy Committee (where it was not changed), and negotiated and drafted the subsequent TUC-Labour Party Liaison Committee statement *A Plan for Private Schools*.

Conclusions

Private Schools is a clear attempt by the party organization to influence the process of policy implementation. It states

> The purpose of this section is to discuss ways in which a Labour government, with the will to do so, could implement this policy ... we are conscious of the fact that successive Labour governments have been faced with powerful and well organized opposition to change from vested interests inside and outside Whitehall. The need for a firm, systematic and practical policy is therefore all the more obvious and it is with this in mind that we set out full policy options together with the implications of those options. (p. 35)

Furthermore, following criticism from the Socialist Educational Association that *Private Schools* did 'not consider the stages through which policy has to be carried — nor distinguish clearly enough what can be done at once, and what needs to be planned in a step-by-step way for carrying out over a longer period' (RD 836, April 1981, p. 10), a schedule for implementation of the policy was included in *A Plan for Private Schools*.

On this issue, the party organization has probably gone as far as it is able along the path of controlling policy implementation. At the levels of both conference and the NEC, intellectuals have successfully translated party ideology into specific policy form. Where they have conspicuously failed and where there has been no activity, is in the translation of both ideology and policy on private schools into a form which could be sold to the electorate. How this could be achieved appears not to have been discussed or seen as a relevant political question. Only Caroline Benn seems to have raised the issue (a decade ago). In her 1973 paper on direct grant, independent and voluntary schools she asked: 'How do we devise a policy which enables support for integration, which undoubtedly exists to be mobilized and so "justify" action by the Secretary of State of this kind?' (RD 653, February 1973, p. 13). For the rest, public opinion is, by default, regarded as immutable or irrelevant. In an electoral party this is a critical omission which must inevitably limit the extent to which the policy can be implemented. While the omission remains the challenge to the private schools is only half born.

The time taken to develop the challenge to its present stage was a product of the ideological ambiguities aroused by the issue, the complexity of the policy measures needed to tackle it and the absence of the appropriate intellectual support. During the 1950s and early 1960s the ideological clashes continued between those who saw the private schools as bastions of class privilege deserving of destruction and those who viewed fee-paying education as the rightful exercising of parental freedom of choice. Even when the conflict was resolved in the favour of the class privilege position, the way forward remained murky indeed. Labour Party policy development on the private sector had to compete with other policy areas for the intellectual resources required to translate conference resolutions into detailed NEC policy. And given the variety of legal, financial and fiscal issues involved, a policy on private schools needed a range of intellectual inputs which were not easily obtainable. The result was that policy development on the private schools during the 1974–79 Labour government was left to the DES which naturally made use of the bureaucratic procedures most readily available to it. In this respect the direct grant schools were the most vulnerable part of the private sector (since organizing their demise did not require legislative time) and therefore they were the first to go. Ironically, it was only when the Conservatives introduced their own policy on private schools in 1979 (the APS) that the Labour party was finally spurred into action and a detailed policy developed. But so long as it fails to translate that policy into a form that can be easily packaged, sloganized and sold to the public, the electoral liability of the policy will severely curtail its chances of full implementation. And so long as the ideological initiative remains with the Conservatives it will be a very difficult policy to sell.

6   The Private Sector Counterattacks: Institutional Cooperation and Ideological Warfare

Introduction

It is part of the general thesis of this book that to understand the process of educational change it is necessary to analyze how the pertinent institutions respond to their social context. We believe that institutions are not inevitable victims, or indeed beneficiaries, of broader social forces. The change process, as well as the consequences of that process, is determined in part by how institutions react to their opportunities and challenges. In this chapter we will be examining how the institutions that represented the private sector of schooling reacted to a dangerous crisis that emerged in the period between the 1944 Education Act and Circular 10/65. The initial response to that crisis was defensive, but slowly — within a context that was increasingly more favourable — the private sector institutions were able to rebuild their political support, to turn the educational debate in their favour and to establish their popularity with a larger number of parents. It is our contention that the key to this success was the institutional regeneration of the private sector for this provided the basis for making a sustained and effective counterattack. We will conclude the chapter by assessing the current political position of the private sector and evaluating how the changes have affected the schools' traditional class reproduction function.

The Growing Critique

From the 1944 Education Act to Circular 10/65 a broad political consensus underlay the system of schooling in Britain so much so that it was not uncommon to think of education and politics as mutually exclusive concepts. As part of a purposeful political strategy Butler, the architect of the 1944 Education Act, had 'side-tracked the public schools issue' and in his own terms 'the first-class carriage had been shunted on to an immense siding' (1971, p. 120). The steady erosion of the political consensus was partly a result of the persistent efforts of those who were determined to shunt the first-class carriage out of the siding and back onto the tracks. Although the main attack upon selective secondary education centred upon the 11+ examination and the maintained grammar schools, it should not be forgotten that many of the independent schools were in fact grammar schools and all of them were selective.

In our chapter on the relationship between independent schooling and the reproduction of class relations we have already examined much of the traditional critique — that the schools recruit pupils from a very narrow segment of the class hierarchy, expose them to peculiar socializing experiences that cement internal loyalties while isolating them from outsiders, and create an old boy network which gives its members unfair job advantages. During the time period 1944-65 a number of developments intensified the political isolation of the private schools, sapped their economic strength and questioned their credibility as centres of learning.

The most significant political development was the change in Labour party policy. Until the late 1950s the dominant faction within the party believed that private schools would wither on the vine as parents abandoned them for a steadily improving state sector. No direct positive action was necessary for the central task was to increase resources for the maintained sector, improving its quality as it expanded in response to demographic trends. With the passage of time it was increasingly difficult to believe that the private sector would simply waste away. The evidence suggested that, regardless of the quality of the maintained schools, the independent schools continued to retain the loyalty of at least some segments of the British middle class. However, the challenge to private schooling emerged within the context of an even more powerful movement within the Labour party against the selective system of maintained secondary schools. Selection rather than independence was the most important target.

In the second phase, notwithstanding the vocal and growing voice of the abolitionists, the Labour party committed itself to integrating the two educational sectors. The Labour minister most closely identified with this strategy was Tony Crosland. Under his auspices the Public

Schools Commission was created which was required, as part of its terms of reference, 'to advise on the best way of integrating the public schools with the State system of education' (Public Schools Commission, 1968a, p. viii). The First Report of the Commission (the Newsom Report) actually recommended that 50 per cent of places in independent schools should be made available to non-fee paying pupils who were in need of boarding education and that the state should at least contribute towards the payment of these pupils' fees (*Ibid.*, pp. 8 and 11–12). But as an indication of how fast opinion within the Labour party was moving, the Report was repudiated in a motion carried at the party's conference in 1968. It was not long before the abolitionists within the party were to have their way; their cause undoubtedly furthered by the Second Report of the Public Schools Commission (the Donnison Report) which recommended that the direct grant schools should be incorporated within the maintained secondary system on a voluntary-aided basis (Public Schools Commission, 1979a, pp. 11-12).

The independent sector was not slow to recognize the importance of the shift in Labour party policy. The first session of the 1965 annual meeting of the Headmasters Conference (held in Christ Church College, Oxford) was devoted to 'The organization of secondary education'. That meeting made a thorough, if conventional, case against the reorganization of secondary education along the lines proposed in Circular 10/65, with the arguments being pitched at both the ideological (a dislike of social engineering coupled with a defence of standards, independence and diversity) and practical (lack of resource input, no research and too hasty changes) levels (HMC, 1965, First Session). Of greater consequence was the emergence of the Direct Grant Joint Committee (DGJC) for it was recognized early on that the direct grant grammar schools would form the independent sector's first line of defence. The 1965 minutes of the Direct Grant Schools Committee (one of the sub-committees of HMC) convey the impression that battle is about to commence. Thus we read of the need for 'quiet watchfulness' and that 'The heads of direct grant schools must be well-versed in political trends but must not get personally involved. Their job is education' (HMC (1965), *Bulletin*, No. 1, February). On a related front the Association of Governing Bodies in Public Schools (GBA) and the HMC established a joint committee, consisting of many of their notables, to consider the government's proposal to set up an educational trust for public schools (the Public Schools Commission).

Whereas at the national level there was time enough in which to engage in lofty debates and to prepare for possible future political moves, at the local level the pressure was more immediate and that much sharper. Local education authorities, invariably controlled by the Labour party, had anticipated Circular 10/65 and were already reorganizing their secondary schools along comprehensive lines. Prior to 1965 these changes did not usually threaten established grammar schools (either there were no such local schools or they were simply excluded from the reorganization plans) and as such they received broad political support. Inevitably the existing political consensus was strained once existing grammar schools were threatened. For the independent sector this challenge took the form of local authorities failing to take up their quotas of free places in direct grant schools. Faced with the latter crisis a direct grant school either had to look to other sympathetic local authorities to fill the available places or finance the places out of their own resources as the direct grant regulations prevented the schools from charging fees for their free places.

The initial response to the disengagement of the local authorities from the direct grant schools was a monitoring of the situation. Thus the 1963 minutes of the Direct Grant Schools Committee refer to a survey of developments with the intention of making the 'results known to the ministry and of sending a summary to all the headmasters of HMC direct grant schools (HMC (1963), *Bulletin*, No.1, February). Later, under the auspices of the DGJC and the Independent Schools Information Service (ISIS), the monitoring was systematized in the form of annual surveys. Much of the early collation of information was undertaken by Peter Mason, former High Master of Manchester Grammar School and one of the work horses of the DGJC. Given the fact that the withdrawal of local authority support could escalate to crisis proportions, a mere review of the trend was clearly insufficient. What was required was a change in the rules. The direct grant schools needed regulations which would mitigate the financial consequences if local authorities refused to take up their quota of free places. The most obvious improvement from the point of view of the direct grant schools would be the removal of the obligation to offer free places at their own expense if the LEAs disengaged. In fact a Labour government, in the 1976 Education Act, restricted the right of local education authorities to buy places in the independent sector. So rather than protecting the schools from the capriciousness of local authority action the central government eventually intervened to control those who were prepared to buy places!

Circular 10/65 intensified the contact between the direct grant schools and the LEAs because it encouraged local negotiations to determine the form of comprehensive secondary schooling and the pace at which its introduction would proceed. At its very first meeting (25 February 1966) the DGJC reviewed the principles that it felt should be defended in such negotiations. A view was expressed that a direct grant school could become comprehensive but still retain its direct grant status. The general tone of the meeting was opposed to such sentiments (one member expressed 'grave concern at this development') for it was accepted that direct grant schools had been built and equipped for a specific purpose i.e. as schools that catered for pupils who had been selected on academic grounds. It was felt that some gesture could be made in the form of a modest expansion in the academic range of the pupil intake (DGJC, *Minutes*, 25 February 1966). Given this position, which was adhered to consistently by both the DGJC and HMC's Direct Grant Committee, clashes between the schools and those local authorities determined to remove the selective basis of secondary school entry were inevitable.

This necessity to be involved in protracted local negotiations forced the independent sector into the political arena in a more forceful, persistent and visible fashion than had been true in the past. In the process internal developments occurred: it had to make explicit those principles which it wished to defend, it had to create institutions which had the competence to monitor developments on the ground and the authority to inform their members as to what their guiding principles should be, and it had to draw upon the lessons it learnt in negotiations to formulate future policy options. In this latter respect it is pertinent to note, for example, that the involvement of the LEAs in the present government's Assisted Places Scheme is minimal.

The independent sector would have felt less threatened by the trend of Labour party policy if it had been assured that the Conservative party could be relied upon to defend its interests. The Conservative party has traditionally advocated the cause of private schooling in the sense that periodically party conferences reiterate their support for the principle that parents have the right to purchase schooling for their children. However, and this is especially true of the time period we are considering, Conservative governments have been much more circumspect in providing concrete assistance. Furthermore, the party's response to Circular 10/65 was highly pragmatic. There was widespread recognition that early selection for secondary schooling, and the 11+ examination in particular, was very unpopular with many parents. To defend the grammar schools could, therefore, tarnish the party's image and possibly harm its electoral prospects. It was also true that the party's chief educational spokesman in the 1960s, Sir Edward Boyle, was convinced by many of the intellectual arguments against early selection (Kogan, 1971, pp. 17–19). Powerful elements in the two main political parties seemed therefore to be maintaining the policy consensus that had been established by the 1944 Education Act.

Although Circular 10/65 did not produce a sharp political divide, the two parties differentiated themselves on the question of comprehensive schooling. The Conservative party incorporated the following provisos: that it should be a matter for negotiations on the part of the local education authorities, that 'botched-up' schemes of reorganization were to be avoided, that large schools were inadvisable, that selection was sooner or later inevitable, that it was possible in places for grammar and comprehensive schools to coexist successfully, and that it was preferable to delay action until research had evaluated the two systems. Indeed Sir Edward Boyle argued at the Conservative party's 1965 conference that neighbourhood comprehensive schools in the large conurbations were unlikely to assist the academic progress of intelligent working-class children and that some grammar schools should be retained for this purpose (Conservative Party, 1965). However, it could be argued that this was policy differentiation at the margins and that its purpose was to increase the party's electoral appeal and to ensure some semblance of party unity. It was unlikely to be of much comfort to those schools which believed that their very existence was threatened.

Perhaps more damaging to the interests of the private sector, than its exclusion from the policy making processes within the political parties, was its isolation from what is usually referred to as the educational establishment. It is widely conceded that since the 1944 Education Act the management of schooling in Britain has been under the control of the Department of Education and Science (DES), the LEAs and the National Union of Teachers (NUT). Not surprisingly, in view of the fact that it draws most of its members from the maintained schools, the NUT can hardly be expected to promote the interests of private schooling. The perspective of those umbrella bodies in which the LEAs were represented obviously varied as the fortunes of the political parties fluctuated but this meant that they were at best uncertain allies.

The position of the DES is more difficult to gauge. Representatives of the independent sector refer to very proper behaviour by departmental officials in the negotiations that preceded the Assisted Places Scheme but relations in the past may have been more strained. One very senior retired official has told us that in the post-war years the Department came to see the independent sector as an anachronism. Apparently there was some resentment at the amount of time that had to be put into its concerns when the Department had more than sufficient work to do in looking after the maintained sector. Certainly the DES did not appear to protest when its power to recognize independent schools as efficient by means of inspections was ended in April 1978. Furthermore, Kogan (1971) (as the informed insider) suggests that the Department — in tune with the political lead set by Boyle and Crosland — gradually came to accept the soundness of the case for comprehensive secondary schooling (pp. 16-25). If this is indeed so, then there would be substantive policy reasons for not supporting the interests of the independent sector, in addition to the feeling that it was a rather irritating left-over from the past.

Whereas it has always been alleged that the public schools provide an education that helps to perpetuate a ruling class, in the 1960s the schools were considered by many to be anachronistic in cultural, educational and social terms. In the maintained sector there were innovations in the design of the schools, the content of the curriculum, the relationship between subject areas, methods of assessment, and authority structures. By comparison the traditional world of the public school appeared to be archaic, more than ready for the spring cleaner's broom. As we argued in our previous book, independent schooling was not in fact immune from progressive educational ideas, and had radically reformed itself in the post-war era. But it was a question of images, and as the headmasters of the public schools knew only too well it was hard to shake off the legacy of the past.

Such attacks would have carried little weight as long as the independent sector was thriving financially. Although some schools have lucrative endowments, and probably all independent schools receive some form of indirect financial aid from the state, they are competing for pupils in the market-place. Failure to compete successfully will sooner or later force most schools to close. Statistics presented by the Public Schools Commission suggest that in the time period 1947 to 1967 many independent schools were experiencing considerable difficulties in remaining solvent.

In terms of gross numbers the independent sector declined between 1947 and 1967. Within that sector the schools recognized as efficient received a steadily increasing share of the market, a reflection of the fact that more schools applied for, and were granted, that accolade. If comparisons are made of the proportions of children in schools then the picture is particularly depressing from the point of view of the private sector. Whereas in 1947 89.7 per cent pupils were in maintained schools and 10.3 per cent in direct grant/independent schools in 1967 93 per cent were in maintained schools and 7 per cent in direct grant/independent schools. Finally it must be remembered that this trend was occuring as pupil numbers increased so the decline in overall numbers in the independent sector represents a decisive vote of no confidence. At the elite end of the market perhaps the schools had little incentive to expand their numbers as they were more interested in maintaining their social and academic exclusiveness. But this would not have been true of the independent sector as a whole, and in any case, the prestigious schools would have welcomed an increasing demand for their services even if they intended to turn down most of that demand. We are under the impression that demand was generally on the wane. Furthermore, it has to be remembered that incomes were increasing in real terms throughout this period. The decline in demand was due, in our opinion, to both educational (the growing prestige of the grammar schools, direct grant and maintained) and ideological (the stigma attached to private schooling) factors.

We have demonstrated previously that the independent schools form a complex sector and that they would not have been equally affected by their generally poor performance in the market-place. For example Table 7 shows that the direct grant schools were over time educating an increasing number of pupils and that by 1962 they had regained their 1947 share of the market following a decline in the 1950s. The fact that non–recognized independent schools were requesting the ministry for inspections in order that they could be registered as efficient suggests that it was the less prestigious end of the sector that was feeling the pinch most acutely. However, even those who were

Table 7: Numbers of Pupils and Schools, 1947–1967

	Pupils (000's)			
	Maintained	Direct Grant	Independent Reg. Efficient	Other Independent
1947	5,034.3	78.0	165.1	332.5
1952	5,970.0	85.3	234.6	254.9
1957	6,776.5	92.5	278.7	220.3
1962	6,965.3	111.6	303.9	185.4
1967	7,328.1	116.2	305.2	129.8

Source: Public Schools Commission (1968b) *First Report, Volume II*, London, HMSO. p. 22

more favourably placed must have experienced some anxieties as they saw the steady erosion of their support base. Both bursars and headmasters have revealed to us that even some schools in HMC struggled to fill their last half dozen places in order to balance the books. The political repercussions of a declining independent sector were obvious for as it shrunk in size, and became less diverse in character, so its political vulnerability increased.

So far we have argued that in the twenty-year period following the 1944 Education Act independent schooling in Britain was losing out in three critical areas: it was on the political defensive as its enemies in the Labour party increased their influence, a problem intensified by the quiesence of the Conservative party; it was ineffective in defending the kind of educational experiences it had to offer; and over time it was educating a declining number of pupils and a shrinking proportion of the school age population. The potential impact of these trends was exacerbated by three parallel internal weaknesses: political naivety; ideological stagnation; and institutional fragmentation.

It is to be expected that the institutions representing the independent schools would purposefully try not to be too closely identified with any one political party. Although we shall later demonstrate more than a simple converging of interests between private schooling and the Conservative party, prominent spokesmen for the former have from time to time made statements in which they stress the need to maintain a separate identity. Furthermore, approaches have been made to all the other main political parties, including the Labour party. In the period prior to the mid-1960s the independent sector did not perceive a need for direct political contacts because the threat from this quarter was undeveloped. Although this posture may be understandable it is far more difficult to appreciate their rudimentary efforts at public relations. It is not until the early 1960s that HMC actually made some positive steps in this direction. A public relations consultant was employed on a short-term contract and he gave his first report in 1963 (HMC (1963), *Bulletin*, No. 2, April). At about the same time a Publicity Committee (soon to be renamed the Public Relations Committee) was created as one of HMC's sub-committees. This was followed by the launching of HMC's own house journal, appropriately named *Conference*. At the 1963 annual general meeting, at which it was agreed to proceed with the journal, Frank Fisher (its main architect) claimed that it would propagate good educational practice and spread their message to a wider audience. Finally, in recognition of the fact that a General Election was impending, HMC decided that it would have to conduct research in order to obtain the necessary hard evidence on which to base the case it would make to the public (HMC (1963), *Bulletin*, No. 4, July).

This frenetic activity of the early 1960s illustrates the extent to which the independent sector, and HMC in particular, was politically unprepared. Within HMC itself a new group of headmasters, in alliance with certain of the more forward-looking members of the previous generation, assumed control. Not much political sophistication was required to realize that thirteen years of Tory government were drawing to a close and that decidedly choppy political waters lay ahead. The schools, even if they wished it, could not remain in their comparatively cosseted worlds imagining that 'education and politics' would forever remain separate. What is also remarkable about this burst of activity is the confidence of its instigators for they believed that if the public was presented with the facts it would be persuaded of the merits of private schooling. Given the alternative of a steady slide into oblivion perhaps there was no other way they could have thought.

In view of the hegemony which protected independent schooling (both in terms of the legal framework and ideological themes) a certain lack of flexibility in responding to the contemporary intellectual trends could be anticipated. Nowhere is this better illustrated than in some of the evidence submitted to the Public Schools Commission. HMC and the Association of Governing Bodies (GBA) created a Joint Working Party to formulate the evidence they would submit to the Commission and to prepare briefs to guide their members in their 'initial public reactions' to the Commission's proposals (GBA/HMC, 1968, p. 1). In its evidence to the Commission the Joint Working Party argued that '. . . we hardly think that we can reasonably be supposed to be the cause of the class system as it exists in this country: that system is a result of the complexities of history and the distribution of wealth, and we are ourselves a product of it' (Public Schools Commission, 1968b, p. 153). Few individuals of any political persuasion would dispute this but it is not much of a response to those who are intent on breaking the established relationship between schooling and the class structure, who are determined that schools should not — as far as it is possible — be one of the agents of class reproduction. This part of the Working Party's evidence smacks of complacency, of a willingness to accept the status quo even if it should be considered undesirable.

Not surprisingly, given that it represented schools universally noted for their academic excellence, the DGJC's evidence to the Commission took up the question of selection. In a sub-section entitled 'The Inevitability of Selection' the DGJC claimed that 'While we agree that on general grounds it is desirable to postpone selection as late as is practically possible, we believe some selection in the secondary stage to be both inevitable and sound' (GBA, 1968, p. 5). Again it is hard to disagree but there would be bitter conflict over what is 'practically possible' and much argument to the effect that if selection were necessary it was better that it should occur within the context of a comprehensive system of secondary education. Of greater significance was the defensive nature of much of the independent sector's intellectual position: 'we merely reinforce class differences we don't cause them'/'selection is sooner or later inevitable'. It was intellectually better equipped to defend the prevailing system of schooling and less able to respond to the central themes of the contemporary debate.

The central problem for those who wished to see a reformed private sector was how to restructure the relationship with maintained schooling. The reformers hoped that a new bridge could be created if the schools provided places for those who needed boarding education. The First Report of the Public Schools Commission gave its official approval by urging the schools to make 50 per cent of their boarding places available to those with such needs. These were to be assisted places with much of the cost being met by the state. The proposal floundered mainly on the antipathy of the major protagonists: powerful forces in the Labour party were opposed to the state funnelling money into schools that they would prefer to see abolished while the GBA and HMC were suspicious of moving ahead 'too rapidly or on too large a scale' at least in the early stages (GBA/HMC, 1968, p. 5). Even this proposal, however, was tainted by more than its fair share of wishful thinking. As Vaizey pointed out in his 'note of reservation' to the Public Schools Commission there is a critical distinction between boarding demand and boarding need (Public Schools Commission, 1968a, pp. 221–4). Although well-meaning liberals may conclude that certain social problems can best be dealt with by providing some children with boarding education, this is far from demonstrating that the individuals involved in the situation see the matter in the same light. Given the importance of the concept of 'boarding need' to those who were trying to build bridges between the maintained and independent sectors through an Assisted Places Scheme, the failure to grapple seriously with the attendant problems is little short of staggering. If defenders of the system can be best described as conservative but pragmatic then the only way to describe the reformers is as well-intentioned but naive.

We have already referred to some examples of institutional

cooperation within the independent sector, but this did not occur to any great extent until the 1960s and what early collaboration took place was invariably between two institutions in pursuit of a specific goal. Throughout the time period we are examining, however, the various segments of the independent sector were represented by separate institutions which were there to defend the particular interests of their own members. Although as independent schools they would have much in common there were always potentially divisive issues. Even within HMC clear status divisions could, and still can, be found. Furthermore, the direct grant schools were committed to a somewhat distinctive ethos as they were concerned with furthering academic excellence rather than educating 'the well-rounded scholar'. Moreover the direct grant schools were themselves split into at least two camps — those who were members of HMC and those who were not. Preparatory and secondary schools could clash over the entry requirements of the latter as preparatory schools had a vested interest in securing good public school places for their pupils while the secondary schools obviously wanted pupils who would fit in and do well. Many of the schools were competing for the same pupils and when this involved members of different institutions the situation was potentially explosive. This became an especially serious internal conflict when HMC schools (which some would say had previously flaunted their masculinity) started to recruit (others would say 'poach') girls (Rae, 1981, pp. 131–43).

The absence of institutional links was less of a problem in maintaining internal harmony than in acting effectively in response to external threats. The internal divisions could be exploited in order to undermine the overall viability of the independent sector. One prominent ex-headmaster, for example, informed us that if matters really came to a head his preoccupation would be to ensure the survival of approximately thirty schools. Besides enabling the schools to present a united front, more permanent institutional cooperation opened up the possibility of the deployment of greater resources in a more effective manner.

In view of what has been written so far it is reasonable to ask why the independent sector was not in fact swept away sometime in the late 1960s. We have argued that over a period of approximately twenty years its overall support base was on the decline, that the traditional attacks were reinforced by contemporary social trends, and that the independent schools were increasingly isolated politically. In response to these trends the independent sector had little to offer: it was politically unsophisticated, it was intellectually defensive, and it was organizationally weak — divided, if not into mutually hostile camps, then into camps which jealously guarded their own sectarian interests and which seemed incapable of sustained institutionally-based cooperation.

At this time the defence of the independent sector depended upon two legacies: the strength of the idea that, no matter how repugnant private schooling might be, parents still had the right to purchase it and the political constraints that affected the Labour party. The right of parents to purchase schooling is part of the more general belief that parents should be as responsible as possible for the upbringing of their offspring. Indeed there are many who would claim some moral superiority for those parents who either educate their own children or purchase private schooling. One of the consistent defences of private schooling is that parents who pay directly for the education of their children are more concerned that they should do well than those parents who use the maintained schools.

It required, therefore, a significant ideological shift to accept the curtailment of individual rights in an area where the restrictions had previously been few. For all its desire to restrict inequalities in our society the Labour party has been unwilling to move in this direction until comparatively recently. Even Crosland, who believed that educational change was more significant to the cause of equality than the Labour party's constitutional commitment to the nationalization of the ownership of the means of production, was reluctant to take this step (Crosland, 1956, pp. 261–2). The party grappled to find its own middle way and sought comfort in the advocacy of positive discrimination and in the move from the weak to the strong definition of equality of educational opportunity. Moreover, there were still those in the Labour party who, with probably one eye fixed firmly on the electoral barometer, found it extremely difficult to cast off the aura of the grammar school tradition. Selection at 11 may have been unpopular but the grammar schools were not. Harold Wilson argued that the comprehensive schools would extend rather than destroy the grammar school tradition (Kogan, 1975, p. 219). And Reg Prentice, whose job it was to oversee the local negotiations that followed from Circular 10/65, was undoubtedly an educational moderate. In his 1965 address to the annual meeting of HMC the Chairman pointed out that Prentice (significantly in an address to the Incorporated Association of Preparatory Schools) had said that, 'The nation cannot afford to lose any good schools'. It was sentiments such as these that led some in the independent sector to believe that a deal could be struck with a Labour government.

One consequence of Butler's 'shunting of the first-class carriage onto an immense siding', coupled with the dominant belief in the Labour party that the private schools would wither on the vine, was an obscuring of the independent sector from the public gaze. It simply did not figure in public discussion. This meant that there was very little serious debating of the relevant issues. The political parties either ignored the schools or retreated into ritualistic party dogmas. The intellectual debates that arose within the educational world were couched in the terms of the maintained sector and there was a lull before they embraced independent schooling. This was why the direct grant schools were the first line of defence, the issue was selection rather than independence.

But the independent sector could not rely upon the old hegemony and the uncertainties within the Labour party to last forever. It was only a matter of time before the mainstream within the Labour party was prepared to argue that the cause of equality is greater than the rights of a comparatively small number of parents. Ironically even the moderate candidate in the last struggle for the leadership of the party displayed his radical credentials by advocating in 1973 that a tough line should be pursued when dealing with the independent schools. Although in fairness to Roy Hattersley he has maintained a consistent policy line on this issue. Equally ironical is the fact that, although the Labour party is now more ideologically consistent on this issue, it has failed to break the old hegemony. If opinion polls are to be believed even a majority of those who vote Labour are opposed to their abolition (ISIS, 1982, p. 1). But in the context of the mid-1960s many of the more sophisticated members of the independent sector quite rightly believed that the tide was running against them and that determined action was required to turn it before they were all swamped.

Institutional Regeneration

In our opinion the independent sector's most significant response to the growing external threats was the move towards institutional cooperation. Although our analytical strategy may give the impression that historical developments unfolded in a neat sequence, it must be stressed at the outset that this was not so. As is so often the case events occurred in a far more haphazard fashion. However we have commenced with examining examples of institutional co-operation because of our belief that organizations provide the critical links between the generation of ideas and the formulation of policy. In other words, without the creation of new representative institutions it is doubtful if the independent sector could have sustained an ideological counterattack, formulated new educational policies, and — most crucially — have linked the two.

We have already noted that in the 1960s there was growing cooperation on an ad hoc basis between institutions in the independent sector. These initiatives have been followed by the creation of umbrella organizations which have varying functions to perform on a con-tinuous basis. The umbrella organizations incorporate a number of the independent sector's differing institutions with power invariably con-centrated in a small controlling committee composed of members who are broadly representative of the organization's constituent institutions. When it has been necessary to form working parties, usually to conduct more specific business, then the same representative principle has been observed. The intention is that decisions will be backed by all the constituent members so that the independent sector pulls in the same direction.

The three best examples of institutional cooperation that have been created within the independent sector along the above lines are: the Direct Grant Joint Committee (DGJC); the Independent Schools Information Service (ISIS); and the Independent Schools Joint Council (ISJC — originally known as the Independent Schools Joint Commit-tee). Of the three, the DGJC is somewhat peculiar as it was formed (very much in response to Circular 10/65) to promote the interests of only one segment of independent schooling. It is important because it was the first such organization to be created (the inaugural meeting was held on 25 February 1966), it gave much greater prominence within the independent sector to the direct grant schools, and it was very active politically. In the opinion of the first Chairman of the DGJC, the very influential Sir Hubert Ashton, it had been established in order to present a united front on basic principles and its purpose (as described by another founder member) was to explain the complexities of the problems to the Department (i.e. the DES) and when possible to give informed guidance to the schools (DGJC, *Minutes*, 25 February 1966). In concrete terms, the Committee's principal initial task was to monitor the local negotiations that had been set in motion by Circular 10/65 and to advise the individual direct grant schools accordingly.

The DGJC evolved quickly into the main negotiating body for the direct grant schools and in the course of its existence it undertook (usually through a small working party) the following tasks: negotiated with the DES on the financial support central government should make available to the direct grant schools; pushed hard to have the direct grant schools included in the Public Schools Commission's terms of reference (which was initially resisted by the government) and then submitted evidence to the Commission; tried to persuade Mrs Thatcher in the early 1970s to reform the direct grant system by means of an Assisted Places Scheme; participated heavily in the political campaign that the independent sector mounted against the abolition of the direct grant schools; negotiated with the DES the terms on which direct grant status was phased out; persuaded the Conservative party to make the Assisted Places Scheme part of its educational programme; and commenced negotiations with the DES on how the Assisted Places Scheme should be implemented. These are considerable testimonials to the persistence and finesse of the Committee. It was surely one of the most effective educational pressure groups.

It can be safely claimed that as a result of the activities of the DGJC the interests of the direct grant schools were more forcefully promoted than ever before within the field of private schooling. This was apt to cause tension within the independent sector as a whole, and perhaps more surprisingly, within the Committee itself. Within the DGJC the Roman Catholic controlled schools were peculiarly placed because their spokesmen knew that few of them could hope to go fully independent if direct grant status was lost and yet they were unable to support an Assisted Places Scheme as they believed it would be unacceptable to their parents, most of whom already held free places. Furthermore, the Church was less interested in preserving the distinctive educational character of the schools than that they should remain Catholic schools. When it came to the crunch nearly all the Catholic direct grant schools joined the maintained sector. In view of the government's intention that the direct grant schools should join the comprehensive system and the willingness of most of the schools 'to go independent', it is doubtful if any alternative outcome could have been negotiated. The respective parties were too far apart to achieve this and the Roman Catholic schools, squeezed in the middle, had to come down on one side or the other. As they were not in middle-class catchment areas (and therefore could not attract sufficient fee-paying parents), and alternative funding (for example, through the Church itself) was apparently unavailable, then they had little option but to join the maintained sector. Conflict with other members of the independent sector came to a head at the

1979 annual general meeting of HMC, which was held at Trinity College, Cambridge. The focus of the conflict was the Assisted Places Scheme which was discussed at a special session of HMC's annual meeting. The APS was very much the brainchild of the DGJC and the anxieties it raised within the independent sector will be analyzed in chapter 8.

Whereas the DGJC was formed to protect the interests of just one segment of the independent sector (even though this involved several different institutions) the Independent Schools Information Service (ISIS) was established to serve almost the entire spectrum of independent schooling. In November 1970 the committees of GBA and HMC had invited their Joint Working Party 'to appoint a sub-committee to examine the present position of the independent schools and to suggest ways in which that position could be strengthened' (GBA, 1971, p. 1). The Sub-committee's main recommendation was that a national information service should be created:

> The independent schools have not in the past been their own best advocates. They have had little common organization, and have left prospective clients to find out about them individually as and when they could. This is a weakness which should be remedied. The GBA must look to its own organization and to its relations with other associations of independent schools; and positive steps must be taken to meet the interest in independent education for children of all ages and both sexes. Information about independent schools must, if it is to be up-to-date and reliable, be supplied by themselves and this points to the need to provide an Information Service to cover schools of all kinds. (*Ibid.*, pp. 9–10)

The function of ISIS has been to operate an expanding and sophisticated publicity machine. In terms of its educational purpose the intention has been to publicize the independent sector to potential purchasers of private schooling and to keep those parents of children already within the system informed of contemporary events. Its political activities are very much in keeping with those of a traditional interest group: it publicizes evidence to repudiate the opponents of independent schooling, it has helped to organize a mass lobby of Parliament, it has attempted to keep the issue of independent schooling to the fore in parliamentary by-elections (probably most successfully in the Crosby by-election that resulted in the temporary return of Shirley Williams to the House of Commons in November 1981), and it now employs a

Parliamentary Liaison Officer whose job is to sensitize members of both houses to the pertinent educational issues. An offshoot of ISIS is the ISIS Association, membership of which is open to parents of pupils in independent schools as well as other sympathizers. This body provides resources, including finance and manpower, for the independent sector's pressure group activities.

The range of ISIS's current activities contrasts very sharply with the independent sector's pre–1970 innocence in the field of public relations. But it must be remembered that it was the product of a definite policy proposal (prepared by Sir Desmond Lee, ex-Headmaster of Winchester College, one of the most forward-looking of the old guard headmasters, and a long-standing member of the independent sector's inner political circle) and was therefore a positive recognition of the fact that action in this area was needed. Moreover, before it was actually launched there were several moves (some of which we have already referred to) to improve the sector's ability to publicize itself. The latter included the mushrooming of regional ISIS organizations which consisted of a number of schools within a particular locality cooperating to make their services better known to local parents. The foundation of national ISIS was the culmination of this trend. It was officially operational on 24 October 1972 with Donald Lindsay as its first Director and a broadly-based Management Committee in control of the general direction of its activities. The ultimate controlling body is the ISIS Joint Council which meets once a year and is composed of forty members who represent all the appropriate associations within ISIS.

There was some discussion within the independent sector as to whether a broad-based policy making body should precede the formation of the publicity machine. The advocates of the latter won the day but the Independent Schools Joint Council (ISJC) was soon to follow in the wake of ISIS. The Council first met on 4 October 1974, with Lord Belstead (who was later to be a member of Mrs Thatcher's first government) in the chair. Following the usual practice, the bulk of the work was undertaken by a smaller advisory committee which was initially headed by Sir Desmond Lee. It is evident that, regardless of the ISJC's formal position as the overall policy making body for the independent sector, it took a while for it to be accepted as such. This is natural given the longevity of the individual associations and the tradition of carefully guarding their own interests. The ISJC's cautious assumption of the policy making mantle is reflected in the time it took to replace the DGJC with its own Sub-committee (the Assisted Places

Steering Committee) in negotiations on the Assisted Places Scheme. There had been occasional contact between the Conservative party and the DGJC from at least the mid–1970s onwards about the possibility of the party committing itself in its next election manifesto to an assisted places scheme. Furthermore, as late as early 1978 HMC committee minutes are noting that, 'It was thought important that ISJC should enlarge its role as a coordinating committee and become a significant voice to speak with authority on matters of policy for independent education' (HMC (1978) *Bulletin,* No. 2, March). While at the same time, in support of these sentiments, the Political and Public Relations Sub-committee of HMC remarked '*In the future,* the role of HMC should be to influence ISJC in political matters rather than to aim at being itself a single political force' (*Ibid.,* our emphasis added).

In spite of the obvious teething difficulties the ISJC has assumed a positive political role: it now monitors, through its Assisted Places Committee, the Assisted Places Scheme; it has drafted the independent sector's official response to the Labour party's discussion document on private schooling; it has sought the opinion of counsel on the rights of parents to purchase schooling under various European and international conventions to which the United Kingdom is a signatory; and it has likewise sought counsel's opinion on the charitable status of independent schooling. Its most overt political activity, and the one which received the most publicity, was undertaken by one of its sub-committees, the Independent Schools Joint Action Committee (ISJAC) which was set up to defend the private sector from the Labour party's attack and to promote the cause of independent schooling in the run up to the General Election of 1983. The Action Committee, chaired by Frank Fisher, spawned some 150 local action committees and in view of the Conservative party's comfortable electoral majority it can rest on its laurels, waiting to be reactivated should the need arise.

It should not be assumed that all of ISJC's policy decisions have strong political ramifications. Much of the Council's attention is directed to the efficient management of the independent sector, and as the schools now probably feel politically secure, at least for the time being, this aspect of its work is likely to take on a greater importance. For example, the ISJC has spent much time and energy in formulating its own 'accreditation and validation scheme' to replace the DES's 'recognized as efficient' label. Furthermore, because it does cover the whole spectrum of independent schooling, it can make the authoritative decisions designed to iron out what internal differences may emerge. The contemporary political climate may be such as to permit both ISIS and the ISJC to return to more purely educational matters, to the promotion of good classroom practice and to the encouragement of the efficient administration of the schools.

It is impossible to calculate the precise pay-offs that have followed from these moves towards greater institutional cooperation. While the independent sector was getting its act together a whole variety of other factors were also changing and these may have had as much, or even greater, bearing upon the subsequent development of independent schooling as the internal moves towards coordinated action. In the next section of the chapter we will examine the resurgence of independent schooling since the phasing out of direct grant status in September 1976. The aim is to show the interplay between internal reforms in the management of independent schooling, political developments (especially changes within the Conservative party) and pedagogical changes. The consequences of this interplay are an independent sector that is relatively secure in financial terms, politically sophisticated, and ideologically on the counter-attack although displaying certain insecurities.

The Empire Strikes Back

The ideological counter attack occurred within, and indeed helped to formulate, a context that started to question the wisdom of many of the educational developments of the post-1944 era. The move towards a universal system of comprehensive secondary schooling was attacked by those who believed that it frequently resulted in the destruction of good schools which had simply been replaced (often in a haphazard fashion) by comprehensive schools that failed to maintain the academic standards and discipline of their pupils. The critique of the reorganization of secondary schooling was accompanied by a vigorous attack on so-called progressive teaching methods which it was claimed were most harmful to working-class pupils, the very children who supposedly would most benefit from them. Several heads of independent schools contributed to this critique through their articles to, for example, the Black Papers and the publications of the National Council for Educational Standards.

The growing debate about schooling in Britain inevitably had a political impact; more immediately within the Conservative party which contained a powerful element that had been less than happy with Sir Edward Boyle's consensual approach. Although there was no consistent drift to the right, Boyle's position was jeopardized in the late 1960s partly by a rank-and-file revolt at the party's 1967 conference (when the platform's motion was only narrowly approved after the indignity of a formal count) and partly by a swing to the right in the Parliamentary Backbench Committee on Education as a result of elections in November 1967 (Richmond, 1975). Boyle's successor, Margaret Thatcher, purposefully made it her concern to shift the educational debate away from the dominant established themes, that is how schooling should be formally organized and how to cope with expanding demand, and onto new territory. She argued that it was important to establish educational priorities and to pay particular regard to what actually takes place in the classroom. In concrete terms, as Secretary of State for Education and Science in Edward Heath's government, her top priority was a substantial building programme to replace the older primary schools. At the more rhetorical level she consistently stressed the need to maintain educational standards, although she gave some flesh to this concern through her appointment of the Bullock Committee ('on the teaching of reading and the use of the English language') and her support for the James Committee proposals (directed at the reorganization of teacher training colleges). The Conservative party, therefore, was not simply responding to the wider educational debate but shaping it to serve its own purposes.

If the ideological counterattack had concentrated simply upon the need to restore educational standards (as powerful a rallying cry as this was in the late 1970s) it would have been narrow in focus and essentially traditional in its concerns. However, two other critical themes were promoted: the desire to increase parental influence in the decisions that affect the schooling of their children, and the desire to relate schooling more closely to the needs of industry. The independent sector was well placed to exploit these themes. Its spokesmen could claim with some justification that many of their schools had excellent academic records, indeed this had been central to their defence to the direct grant schools. Independent schools made parental choice more of a reality and although that choice was restricted to only a limited number of families the state could make the resources available to change that situation. Increasingly the schools were prepared to expose themselves to the public gaze, to reveal that they were no longer fossilized institutions. They had radically revitalized their experience of schooling so that it was in tune with the needs of contemporary society and, even if the Labour party failed to realize this, parents certainly did as reflected in the schools' steadily improving pupil intakes.

A causal link could be drawn between the changing nature of the experience of schooling within the independent sector and the fact that the schools were subject to the pressures of the market-place. They were forced to change in response to parental demands for failure to do so would lead to their demise. In other words it was parental choice that had made them more relevant, so tying in with a growing strain within Tory educational thinking which claimed that so much had gone wrong in the maintained schools because of the exclusion of parental influence. Two main policy proposals were formulated by the Conservative Party to expand parental influence: a parents' charter and an Assisted Places Scheme. Besides increasing parental power it was hoped to restrict the authority of what was commonly referred to as the educational establishment, on whose doorstep the Tories placed much of the responsibility for the alleged ills of the maintained schools. For example, Norman St John-Stevas, while Opposition spokesman on education, was moved to write (1974): 'Mrs Thatcher fought gallantly for parental rights against an educational establishment which was hostile to all that she stood for' (p. 1).

Parental decisions are not made in a vacuum and the purpose of the recent debate about schooling has been to reshape the educational climate within which parents make their choices. Even if one accepts that the British economy should be organized along capitalist lines, there is no objective answer as to what form of schooling best suits the reproduction of British capitalism. This has to be politically defined and politically imposed. In view of the decentralization of educational power, integral to such imposition is the need to conduct ideological warfare; to make sure that those whose decisions cannot be controlled centrally are fully aware of what is considered to be desirable practice. And for some of the most influential Conservative ideologues it was the independent sector that constituted the best model of acceptable educational practice (Boyson, 1975, pp. 144–9).

Although the independent sector has benefitted considerably from the recent changes in the educational climate, it is not without its attendant dangers. We have argued elsewhere that the changing character of schooling within the independent sector has been more of a response to its institutional links rather than to pressure exerted by the market-place (Salter and Tapper, 1981, pp. 178–86). In either case it is legitimate to ask what this means for the integrity of the private schools. At what price will they sell their souls? One response has been simply to camouflage the problem, so that the answer is composed of either sweet moderation or banal generalizations. While this may mean that no sensible person could object to the values that private schooling tries to inculcate, likewise it is impossible to fathom out what is the distinctive message on sale. Perhaps that is the answer — the private schools do nothing different, they simply do the same things better. Some discussion, invariably in relation to very pragmatic issues, has taken place within the independent sector on this very problem: the merits of the smaller boarding school, the danger of stressing academic success too strongly, and the wish to select some assisted place pupils on grounds of special educational needs or boarding needs.

Probably the most direct consequence of the private sector's institutional cooperation has been a very marked increase in its political sophistication. The attempt to influence public opinion at large has been largely due to the work of ISIS. Whereas not so long ago the private schools shunned publicity now it must appear to some that they court media attention. Without being relatively assured that the viewers would respond favourably, it is inconceivable that the ten-part series on Radley College would have been shown on BBC television. Policy negotiations have brought the independent sector into much closer and more continuous contact with the DES. For example the Department was involved in lengthy discussions with the DGJC on both the phasing out of direct grant status and the implementation of the Assisted Places Scheme. It is possible that the private sector institutions will be accorded a more permanent place in the management of the educational system as the Thatcher government looks for means of undermining the old establishment and replacing it with structures that it finds more acceptable.

Although building bridges to the DES may raise few qualms within the world of independent schooling, the growing ties to the Conservative party cause considerable unease. The links are much more tangible than the ideological convergence to which we have already referred. Lord Belstead gave up his vice-chairmanship of ISJC on becoming a junior minister in Mrs Thatcher's government, while the present Chairman, Sir George Sinclair, is a former Conservative Member of Parliament. There is a Conservative Independent Schools Committee (CISC), currently chaired by Mark Carlisle, which has compiled notes that are 'primarily intended to assist Conservatives when called upon to speak in support of the independent schools, and to defend those schools against attacks from the Labour Party and others' (CISC, n.d., Foreword). The Committee, as it acknowledges, has relied heavily upon ISIS in the compilation of its notes. The closest links between the Conservative party and the independent sector were forged by the Assisted Places Scheme. There were lengthy discussions between representatives of the party and the DGJC before it became one of the party's policy commitments and was incorporated in the 1979 election manifesto. These contacts were further extended by the intense three-party talks (i.e. between the DES, government and the APSC) that resulted in the implementation of the scheme. Finally, the links to the parliamentary wing of the Conservative party are maintained in good working order by the ISJC Parlimentary Committee and the ISIS Parliamentary Liaison Officer.

In.view of the political climate perhaps the independent schools had little choice but to ally themselves much more closely to the Conservative party than in the past. It could be read as a sign of political maturity; the realization that education and politics are closely entwined and that the best defence against attack is to find reliable political allies. As the Labour and Liberal parties were by and large both unsympathetic to private schooling, it was impossible to do little more than make a show of spreading one's political feelers. Such developments have not been universally welcomed within the independent sector even if it has been widely believed that the schools had few viable options.

The desire to broaden the independent sector's political support is reflected in the tentative overtures that have been made to the Social Democratic Party. Although the party is prepared to accept the principle that parents have the right to purchase private schooling, it also believes that what financial backing the state gives the private sector should be withdrawn. Inasmuch as this would mean the loss of valuable concessions, which the Conservative party is prepared to continue, this is not much of an incentive for the independent sector to shift its political ground. In the meantime it may be tactically worthwhile to continue with negotiations, especially as the Alliance may succeed in widening its political base.

Even the Labour party may not be beyond redemption. Current party policy envisages a two-pronged attack: in the initial phase various alleged state subsidies to private schooling will be removed while in the second phase the right to charge fees will be prohibited (TUC-Labour Party Liaison Committee, 1981). Not only can a lot happen in the move from opposition to government but also the implementation of party policy is fraught with danger especially when such a long time span is envisaged. The issuing of a discussion document may signify the strength of the party's commitment to action (including the determination that the civil servants will not be allowed to dilute the initiative) but it can also be legitimately interpreted as a sign of insecurity. Perhaps those in the party who are committed to action are either trying to convince the waverers or, more likely, they are trying to establish party policy before the doubters can mobilize themselves. The situation, regardless of how we interpret it, offers the independent sector the chance to explore and exploit differences within Labour party ranks. Not surprisingly this opportunity has been seized; thus there is a courteous wooing of Lord Lever and the revelation in an ISIS Association poll of Labour MPs that a sizeable minority of backbenchers appear to be either confused about party policy or opposed to it (ISIS, 1983a, p. 1, and 1983b, p. 1).

Although ISIS is an effective publicity machine it is impossible to say how much of the credit it deserves for the comparatively healthy state of the independent sector in recent years. There is no reason to suppose that ISIS has exercised a decisive influence in many individual decisions to use the private sector. As with the clashes over educational values and political strategy, the health of independent schooling is partially dependent upon the general social context within which it is located. For example, the decision of the Labour government to phase out direct grant status from September 1976 persuaded approximately 120 schools to go independent. Furthermore, the independent sector was undoubtedly boosted by the move towards comprehensive secondary schooling in the maintained sector. Regardless of what the facts may have been, some parents did not want their children to attend comprehensive schools and were prepared to purchase independent schooling if no alternative was available to them. However, it is vital not to forget the ability of the private sector institutions to affect the climate of opinion. ISIS may not have influenced individual decisions but it certainly helped to reshape the general image of independent and comprehensive schooling. Furthermore, without effective action by the DGJC it is doubtful if such a high percentage of direct grant schools would have resisted government pressure to join the maintained sector.

In recent years, in spite of the declining school age population, the independent sector has managed to increase both its number of pupils (although the 1982 and 1983 ISIS censuses showed a slight downturn) and its share of the school age population. The ISIS publications, not surprisingly, exude an air of confidence:

This drop (i.e. of 2 per cent in pupil numbers over the past two years) is very small particularly when compared with the drop in pupil numbers at maintained nursery, primary and secondary schools over the same period. Provisional figures from the DES for England show that total numbers in the maintained sector dropped between January 1981 and January 1982 by 470,000 (5.4 per cent). Between January 1982 and January 1983, provisional figures indicate a drop of some 252,000 or 3.25 per cent, so the independent schools are gaining and increasing share of a declining total school population. (ISIS, 1983c, p. 3)

And in the 1984 annual census we read that 'For the first time since 1981 pupil numbers at independent schools are on the increase. The results of the 1984 census are most encouraging for schools in membership of the leading associations of fee-paying schools in Britain. . . . This welcome news could herald the end of the recession as far as independent education is concerned' (ISIS, 1984, p. 4).

Class Reproduction and Political Visibility

The weak position in which the private sector found itself in the mid-1960s has been turned around by purposeful action. The values which protected independent schooling were steadily crumbling and the Labour party was bound to exploit this at some point. Probably more in response to the assumed merits of grammar school education than ideological and policy shifts, the middle classes were slowly deserting the independent sector. Certainly it is accurate to describe the private schools as stagnant in the sense that they were trapped within a very confined social base. We have examined various facets of how this slide into oblivion was first halted and then reversed. Institutional regeneration is in our opinion the key to the revival of the fortunes of private schooling. From this has flowed considerable political sophistication (at both the levels of elite negotiation and the shaping of public opinion) and the ability to launch a sustained counterattack in terms of educational values. As a consequence the fortunes of the independent sector have blossomed which is a sure sign that the message has been successfully attuned to the values of the potential customers, and in some instances the message may have actually changed the values of parents.

It is our contention that the old hegemony has not merely been shorn up by sustained institutional action but has in fact been reformulated. The critique which argued that independent schooling offered experiences that were out of tune with contemporary needs (indeed that the schools were partially responsible for the nation's seemingly endless economic decline) has been countered by a successful restructuring of their image. This image portrays the schools as very relevant indeed, imparting in a disciplined manner those skills that are vital to the economic regeneration of Britain. The message has been picked up by discerning parents who are prepared to pay the fees that ensure their children receive the desired schooling. As a consequence independent schooling has been able to retain its role in the reproduction of class relations. Although the schools now fulfil that role in a different manner they are still perceived by many middle-class parents as a vital link in the opportunity chain that they can make available to their children. The actual pay-offs of independent schooling may be different from parental perceptions but it cannot be denied that the schools have successfully retained their grip upon a large segment of middle-class consciousness.

In September 1973 Roy Hattersley, then Labour Shadow Minister of Education, appeared to cause panic in the ranks of the private schools when in a speech to the Annual Conference of Incorporated Association of Preparatory Schools he said: 'If I am to give you an accurate picture of both the policy of the Labour Party and the prospects for independent schools during the lifetime of the next Labour Government, I must above all else, leave you with no doubts about our intention initially to reduce and eventually to abolish private education in this country' (ISIS, September 1973, p. 1). Ten years later much the same message is echoed by the Labour party but who can doubt that the ring of self-confidence is missing. The party has been chastened by the ability of the independent sector to counter the phasing out of direct grant status, been forced to acknowledge — most dramatically through Callaghan's sponsorship of the Great Debate — that many parents are fearful of the quality of schooling in the maintained sector, and has still failed to convince the electorate that its case against private schooling makes sense. Its present two-phase strategy can be interpreted as an admission of the party's continued vacillation rather than of its continued determination. It is perhaps as good a manifestation as any that the ideological challenge that grew in intensity in the two decades after the 1944 Education Act has been met and rebuffed.

The restructuring of the institutions of private schooling succeeded in fortifying the defences of the independent sector, for example, ironing out some internal conflicts, building morale and improving the management of the schools. For those institutions to move onto the offensive (for example, propagate their educational values, promote policy initiatives, and make sustained political attacks) they needed to build alliances with other institutions. Much of the broader institutional contact has been established through the connections of particular individuals and has tended to be both informal and intermittent. This is as far as many of the more influential figures in the world of independent school politics wanted to go, and in view of their present comparative security a loosening of the bonds can be expected. This may, however, prove difficult to realize for the institutional bridge-building that occurred in the past decade was not a one-way process. We have referred to the policy shifts within the Conservative party and how the existence of an independent sector helped facilitate its rethinking. The cost of edging away from trusted allies could be unacceptably high and in any case the independent sector may simply not be permitted to lower its political profile. But these are matters for the future.

7   Towards a New Ideological Consensus

Introduction

All policy making in Britain takes place within a general ideological context which welcomes some policies and discourages others. Within this dominant system of ideas, or hegemony, as it is known organizations such as political parties and interest groups pursue policies which will mesh more and less well with the prevailing ideological climate. For political parties dependent upon electoral success, susceptible as they are to public opinion for their power, the nature of the hegemony is a constraint on policy-making. Basically, parties can adopt any combination of four options in their response to hegemony: they can ignore it; they can adapt their policies to suit the dominant ideology; they can seek to change it; or they can hope that it shifts spontaneously in the direction of their own ideological preferences. Whatever weighting of these options is adopted, intellectuals will be needed by parties to shape and present ideas.

We have seen in Chapter 5 how intellectuals within the Labour party assumed a number of roles in the production, translation and dissemination of ideology during the three decades it took to develop a cohesive policy on private schooling. For the most part these paralleled the formal policy-making procedures of the party. Intellectuals concentrated on the translation of ideology into conference and NEC policy with the intention by the late 1970s of influencing and possibly determining the details of policy implementation when Labour was returned to office. What they ignored was the translation of party ideology on private schooling into electoral appeal: that is, they did not seek to change those parts of the prevailing hegemony relevant to this issue. Precisely why they neglected this intellectual role is not clear.

Internal feuding has long been an absorbing career path in its own right in the Labour party and it may be that this obscured the need for another dimension to be added to the existing range of intellectual activities. Perhaps the presentation, packaging and selling of ideology offended the purists.

To an extent, Labour's electoral successes of the 1960s and 1970s may have fostered the belief that the external climate of opinion could be taken for granted. In the 1960s, the Conservative party's attachment to the dominant consensus ideology of 'Butskellism' with its commitment to the welfare state and neo-Keynesian management of the economy had meant that the opposition to Labour's policy of comprehensivization in secondary education, to the abolition of the grammar schools, and to the beginnings of the attack on the direct grant schools was only weakly orchestrated. At that stage, the Conservatives did not have the ideological weapons with which to resist the march of educational progressivism. Thus Labour intellectuals may have been lulled into a false sense of security by a dominant ideology which, in the educational field at least, was reasonably sympathetic to their point of view. Whether this ideology would have tolerated an attack on the independent sector which extended beyond the direct grant schools is something we will never know, because by the time the Labour party formulated the policy for such an attack with the publication of *Private Schools* in 1980 the nature of the dominant consensus had changed.

By the late 1960s influential sections of right-wing intellectuals had come to the conclusion that the existing hegemony was not to their liking and would have to be reshaped. In this chapter we examine their analysis of what needed to be done and why, the means employed to achieve their objectives, the relationship between what they were doing and Conservative party policy making, the form of the new hegemony particularly so far as education is concerned and the implications of these developments for policy on private schooling.

The Right's Analysis

Although the Right is no more ideologically homogeneous than the Left a common understanding developed among its ranks of what had gone wrong. The Conservative party was seen as having failed in the 'battle for ideas' and, indeed, as having abdicated the battlefield to the Left. 'In the last thirty-five years', argues Cowling (1978) in *Conservative Essays*, 'the intelligentsia has been vital in constructing a Labour platform, in validating it once it had been constructed and in making Conservative criticism seem morally or intellectually disreputable' (p. 12). No similar task had been undertaken on behalf of the Conservative party with the result that politicians who, Cowling observes, are 'victims as much as they are initiators', were 'parasitic' in what they thought and said upon a liberal-left public doctrine (*Ibid.*, p. 20). Because Conservatives had failed to join the intellectual battle, maintains Lord Harris (co-founder with Arthur Seldon of the Institute of Economic Affairs), they had by default been forced to fall back into a rearguard action of slowing the pace of unwelcome socialism (Harris, 1980, p. 4). This 'failure of the intellectuals' accusation is matched by the belief that the elite (variously defined) had been seduced into the woolly ways of liberal-left thinking. Harris continues: 'They (the Conservatives) have failed to see that fashionable consensus is no more than a complicity of ruling elites in growing government, taxation, bureaucratic trade union power that the majority resent or reject' (*Ibid.*, p. 6).

Here we see the conviction of members of the Right that it is they, not the Left, who are in touch with the people. The most powerful and consistent originator of this populist element in the Right's analysis has been Enoch Powell. Long before it was fashionable to do so, Powell maintained that a deep and dangerous gulf had opened up in the nation between

> . . . the overwhelming majority of people on the one side, and on the other side, a tiny minority with almost a monopoly hold upon the channels of communication who seem determined not to know the facts and not to face realities and who will resort to any device or extremity to blind both themselves and others. (Powell and Woods, 1969, p. 300)

Worse than the existence of the gulf itself was the fact that the Conservative party connived in its perpetuation through a failure of philosophy which produced 'a battle-weary resignation, a conviction that in the end collectivism was *bound* to win, although a few cunning ploys and wordly wise manoeuvres would delay the process' (Howell, 1980, p. 8). Continual pragmatic adjustment by the party to the dominant consensus had alienated it from the values of the middle bourgeois layers of society.

There is some confusion in the Right's analysis over what exactly constitutes 'public opinion'. If large sections of the population hold values which differ from the collectivist consensus of the elite do not these values themselves form part of public opinion? If they do, then why are politicians not responsive to these values? The answer is probably that the Right regarded this opinion as latent and unarticulated as a result of the Left's dominance of the media. In any case, the Right was quite definite as far back as 1967 that, as Angus Maude put it then, 'the lack of philosophy was at the root of the current Conservative malaise. Philosophy would tell Conservatives what it was they wanted to conserve' (Gamble, 1974, p. 104). Without a clear philosophy the Conservatives could not hope to regain the ideological initiative which they had so clearly lost and therefore would have no chance of challenging the existing hegemony (Boyson, 1970). Lord Blake spells out the implications of this ideological subordination in discussing the 1970 Heath government's lack of a 'clear intellectual mandate' and the lack of a guiding purpose in its policies in pursuing a course which did not at that time appear intellectually reputable.

> Nevertheless, it is hard to believe that an administration which felt that it had a firm doctrinal base and an intellectually legitimate ideology (by which I mean one that was accepted by a substantial section of the opinion formers), would have diverged quite so far from the principles which it had been proclaiming before it came back into power. (Lord Blake, 1976, p. 2)

The agreed diagnosis was that the Conservative party needed to develop a strong philosophy for both internal and external reasons: internally a philosophy was needed to maintain policy directions over time and resist the pragmatic pressures of politics; externally it was needed as a force with which to shape public opinion.

The Right's analysis of the role of intellectuals in shaping public opinion is one which Gramsci would applaud since it is expressed in terms of the political function of intellectuals (see, pp. 30–4). According to Lord Harris their importance 'stems simply from their roles as writers, teachers, preachers, broadcasters, producers, in spreading ideas until they come to dominate public opinion' (*Ibid.*, p. 4). They are not, he argues, predominantly seminal thinkers but are what Hayek calls 'second-hand dealers in ideas' — a phrase guaranteed, and probably intended, to irritate the liberal intelligentsia. Differences exist over which group of intellectuals are most influential and therefore most important to recruit to the cause. Gale plumps for the media, maintaining that it 'mediates between the politicians and the public. It creates political reputations and climates of opinion; it transmits and transmutes politicians' views; and it decides what and how to tell the public' (Gale, 1978, p. 189). Roger Scruton, columnist in *The Times*, on the other hand, thinks it is a mistake to assume that the media is politically important seeing it as ineffective in the battle of ideas. While it is useful to control it 'It is far more useful to control the universities and the professional societies — for these channels, while narrow, are more firmly connected to the instruments of power. Ideas which gain currency among professors, lawyers, doctors and literati, soon gain currency in Parliament' (Scruton, 1983, p. 12).

Obviously the question of ideological influence is directly related to the question of political power. Exercising ideological influence over the masses is a pointless pursuit if the masses have no power. In this situation it makes much more sense to try and influence intellectuals who, directly or indirectly, help determine the views of those who do have decision making power. In British political society with its combination of elite and pluralist institutions the most sensible strategy is a multi-faceted one. Electoral politics means that the shaping of public opinion is important because, as Peele (1976) remarks with regard to the Right, 'even the discussion of the most bread–and–butter issues of politics takes place against a background of assumptions and generally held ideas'. Thus, 'by attempting to mould, or at least prevent the distortion of, the intellectual milieu a party is contributing to the next generation's capacity to pursue certain strategies or policies' (p. 18). At the same time, many elite institutions are well insulated from the hurly-burly of party politics and require a different and more selective approach from those wishing to influence them.

The Right is quite clear about how institutions support and promote the influence of particular groups of intellectuals. In his examination of the economic policies prevalent in the early 1970s, for example, Pringle (1977) discusses how the 'dominant ideology' of neo-Keynesianism was actively supported by 'the Treasury, the Bank of England, the press and members of the Cambridge University Economics faculty. Together they created a climate of opinion which gave birth to misshapen policies' (p. 3). Taking on board the same point in his introduction to Pringle's book, Sir Keith Joseph discusses how the Bank of England *Quarterly*, the *Review* of the National Institute of Economic and Social Research and *The Economist* helped to orchestrate to the public discussion of economic management in Britain over the past two decades (*ibid.*, p. viii). Institutions are seen as organizing and channelling intellectual effort to appropriate targets.

For all its internal divisions and rivalries, by the early 1970s the Right had developed a common understanding of how it had let slip the reins of hegemony. Lack of political will and a pervasive complacency were seen as having caused a withdrawal from the ideological battlefield which the Left was then able to occupy by default. Right-wing intellectuals had failed to challenge the advance of the liberal–Left with the result that this had become the 'natural' ideology of British political culture; the consensus within which new policies were framed. Even the elite, particularly the Whitehall elite, had fallen prey to the insidious appeal of the consensus as had the organs of the media and acadaemia. Yet at the same time the Right felt sure that large sections of the ordinary population remained immune to the consensus ideology of Butskellism and awaited a trumpet call from the Right.

Implicit in the Right's analysis is a strategy for an ideological counter-attack. Intellectuals have to be recruited and trained in a variety of roles in the production, translation and dissemination of ideas and their work directed through appropriate institutions. Ideological themes have to be identified and packaged in order to appeal to different types of audiences. Although to begin with this strategy may not have been a conscious one, but rather a logical consequence of the analysis itself, there is little doubt that it did subsequently become quite explicit as it was translated into resource needs and organizational forms. One of the main, and natural, targets of such a strategy was bound to be the policy making process within the Conservative Party. Before examining how the strategy for obtaining control of the dominant ideology was implemented we will therefore briefly outline the nature of this policy making context focussing in particular on the role of intellectuals within it.

Intellectuals and Conservative Party Policy Making

Pinning down the role of intellectuals in the Conservative party is no easy task. Unlike the Labour party, the Conservative party does not have a formal democratic machinery of policy making to which intellectuals can make inputs at different points. There is no set hierarchy of committees through which ideas must journey in order to evolve into policies. As Robert McKenzie (1963) pointed out in *British Political Parties,*

> The Conservative leader, whether in power or in opposition, has the sole ultimate responsibility for the formulation of the

policy and the electoral programme of this party. The resolutions of the annual conference and the other organs of the
National Union (the federation of constituency Conservative
parties) are 'conveyed' to him for his information; however
emphatic these resolutions may be, they are in no way binding
upon him. (p. 21)

Furthermore, it is a responsibility firmly supported by an impressive array of administrative controls. The leader directly controls the
entire Central Office Party organization with its research and policy
forming committees, its educational and propaganda functions, and the
spending of party money. It is thus effectively the personal machine of
the leader who appoints all its senior officials. The leader also appoints
the Chairman and Deputy-Chairman of the Advisory Committee on
Policy, the Chairman of the Conservative Research Department (recently absorbed into the Central Office organization) and the Head of
the Conservative Political Centre. All of them are responsible to the
leader alone (*Ibid.*, pp. 65–6).

However, the fact that the party leader has more or less complete
formal power over the policy making process does not obviate the
need for intellectuals to undertake the construction of policies. The
leader obviously cannot do so alone but must draw on a pool of
expertise. While there is no logical reason why this expertise necessarily
has to be housed within the party organization it clearly makes
administrative sense if it is, since this both makes use of existing
resources and avoids the possibility of in-house versus out-house
frictions. Precisely how the leader uses the available intellectuals in
forming policy, or drafts in fresh ones if those available are unsuitable
for some reason, is where the power of the leader is important, because
it provides the freedom of manoeuvre to shuffle intellectual manpower
until the right (i.e. most sympathetic) combination is achieved. If the
leader does not use his power in this way then he is failing to fulfil
adequately his constitutional role of taking responsibility for the
formation of policy. That, presumably, is what the power is for.

But exercising power, particularly the power of appointment, in
order to harness intellectual manpower to policy making not only takes
time but is also constrained in a number of ways: by the limits on
power experienced by any Tory leader; by the leader's own conception of policy making and the place of intellectuals within it; and by the
availability of networks of intellectuals who fit the bill. It is out of the
interplay of these factors that the role or roles of intellectuals in the
Conservative party emerges.

To illustrate this point it is useful to compare the ways in which Heath and Thatcher have employed intellectuals in policy making. Both spent the first part of their leadership in opposition, Heath 1965-70 and Thatcher 1975-79. This is important because policy making in opposition is quite different from that in government and provides different opportunities for intellectuals to make an impact. In opposition the part played by the party organization is much more significant than in government when policy 'emerges very largely from reactions to events, from tackling the problems of governing the country' (Patten, 1980, p. 10). Burch identifies two models of parties in opposition. First, the critical approach where the leader concentrates resources upon criticizing the government party. Second, the alternative government approach where the leader concentrates resources upon presenting the opposition as a real, responsible and viable alternative to the existing administration (Burch, 1980, pp. 161-2). Heath emphatically adopted the latter. From 1965 onwards he launched a systematic review of policy which had as its aim the identification of particular answers to particular policy problems. He was interested, not in the generalities of Conservative philosophy, but in the way in which forward planning could be used to pave the way for policy management once returned to office (*Ibid.*, p. 166).

In order to carry out this exercise Heath effectively created a new policy making machinery and, as part of this, new roles and new demands for intellectuals. Approximately thirty policy groups were set up consisting of a chairman (usually from the Shadow Cabinet), six backbench MPs and six industrial or academic experts from outside the party, all personally appointed by Heath himself. Each group was serviced by a Conservative Research Department (CRD) officer who liaised with the relevant backbench committee (Patten, 1980, p. 15). The new machinery necessitated a conscious effort to recruit the intellectual manpower required to make it work. Networks of intellectuals had to be established and maintained. Ramsden notes how from the summer of 1965 Heath regularly visited universities in order to make contact with sympathetic academics; and in 1966 Fraser and Spicer of the CRD conducted a series of fifty visits to universities and colleges (Ramsden, 1980, p. 239). A card index was evolved listing academics who were prepared to help the Conservative party in some specific area of policy (*Ibid.*).

It was during this period that the Research Department developed a key role as broker between the Party's needs for ideas and information on the one hand, and expertise in the universities, business, industry, the professions and trade unions, on the other, Obviously the expression of these needs was only partly spontaneous and could be stimulated and guided by the setting up of new policy groups which the CRD then obligingly serviced. Given that Heath was himself Chairman of the CRD between 1965 and 1970 it is not altogether suprising that the emphasis during this period was on the political education of the Party into the ideas of a post-Beveridge, post-Keynes epoch (Patten, 1980, p. 14). Policy formation on this scale, ably coordinated by the CRD, thus became the vehicle for disseminating throughout the party an ideology which was anathema to the Right. The Right's only recourse at this stage, until it could fight its way back into the networks of intellectuals orchestrated by the party machine, was to publish and campaign from a distance. It must have felt very despondent.

In creating a new policy making structure Heath had also created new intellectual roles within the Party (or perhaps more accurately, he had formalized existing but little-used roles), in particular those of broker and expert adviser on policy detail. One of the main motivations of those who supported this initiative was the feeling, as Patten reports, that after thirteen years in office the Party had 'exhausted its intellectual capital' and had 'been captured by the Whitehall machine, which is usually more conscious of the difficulties of any departure from the existing way of doing things than of the benefit of new ideas' (*Ibid.*, p. 15) — a sentiment which echoes certain Labour Party comments. Thus, one of the tests of these new roles was how far they succeeded in producing policies which were 'blueprints for legislation' with the administrative sophistication that Whitehall would respect. Like the Labour party over private schooling, the Conservative party was here concerned with how intellectuals assist policy implementation. But what the Conservatives were not clear about was what ideas were being translated by intellectuals into policy details. Heath's problem-centred approach to policy making and his deliberate avoidance of philosophical discussions meant that the ideological basis for a policy was not clearly stated. The result was that actually producing a document proved to be very difficult. Noting this, Ramsden (1980) comments, 'The 1945 policy exercise had proceded from a philosophical base to more detailed policies; the 1964–70 exercise had begun with more details and it was therefore extremely difficult to establish the common cause afterwards' (p. 269). He cites the example of the agonizing and the six drafts which marked the passage of the policy document *Make Life Better* produced in 1968 for the Conservative conference that year. If the role of intellectual as producer of 'blueprints for legislation' can scarcely be said to have worked satisfactorily, the role of intellectual as translator of policy into electoral appeal appears to have gone largely unrecognized by Heath during this period. (It of course formed a central part of the Right's subsequent critique of what had gone wrong.)

Nonetheless, although the external effect of this use of intellectuals was unconvincing, internally it undoubtedly helped Heath to maintain his ideological dominance of the Party and so minimize the murmurings of dissent. As McKenzie argues throughout *British Political Parties*, the Conservative leader's authority rests on the support of MPs and the party organization and this support is in turn dependent on the leader's perceived ability to win elections. But with sufficient intellectual resources at the command of the Leader it is possible to influence the way in which such perceptions are shaped by dominating any given area of party debate. While these intellectual resources do not remove opposition and factional in-fighting, they do limit the damage. Furthermore, they allow consultation between Leader and led to take place on the leader's terms. Unless he loses an election, that is.

It is the case for both the Conservative and Labour party organizations that the winning of an election places a greater distance between themselves and their leading MPs and ministers. We have already seen how the activities of some Labour party intellectuals have been geared exclusively to closing that gap (see pp. 103–10). If a group of intellectuals of either party has been closely involved in policy formation with its leaders whilst in opposition it is not unnatural that it should feel neglected and frustrated if it is excluded from policy-making when the party forms the government. There is no reason to assume that Conservative and Labour party intellectuals are any different in this respect.

With the election of Heath to office in 1970 Conservative party intellectuals, and in particular the 'in-house' intellectuals of the CRD, had to adjust to having only limited access to party leaders and to competition with the Civil Service. Although a number of party professionals moved into Whitehall to temporary posts in the Civil Service, positions as political advisers to ministers, to the Cabinet Office, and to the Prime Minister's personal staff, they did not act as links between the party organization and the government. Ramsden (1980) points out that

> The advisers might be used as channels of communication in an emergency, but their role in Whitehall was sufficiently anomalous to make them ever mindful of the terrors of the Official

Secrets Act. As Douglas Hurd wrote, 'the Official Secrets Act and (far more important) the entrenched habits of Whitehall turned the familiar friend into an occasional acquaintance'. (p. 287.)

Thus was the party distanced even from its former employees. In addition, the Central Policy Review Staff (CPRS) was established as a further source of intellectual support for the Cabinet divorced from the party. As usual, Conservative policy was to be found in whatever the Conservative government was doing and the intellectuals with an influence over policy making were those in some way involved with what the government was doing.

With Heath's defeat at the 1974 election the whole system of policy making which he had sponsored whilst in opposition came into question. A CRD weakened by the atrophying effect of four years of policy making neglect between 1970 and 1974 was in no position to instantly reassert the dominance of Heath's problem-solving approach to policy formation. The structure remained in position but its legitimacy was diminished. It would take time for the officers of the CRD to become once again the central brokers in a web of intellectuals contributing to policy. As it happened they were out of luck.

When Thatcher was elected leader in 1975 she inherited a policy-making structure which, though no longer the force it once was, was nonetheless a product of the Heath years and therefore unsympathetic to a right of centre leader. The limits of a new Conservative leader's powers, certainly in the short term, must have been very apparent. She could, and did, use the leader's power of appointment to change the top stratum of the party organization: for example, in March 1975 Angus Maude was made Chairman of the Research Department in succession to Sir Ian Gilmore and Sir Keith Joseph became Chairman of the Advisory Committee on Policy and took special responsibility for the development of party policies (Ramsden, 1980, p. 308). But below this level, it was obviously going to take time to change both the 'in-house' intellectuals recruited, or self-selected, during Heath's rule and the external networks of intellectuals who serviced the policy groups. (The same problem will face any successor of Thatcher who is not in the same ideological mould as she is.) The new leader clearly needed a mechanism for generating a fresh and immediate ideological impetus sympathetic to her own views and capable of overcoming the climate of opinion embedded in Heath's policy making machinery.

One of the predominant characteristics of the policy-making process in the Conservative party is that it is the personal creation of the leader. Although certain elements in that process are given — for example, the CRD and Central Office — precisely what weight they carry will vary depending on the political needs and strategy of the leader. Other elements such as policy groups come and go for the same reasons. There was nothing sacrosanct about Heath's policy-making structure. Thatcher approached the task of establishing her control over the role of intellectuals in policy-making in three ways. Firstly, she kept the policy groups but downgdraded their status. Secondly, the Research Department's influence was allowed to wane and its independence gradually undermined until eventually it was moved from Old Queen Street into the Central Office building in Smith Square in May 1979. At the same time the function of the CRD Chairman was added to that of the party Chairman and the new CRD Director was appointed from the party Chairman's Central Office staff. These were negative actions to limit the influence of the Heath legacy of intellectuals. A third, positive and immediate action was to create new intellectual networks and, where appropriate, link them through the work of the Centre for Policy Studies (CPS).

The CPS was set up by Sir Keith Joseph and Margaret Thatcher in December 1974, a few months before Thatcher became the new party leader. Whether this timing was purely fortuitous is impossible to know but suffice it to say that if the CPS was not already there it may well have had to be created. It arose from dissatisfaction with the Heath regime and from the feeling that the intellectual climate in the Conservative party with its problem-solving adherence to Butskellism should be challenged by arguments rooted in a common philosophical position. Since such arguments could not easily be developed within the existing party machine they would have to be developed outside and imported into the party. Once Thatcher became leader, the need of the new leadership for ideas with which to establish its identity and challenge the existing intellectual interests was acute. As we have already discussed, party policy making is also party political education and until she gained full control of the party organization it was essential that she had alternative intellectual resources with which to generate policies. These the CPS and others supplied.

Thatcherism and the Right

It was a vital coincidence of interests that Thatcher needed the intellectual networks of the Right as much as they needed a political vehicle for their ideas. On the one hand, Thatcher could not oust the intellectuals of the ancien regime without a steady flow of ideas across the policy spectrum and, on the other, the various shades of Right-wing ideology, no matter how sophisticated their analysis, <u>could not mount a sustained attack on the existing hegemony without a national political figure to focus their efforts, gloss over their differences and translate their ideas into political appeal and party policies.</u> Precisely who harnessed whom it is difficult to say. (What may be more interesting is who unharnesses whom first!). But if the mutual interests were to be successfully brought together and a new hegemony established particular intellectual roles with institutional back-up were required over time. Overlapping social networks had to be created to transmit information and ideas to appropriate target audiences on a routine basis.

Studies of the dynamics of social networks show the importance of particular characteristics of the networks in shaping what happens within. For example, the size of the network, the frequency of communication and amount of overlap between different parts of the network (hence its coherence) and the multiplicity of different sets of relationships within the network (for example, occupational, political, cultural) will guide, assist or constrain flows of ideas (Coleman, *et al.* 1957; Katz, 1958; Rees, 1966; Turk, 1970; Granovetter, 1973). Such characteristics will influence how the intellectual receives the information, what he/she does with it, how he/she interacts with other intellectuals, whether this interaction is maintained over time and socially consolidated, and so on. Similarly, the intellectual's position and career background will influence the way in which he/she enters the network and subsequently forms, or does not form, part of it. (These issues and their relationship to belief systems are discussed in an article by Erikson in Marsden, P.V. and Lin, N. (Eds.), 1982). What these studies thus show is that in 1975 Margaret Thatcher had a large and complex task on her hands if she was to challenge the established networks effectively. And if new networks were to be brought into being, or existing ones linked together, what intellectual roles were required and where would the individuals concerned be based?

In 1975 Thatcher needed the full range of intellectual producers, translators and disseminators as well as intellectual brokers to bring the relevant social networks together and particular institutions to act as 'clearing houses' for the ideas (see pp. 31–4). Within the Conservative party these roles were normally carried out by the CRD and, to a lesser extent, the Conservative Political Centre, both of which were for the time being in the hands of the Heathpersons. Intuitively or otherwise, her strategy for developing counter-networks was to encourage competition for her attention among the brokers, entrepreneurs and 'clearing houses' of the Right thus acting as a catalyst for the production of the new ideology by continuously stimulating a demand for ideas. A full understanding of what happened would require a study in its own right and our intention here is simply to identify the main institutions and some of the key actors involved to illustrate the nature of the process.

Between 1975 and 1979, under the guidance of Alfred Sherman as Director of the Centre for Policy Studies, a series of policy groups worked on the main policy areas and, in the course of their work, sought out and brought together like-minded intellectuals of the Right with an interest in using their ideas to make an impact on Conservative policy. Once established, the policy groups naturally became the focal point for maintaining interlinked sets of social networks with a dynamic of their own. Although Alfred Sherman was the intellectual broker who made the CPS work, the inspiration behind it belonged to Sir Keith Joseph.

Like others on the Right, Sir Keith Joseph had come to the conclusion that the key to the party's and the country's problems lay in its obsession with 'the middle ground'. This, as he argued in a speech to the Oxford Union on 6 December 1975, 'was the lowest common denominator obtained from a calculus of assumed electoral expediency, defined not by reference to popular feeling but by splitting the difference between Labour's position and the Conservatives' and thus resulting in a progressive move to the left (Sir Keith Joseph, 1976, p. 21). Echoing Enoch Powell, he maintained that the middle ground was a compromise between politicians, unrelated to the aspirations of the people who did not want it 'But because we ceased to fight the battle of ideas, and told the public instead what we thought they wanted to hear, we tended to hear what we were saying, rather than what they were saying' (*Ibid.*, p. 25).

Such a supine attitude, he argued, guaranteed the effect of the famous 'left-wing ratchet'. However, his analysis is less important than the fact that he was prepared to act on it and, as a prestigious and respected member of the Conservative party hierarchy, possessed the intellectual and political resources to support his action. He happened to combine the roles of both intellectual and politician and, in both capacities, was able to initiate through the CPS one of the most important of the early brokerage operations between the Conservative party and intellectuals of the Right.

In 1975 and 1976 Sir Keith Joseph made sixty speeches in universities and polytechnics alone advancing the moral case for capitalism (*Ibid.*, p. 8). Many of these speeches, a number of which were written by Alfred Sherman (Hodgson, 1984, p. 49), drew on ideas about the various benefits of the market order which had long been advanced by the Institute of Economic Affairs (IEA). Hanging on the wall of the IEA's waiting room at 2 Lord North Street is a framed quotation from John Maynard Keynes:

> The ideas of economists and political philosophers, both when they are right and when they are wrong, are more powerful than is commonly understood. Indeed the world is ruled by little else. Practical men, who believe themselves to be quite exempt from any intellectual influences, are usually the slaves of some defunct economist.

Since its inception in 1958, the IEA has always been clear about the decisive influence of intellectuals and their ideas and about its own role as a clearing house for ideas. It has deliberately 'sponsored, produced, refined and timed the ideas' through an assiduous and prolific publications policy (Seldon, 1981, p. xxxii) and, in performing that role, clearly represented a valuable potential resource for Margaret Thatcher. Its networks had been painstakingly built over many years from a position well outside the dominant ideology which reigned in the 1950s and 1960s when as John Woods, who has been with the IEA since 1963, puts it 'to argue for the use of the market (or for the price mechanism as it was more usually called), was to put yourself outside serious discussion into an archaic and isolated no-man's land where, incidentally, few British academics were to be found, even as explorers'. But, he continued, 'there were a few, and the IEA soon met them' (Woods, 1981, p. 260). Because the Institute had for so long been the only broker in this part of the ideological market it acquired a virtual monopoly of the social networks which were available.

Unfortunately, monopolies are of little value unless there is a demand for the product which, in this case, was ideas on the role of the market in social policy: ideas which 'emerged from disillusionment with Keynes, with Beveridge and with Titmus' (Seldon in Hodgson, 1984, p. 49). Consigned to the wilderness for a decade, Seldon and Harris began to move towards a kind of respectability in the later 1960s when first Hayek, in 1968, and then Milton Friedman, in 1970, wrote papers for the IEA and an upswing began to register in the demand for the Institute's ideas. Thereafter, their move from not even being in the theatre to a prominent position on stage was a steady one. Their explanation of this reversal of fortune is suitably modest. 'Chance', said Seldon when interviewed by us, 'is a key factor. We found ourselves at a concourse of influences (*Interview*, 6 July 1983). Alfred Sherman was equally philosophical about his role and impact: 'Circumstances were propitious. Is it Sherman the hero? Or was the situation awaiting Sherman' (Hodgson, 1984, p. 49). Perhaps so. But their careful cultivation of MPs of all parties over a long period indicates their determination to maximize their chances of being the right brokers, at the right concourse, at the right time. Even after the tide had turned, they became well used to being told by politicians that the ideas in IEA papers though attractive were not 'politically possible' and likened this reaction to the response of a sales manager to a new product — that it would not sell because the public had not heard of it (Harris and Seldon, 1977, pp. xi-xii).

As we discuss below, other intellectuals were bent on making sure that the public did know about these and other ideas. In the meantime, Margaret Thatcher for one decided that the IEA commanded an intellectual network to be valued. Hodgson (1984) quotes her ringing endorsement of IEA thinking: 'All policies are based on ideas. Our policies are firmly founded on those ideas which have been developed with such imagination in the *Journal* (of the Institute)' (p. 49). The Institute had found an appreciative audience in the Conservative party leadership which gave some substance to their claim, or more accurately their advertisement, in 1977 to have won one kind of intellectual championship by supplanting Fabian tracts and PEP pamphlets with Hobart and other papers as 'the largest source of authoritative, up-to-date economic analyses of the recent and current scene' (Harris and Seldon, 1977, p. xi). Even if they are only half right, their links with the Conservative leadership gave them a credibility as intellectual brokers undreamt of in 1958.

One of the difficulties of identifying the key intellectuals in the ideological shifts of the 1970s is that by no means all of them would describe themselves as members of the Right. This is certainly true of two of the most influential financial journalists in this process: Peter Jay and Sam Brittan. They were to take the ideas of monetarism and sell them to a far wider audience than the IEA could ever reach and at the same time deny that they were Conservatives. As economic editors at *The Times* and the *Financial Times* respectively they were disseminators of ideas not only to a broad middle class audience but also to members of the political and civil service elite who formed part of their social networks. (Peter Jay, for example, was son-in-law to James Callaghan.) Both became disenchanted in the late 1960s with the Keynesian assumptions of economic management through the manipulation of demand and convinced instead by Friedman's ideas on the control of the money supply. One of their most important converts was Sir Keith Joseph who, as Hodgson notes in discussing this issue, was able 'to play a crucial role as an intermediary between the world of ideas and the world of practical Conservative politics' by converting Mrs Thatcher to monetarism. (For a detailed, if partisan, analysis of the arrival of monetarism see Congdon (1978). Congdon claims that by 1975 there was a virtual unanimity in the financial press that the money supply must be brought under control (p. 11).)

By no means all of the intellectuals competing for Mrs Thatcher's attention and political support were advocates of the free market either in economic or in social policy. Following her election as party leader the Conservative Philosophy Group (CPG) was formed in the spring of 1975 by John Casey and Roger Scruton, then two academics of Peterhouse, Cambridge and colleagues of Maurice Cowling, with the help of Sir Hugh Frazer. Founded as a forum in which right-wing philosophers can discuss their ideas with Conservative MPs, the CPG's interests are only rarely directed towards economics. In common with the academic journals the *Cambridge Review* (initially, though no longer, edited by Casey) and the *Salisbury Review* (edited by Scruton) the CPG's discussions tend to be concerned with a conservatism based on a respect for order, authority, nation and traditional institutions such as the Church which is a long way from the liberal economics of the IEA (see Stothard, 1983; and Walker, M, 1983). They are quite explicit about their search for a new hegemony. In the first issue of the *Salisbury Review*, for example, Scruton stated,

> It is necessary to establish a conservative dominance in intellectual life, not because this is the quickest or most certain way to political influence, but because in the long run, it is the only way to create a climate of opinion favourable to the conservative cause. The importance of regaining the commanding heights of the moral and intellectual economy has got to be clearly perceived by the partisans of conservatism.

(In fact, as we have seen, rather a lot of people on the Right saw the need to regain 'the commanding heights'.) The dominant ideology which this group have in mind would be highly suspicious of any conservatism which puts the free market first. It has more in sympathy with Edmund Burke than Hayek (Hodgson, 1984, p. 52). Like the free marketeers and monetarists, these conservatives too have intellectuals prepared to translate their ideas into wider appeal. T.E. Utley and Peregrine Worsthorn of the *Daily Telegraph*, for example, have been doing it for years and that multi-functional intellectual, Roger Scruton, now has a regular column in *The Times*.

There was clearly no shortage of new Right intellectuals in 1975 prepared to supply the new Conservative leader with a steady flow of ideas. Some social networks to support such an exercize were already in being, dormant ones were reactivated and new ones swiftly developed once it became clear that there was a national focus and opportunity for political influence. Mrs Thatcher's general ideological presuppositions coupled with her exposed position as new leader meant that it was very much in her interest to stimulate such a flow of ideas. No doubt hindsight adds a liberal amount of lubricant to what was probably a difficult and risky business, certainly to begin with. But at the same time there can be little doubt that the appropriate intellectual roles of broker, entrepreneur and popular translator did emerge to man the ideological vehicle. In the final chapter we will return to this issue and discuss the way in which the roles of new Right intellectuals, and Thatcher's use of them, has changed as a result of the Conservative party's sustained period of office. Now we turn to examine the form the new hegemony has taken in education.

Education and the New Hegemony

In *Unpopular Education* (1981) the left-wing Centre for Contemporary Cultural Studies pays due recognition to the success of the *Black Papers* in changing the parameters of educational debate (pp. 200ff). This should be reassuring news for C.B. Cox, joint author of all the *Black Papers*, who, writing in the same year, expressed himself less than convinced that the battle had been won. The left-progressive hegemony established in the 1960s, he believed, is still very much with us in the 1980s (C.B. Cox, 1981, pp. 7–11). But although disagreements exist about how far the Right has had an impact on the dominant educational ideology, there can be little doubt about the extent of its ambition back in the grim days of the late 1960s and early 1970s. In common with the new Right in general, right-wing educationalists developed a critique, partly one suspects as they went along and partly intuitively, of what had gone wrong and therefore of what needed to be done to put things right.

The first task was to stand up and be counted, to throw down the gauntlet rather than allow progressive opinion to dominate by default. Taking the fight to the left consensus was seen as a necessary antidote to right-wing passivity. Thus the first *Black Papers* have almost a crusading tone about them as they mount the ideological challenge. Cox and Dyson, writing in 1971, saw it as 'perhaps the Black Papers' major achievement to have broken the fashionable left-wing consensus on education, and to have initiated a reappraisal of progressive assumptions' (p. 11). One of the characteristics of any ideological hegemony is that it discourages and devalues ideological challenge. Thus the Right's critique of what needed to be done had necessarily to be founded on the realization that something *should* be done.

The educational Right recognized that any challenge to the prevailing consensus would, perforce, have to take on what it called 'the progressive Establishment' composed of the Department of Education and Science (DES), Her Majesty's Inspectorate (HMI), the teachers' unions and sometimes, though not always, the local education authorities. It was in the ranks of education's officialdom that the Right saw the progressive ideology as most intractably ensconced. Inevitably, therefore, the DES was not to be trusted: *Black Paper 1977* quotes a speech by Viscount Eccles to the House of Lords on 7 October 1976 where he said, 'It is a very sad thing for an ex-Minister of Education to say but you cannot trust that Department not to be biased' (Cox and Boyson, 1977, p. 25). A more recent example of this part of the Right's analysis of the obstacles to change comes from, identifiably, a professor of sociology, Stanislav Andreski, who writes: 'Under the smokescreen of ultra–egalitarian phraseology, the bureaucratic — educational complex pursues its own interests with an almost total disregard for the long-term interests of those whom state education is supposed to serve' (Cox and Marks, 1982, p. 11).

Unlike the progressive establishment, the Right saw itself as being uniquely in touch with the general will of the people and therefore able to act as its champion. This was obviously a basis for some optimism. Writing in the 1975 *Black Paper*, Ronald Butt argues that although the Left has monopoly in places of power, the Right has 'a great deal of inchoate public support and disquiet on which it can draw' (p. 45). But it was an optimism which had to be tempered by a knowledge of the problems of gaining access to that public support, as Butt admits. The problem was that a 'climate of fashion' had been created by an 'opinion forming' establishment consisting of officials, academics, professionals and the media 'who will endorse, reflect and magnify' that climate of fashion (*Ibid.*, p. 43). So it was a question of taking on not only the power structures of the progressive establishment (DES, HMI, unions and LEAs) but also the numerous groups of intellectuals who propagated and legitimized the establishment line. Add to this the inertia of the Conservative party in failing to advance a critique to oppose the prevailing orthodoxy and the task becomes doubly difficult (*Ibid.*, p. 44).

The initial vehicle for the ideological counter attack in education were the *Black Papers*, five editions of which, plus a compendium, were published between 1969 and 1977. Constructed as a series of essays and beginning with a letter to MPs, the *Black Papers* clearly set out to draw together authors from various walks of life who would give the publications a wide appeal, certainly beyond the narrow ranks of educationalists and teachers alone. Academics such as H.J. Eysenck and Cyril Burt (professors of psychology), writers such as Kingsley Amis and Iris Murdoch, politicians such as Angus Maude, and teachers from both state and independent sector schools, gave the books both variety and, eventually, credibility. In terms of sales it was a sound strategy: by 1971 80,000 copies of the first three *Black Papers* had been sold (Cox and Dyson, 1971, p. 9). The Institute of Economic Affairs supported the venture having already had some thoughts on the role of the market in education during the 1960s. (see, for example, Peacock and Wiseman, 1964; Prest, 1966; Ferns, 1969) In particular, Professor Ferns' 1969 IEA Occasional Paper 'Towards an independent university' was closely followed by a meeting organized by IEA of academics and others to discuss the practical steps in establishing such an independent university. Out of this, eventually, and with the assiduous help of Ralph Harris, General Director of the IEA, came the independent University of Buckingham. So the Institute, as was its wont, was already active in this field and sympathetic to ideas contained in the *Black Papers*. (Ralph Harris wrote a paper for *Black Paper Two*.)

As intellectuals with an educational cause to sponsor, the Right needed an institutional focus to coordinate an otherwise fragmented network of individuals and to make the best use of whatever ideological momentum was generated by the *Black Papers*. In other words it needed an institutional broker. This task was initially performed by the National Council for Educational Standards (NCES) and subsequently by the Centre for Policy Studies as well. The NCES was set up during a special conference at Pembroke College, Cambridge, in January 1972. Of the nine signatories to the announcement of its formation, six had already contributed to the first three *Black Papers* and the proceedings of the conference were published by the Critical Quarterly Society which also published the first three *Black Papers*. The address of the NCES was given as 2 Lord North Street, London SW1, which just happens to be that of the Institute of Economic Affairs as well (NCES, 1972). Not surprisingly the aims of the NCES mirrored themes from the *Black Papers* — standards, choice, diversity etc. More revealing of its intended function is the statement in the announcement that 'Associate members will be encouraged to form local groups, write to newspapers, MPs etc., to undertake local initiatives, and help in every way to further the aims which they share with the Council' (*Ibid.*) — in other words provide the support structure for the ideological push. Whether the NCES in fact performed this function to the extent its founders intended seems doubtful. Nonetheless, it provided an initial focus for otherwise isolated intellectuals to vocalize and articulate their common concerns.

The position of the independent schools in these developments was discreet but evident. Private school headmasters contributed articles to the *Black Papers* and were involved in the setting up of the NCES: the list of participants in the inaugural conference at Pembroke College included the headmasters of Eton, Harrow and St. Paul's and officers of the Headmasters' Conference and the Independent Schools Association (*Ibid.*). It can also be no coincidence that the only non-university signatories to the IEA declaration supporting the setting up of an independent university were the headmasters of Harrow, Tonbridge (Michael McCrum, subsequently Headmaster of Eton), and Manchester Grammar School and the Provost of Eton. There was clearly nothing wrong with *their* social networks. In closely allying themselves with the Right's ideological counter attack in education, the private schools were deliberately helping to sponsor ideas and values which, presumably, they saw to be politically advantageous. So what was the nature of the new ideology and how did it help the independent schools?

In *Education, Politics and the State* we developed a framework for the analysis of educational ideology. It has four components: the desired social order; the desired type, or types of individuals (the educational product(s)) necessary to achieve that social order; the educational means necessary to achieve that educational product; and the conception of human nature which limits what is educationally desirable and possible (pp. 63–5). By the late 1960s the Right was firmly convinced that it did not like the social order which, willy-nilly, was evolving around it.

Furthermore it believed, as the Marxists Bowles and Gintis (1976) were to argue later, that there was a direct 'correspondence' between the social relations inculcated in the school and the social relations of the wider society. Judged by the *Black Papers,* the Right wanted a more stable social order characterized by the meritocratic ethos, inequality and a slower and more predictable rate of change. Such a society required an appropriate distribution of types of individuals with a due respect for authority, discipline, 'civilized' values (usually undefined) and conservative social mores (for example, with regard to the family, church, sex). As can be gathered, this part of the educational ideology is rather vague and can sometimes only be inferred from reactions against such items as student unrest and the 'permissive society'. This is not unusual, for as we pointed out in *Education, Politics and the State* one of the more useful aspects of educational ideologies is their claim to be apolitical and to be concerned solely with education. (It is worth noting that in the announcement of its foundation, the NCES included the statement: 'The Council is organized by men and women actively engaged in education, and is wholly non-political'.) This characteristic helps to disguise the kind of social order the ideology seeks to legitimize (Salter and Tapper, 1981, p. 63). However, where the ideology is much clearer is on the educational means necessary to achieve the desired educational products.

An ordered society, argues the Right, requires an educational system which is equally ordered in terms of the way in which knowledge, skills and attitudes are organized, taught and accredited. Therein lies predictability as opposed to the Pandora's box of progressive education. In terms of the overall educational structure, grammar schools, direct grant and independent schools are favoured by the *Black Papers* because they provide a visible demarcation of quality and are the repository of traditional moral and cultural values and educational standards. In an ordered world it is essential to have high status models to which others can aspire. Examinations and testing (usually popularized as 'standards') are important for several reasons: first, because they are the cement which bind the educational structures together giving them strength, cohesion and direction. They can be linked to classroom organization and teaching method through the argument that formal, traditional teaching methods, coupled with good classroom discipline, give the best exam results and should therefore be encouraged. Mixed ability teaching is obviously viewed suspiciously because it destroys the rigid ability hierarchy necessary for specific exam training. Secondly, examinations provide order by giving individuals labels which indicate their educational, and by inference their social, worth: the educational products thus have specific values assigned to them. Underlying this ideology is the assumption about human nature that children require a system of firm educational definitions and controls if their full potential is to be developed.

The descriptive coherence of the Right's educational ideology was matched by an awareness that the mechanisms for educational change, for implementing the ideology in practice, should form part of the campaign against the existing hegemony. So an extra theme was included which insisted, to quote Rhodes Boyson (1975), that schools should be *accountable* 'to some authority outside them'. 'The necessary sanction' he continued, 'is either a nationally-enforced curriculum or parental choice or a combination of both' (p. 141). The use of parental choice as a change strategy is a logical result of the Right's analysis of what is wrong in education. If the 'inchoate public support and disquiet' about education is to be mobilized and the education establishment circumvented then parental choice is the natural mechanism with which to do it. 'Parental choice' neatly links the emphasis on the role of the market in education with the pragmatic need for political influence. The convenient assumption on which this strategy is based is, of course, that parental wishes are in reality the same as those of the Right and that if parental choice was introduced then the William Tyndales of this world would, in Cox and Boyson's (1977) vision of the future, be 'denuded of their pupils' (p. 19).

There does not appear to be any scepticism in the ranks about this assumption. So the parallel advocacy of national controls of the curriculum using monitoring and inspection, which is obviously inconsistent with a pure market in education, can be seen as a different but complementary strategy for getting the same thing: a change in the educational hegemony. The test of the status of parental choice would be the Right's reaction to the horrifying situation where parental choice created more, rather than less, William Tyndales. What if the majority of parents were in favour of progressive education? Would the Right still support their right to choose? One suspects not: because parental choice is a means to a particular ideological end. It is not an end in itself and therefore has a subordinate ideological status.

Throughout the *Black Papers* and other right-wing commentaries on education there is consistent support for the independent schools. As schools which have always been in the educational market, always exposed to and sensitive to parental choice, in the eyes of the Right independent schools assume the status of market leaders. They are perceived as glowing examples of how parental choice, on the one hand, and high academic standards and civilized values, on the other, go hand in hand. They are models of what might, and could, be in the state sector. Given this view, the issue then becomes one of how the model which works so well in the private sector can be transferred to the state sector; and this is where policies about loans and vouchers come in. From the point of view of the independent schools themselves, an ideology which bestows the ultimate legitimacy of high status models to be emulated wherever possible is obviously an ideology to be supported against the progressive consensus which invited the destruction of private schooling.

While the independent schools were no doubt gratified by the emergence of a coherent educational ideology sympathetic to their cause, this was clearly only a first step. An ideology is of little use unless it is taken up and implemented by those in positions of power. Merely because an ideology exists, even if it is publicly paraded, is no guarantee that it will have an impact on political decision-making. It has first to be translated into a form which can exercize political influence. The main vehicle for this translation process has been the Conservative party.

The significance of the *Black Papers* for those on the right of the Conservative party interested in education is that the *Papers* brought together, organized and disseminated disparate ideological themes which had for a long time been simmering beneath the surface. Annual conference reports of the 1960s frequently reflect speakers' concern with issues such as parental choice, vouchers and selection but the speeches have a defensive tone in the face of what was then the apparently inexorable march of progressive education. But not only did they lack a clear-cut and systematic alternative, until 1969 they also lacked a champion. As Minister for Education and then Shadow Minister between 1962 and 1969, Sir Edward Boyle was always too wet for the Right. Many of his winding-up speeches at annual conference consisted of the pouring of oil on troubled waters, particularly once Labour's comprehensivization programme got under way. He would not condemn the comprehensive principle per se, only the 'botched-up' schemes. He would argue in favour of avoiding a doctrinaire approach to education and on selection would maintain, as he did in 1967, that though there has to be selection it does not have to be into different institutions. In many ways he epitomized the charge subsequently made by the Right that the Conservative Party had allowed the Labour Party to capture the ideological middle ground of politics by default. He was therefore a natural target.

It is an interesting, but no doubt fortuitous, coincidence that the first *Black Paper* was published in 1968 and Boyle departed as Shadow Minister for Education in 1969. With Margaret Thatcher's arrival in the post there was a marked change in both content and style. Her speech to the 1970 party conference emphasized the importance of the quality of the schooling experience, the need to retain the direct grant schools and the role of independent schools in acting as a safeguard against a state monopoly in education (Conservative Party, 1970, pp. 18-20). Although a more sympathetic minister was a necessary beginning the promulgation of the Right's ideology in the Party had to take place at a number of levels. One important arena was the Conservative Political Centre (CPC) which publishes discussion documents for use both nationally and locally. Rhodes Boyson was active here and acted as a link between the *Black Papers* and NCES, on the one hand, and the Conservative party activists on the other, publishing *Battle Lines for Education* in 1973 and *Parental Choice* in 1975 through the CPC. Norman St John-Stevas, Opposition Front Bench Spokesman on Education from 1974, also published three CPC papers redolent with *Black Paper* themes between 1974 and 1977 though this may say more about the political commitment of his advisers than about his own.

One might suspect that the Conservative Research Department would be more resistant to the overtures of the Right given that it had at one time been an integral part of Heath's party apparatus but by 1975 its journal, *Notes on Current Politics,* was echoing *Black Paper* ideas. A special edition on education in April of that year argued strongly for the setting of national standards for reading, writing and mathematics, the strengthening of the Inspectorate, the thorough evaluation of new teaching methods, more stress in teacher training on how to teach basic skills and maintain discipline, the importance of parental choice, and so on (Conservative Research Department, 1975). An early example of formal success in the Right's campaign to translate their educational ideology into party policy was the Parents' Charter. It first appeared in the October 1974 election manifesto under the heading 'A Charter of Parents' Rights'. It had five components: the state and local authorities should take account of the wishes of parents; there should be a local appeal system for parents dissatisfied with their allotment of schools; parents should be represented on school boards; headteachers should be obliged to form a parent teachers association; and schools should be encouraged to publish prospectuses about their record, existing character, specialities and objectives. At the following year's conference it was announced that a committee had been set up, chaired by the ubiquitous Rhodes Boyson, to report on the practicalities of realizing these objectives. From then on, the Parents' Charter became a highly visible and useful symbol of the new ideology and was subsequently formally linked to the issue of standards, as in the 1979 manifesto: 'Extending parents' rights and reponsibilities, including their right of choice, will also help raise standards by giving them greater influence over educa-tion' (p. 25). The final hurdle was passed when it was embodied in the 1980 Education Act.

The phasing out of the direct grant schools by the Labour party which began in September 1976 gave added momentum to the advancement of the Right's educational ideology. It apparently showed that its analysis of the progressive effects of the loss of hegemony was correct: the educational models the Right valued — grammar, direct grant and independent schools — were in turn falling victim to the Left's dominance of the consensus ideology. The independent schools would be next and with them would go the last bastions of sound educational practice. This obviously had to be opposed in policy terms and so Labour's action gave focus to one aspect of the ideology — policy translation process: a focus which was to result in the Assisted Places Scheme (see Chapter 8).

Conclusions

By the end of the 1970s and early 1980s right-wing thought on education had assumed a visibility and respectability undreamt of in 1968 when the first *Black Paper* was published. The new ideological consensus may not have fully arrived but the parameters of the debate and the issues which appeared regularly on the educational agenda had changed significantly. The attack on the left-progressive hegemony in education formed part of a wider challenge by the new Right to the consensus ideology of Butskellism: a challenge which was characterized by a conscious analysis of the roles of intellectuals and institutions in generating and maintaining ideologies. The Right clearly recognized the need for intellectual entrepreneurs, brokers and popularizers to promote and disseminate its ideological themes to mass and elite audiences alike.

One audience in particular with which it was concerned was the Conservative Party since ideology is only useful to the extent that it can be used, directly or indirectly, to influence those with the power to implement its objectives. Here the various and different networks of Right intellectuals forged a fortunate alliance with Margaret Thatcher based on its need for a national figure to promote its ideas and her and her supporters' need for a steady flow of policy ideas with which to consolidate her initially weak position as party leader. Intellectual brokerage institutions such as the Institute for Economic Affairs and the Centre for Policy Studies swiftly developed as linking agencies between the networks of Right intellectuals and the Conservative party. However, the links were never allowed to become too permanent and too predictable: Thatcher encourages competition as much among her groups of intellectual supporters as elsewhere.

The general ideology of the new Right is by no means homogeneous. One significant tension is that between the advocates of the free market mechanism in economic and social policy, on the one hand, and the proponents of social order, authority and traditional values on the other. The former may have unpredictable consequences for the latter. In the Right's educational ideology the tension has been superficially resolved by presenting the operation of the market (parental choice) as one of the means by which the traditional educational goals of order and discipline, high academic standards and formal teaching methods can be achieved; the other means being state controls. However, the theoretically open nature of the market could mean that parents at some point choose alternative educational goals, perhaps even progressive ones. In practice this seems unlikely given the ideological dominance of the Right.

The initial impetus for the attack on progressive education came from the *Black Papers* with the National Council for Educational Standards as the institutional broker, and individuals such as Rhodes Boyson acting as facilitating links with the Conservative party. There is no sign that the ideological momentum is slowing down. Since 1980 additional support has been forthcoming from the education study group of the CPS chaired by Mrs (now Baroness) Caroline Cox. Together with John Marks, Secretary to the Group, she has published several books including *Real Concern*, (an attack on the National Children's Bureau's study of comprehensive schools) and *Sixth Forms in ILEA Comprehensives: A Cruel Confidence Trick* — which is self-explanatory. Members of the education group publish frequently, both for the CPS and the older NCES — a convenient but not suprising continuity given that John Marks is also the administrator for NCES (Passmore, 1981, p. 6).

If the Right's challenge to the left-progressive hegemony in education had not taken off the independent schools would have been ideologically exposed and more vulnerable to political attacks from the

Labour Party. Instead, they have been given authority and legitimacy by an ideology which sees them as models to be followed both in terms of the quality of the education they provide and the way in which they provide it through their responsiveness to consumer, i.e. parental, demand. The longer that ideology is sustained the more embedded in the public mind it becomes and the more difficult it is for the Labour Party to sell, let alone implement, a policy which challenges the existence of these schools. Given the limited interest and skills displayed by Labour Party intellectuals in the translation of their private school policy into electoral appeal, the new hegemony of the Right in education is not likely to suffer from that quarter.

It was fairly inevitable that the independent schools would play a supportive role in the development of an ideology which so categorically legitimizes them: obviously it was in their political self-interest so to do. For the most part they have carried out this task discreetly since political visibility means that you are that much of a clearer target. But however discreet they were in the promotion of the ideology it was unavoidable that once the ideology was translated into policies which benefitted them specifically they would become politically visible and would have to develop the means to cope with that fact. Precisely how they did this in the case of the Assisted Places Scheme is dealt with in the next chapter.

8 Phoenix or Damp Squib: The Assisted Places Scheme

A Case Study in Decision-Making

Not so long ago political sociologists were deeply involved in the analysis of power through case studies in decision-making. The purpose was to discover 'who rules', usually in a particular community, by discerning how varying issues were resolved — that is whose will prevailed (Dahl, 1961). The most potent critiques of decision-making have concentrated upon its limitations as an approach to the study of power (Lukes, 1974). Power can assume forms other than control of the decision-making process. How is the agenda for action decided? Certain pressing issues may be excluded from the agenda and if included only 'safe' solutions may be considered acceptable. It has been argued that to control the agenda is partially dependent upon the management of society's dominant ideology so that only some issues are perceived as problems and only some solutions are deemed feasible.

In response to this aggressive critique case studies in decision-making have dwindled rapidly. It is our intention in this chapter to revive the tradition. Although we accept the view that to analyze decision-making is to examine merely one level of power, we are nonetheless of the opinion that it should remain a substantive area of concern for political sociologists. Policy making debates are often fiercely contested and the outcomes can have a significant bearing upon the quality of people's lives. Furthermore, although there may be an analytical distinction between the varying forms of power, it is our contention that in practice they will inevitably interact with one another. To analyze the decision-making process, therefore, is to discern what is the political agenda and how it was formulated.

In several of the previous chapters we have illustrated how the organization of schooling in Britain, at least since 1965, has been subjected to a partisan political infighting accompanied by intense ideological struggle. The proliferation of ideas has been so broad-ranging that it is conceivable that governments could have implemented almost any policy. For example, in terms of private schooling if party statements have any credibility then governments could have either prohibited the charging of fees or legalized a voucher system embracing both the maintained and private sectors. The question then is why particular policy options have succeeded whereas others have failed? The simple answer is that those policies which have prevailed have been sponsored by governments and state apparatuses sufficiently powerful to ensure the prevalence of their preferences. Although this may account for the success of some policy options as opposed to others, it fails to explain why the state should have been so persuaded. In concrete terms one has to know what constitutes being placed on a government's policy agenda and how this is achieved.

To resolve these problems we must analyze how institutions interact to formulate policy. It is self-evident that socio-economic change is the stimulant of ideological conflict. The translation of ideology into policy, like much of the manufacturing of ideology itself, takes place within an institutional context. Although policy change may be the consequence of socio-economic trends, the two are linked together by both the struggle for power (in which the ultimate goal is to win control of, or the support of, the government and state apparatus) and the process of legitimation which embalms decisions with the appropriate ideology.

The Assisted Places Scheme was placed on the statute book by a composite bill, the 1980 Education (No. 2) Bill, which passed its second and critical reading in the House of Commons on 5 November 1979. In September 1981 some 4000 pupils acquired a place at an independent school with the aid of a means-tested scholarship granted under the terms of the Assisted Places Scheme. Thus a small, but highly controversial, educational innovation — and indeed venture in social engineering — was launched. Three main institutional forces were responsible for the successful conclusion to an initiative that had been a long time incubating: the private sector of schooling; the Conservative party; and the Department of Education and Science. The purpose of this chapter is to analyze the interaction of these three institutional forces, including some discussion of their own internal stresses and strains. Although the concern is with policy implementation, the chapter will conclude with more speculative thoughts on the wider educational implications of the Assisted Places Scheme as well as its lessons for the future policy making process. In view of our particular focus within the process of educational change we have a purposefully limited view of why and how policy emerges. We will not review the changing socio-economic context but instead will examine the mysteries of policy implementation through the dynamics of institutional interaction.

Pressure Group Politics — The Private Sector in Action

The private sector's advocacy of the Assisted Places Scheme is perhaps perplexing in view of the fact that those direct grant schools which had decided to go independent rather than join the maintained system (that is approximately 120 schools out of some 175) had successfully survived the transition in status and by the late 1970s numbers in the private schools as a whole were picking up. Many direct grant schools had feared that without financial sustenance from the state they would be forced either to close or join the maintained sector. Later those schools which were to offer assisted places were in no such precarious position for they were responding successfully to market forces. The private sector's support for the Assisted Places Scheme was not a product of financial exigency. Although the private sector has always valued its independence in modern times it has consistently desired to be closely associated with the maintained schools.

The disadvantages of isolation are potentially menacing for it can foster stereotypical images, heighten suspicion and increase political hostility. Through association the benefits of independent schooling can be more widely dispersed enabling the schools to substantiate their claim that they are not so much interested in whom they teach but in preserving a form of schooling which owes its character to their independence.

Because association has taken the form of independent schools educating selected individuals — usually at the expense of the state — the benefits have in fact been tangible. The majority of selected pupils have been either academically gifted or have had specialized talents (for example, in music) so enabling the schools to enhance their scholarly and cultural reputations. If this can be achieved at the expense of the state then so much the better for market forces are not always favourable. In reality the association between the independent sector and the maintained schools remained comparatively restricted until the

Assisted Places Scheme. Few local education authorities have been prepared to deprive their own schools of talented pupils at some cost to themselves. Until the phasing out of direct grant nearly all the association was confined to the direct grant schools which, in a much used metaphor, formed a bridge between the independent and maintained sectors. But like all bridges it had its own particular character for the direct grant pupils (a minimum of 25 per cent in each school) were usually selected according to stringent academic criteria.

Although the bridge may have been narrow, it was nevertheless in place and as such had to be defended. Several of the direct grant schools had a reputation for academic excellence. It was claimed, most forcefully by the former high master of Manchester Grammar School, Lord James (1967), that gifted people were more likely to develop their talents to the full if they were educated in a critical mass. Direct grant schools brought together both able pupils and staff, although they educated fee-paying pupils all of them had to satisfy the requirements of a rigorous entrance examination, merit not money secured acceptance. At the same time the presence of pupils whose fees were paid by the local education authorities ensured that the direct grant schools were socially diverse. Indeed, the schools were a social mobility channel for their many working-class pupils. The direct grant schools represented a viable model of association between the maintained and independent sectors and their sympathizers wanted to see it more widely applied.

However, some time before the bridge was blown up by the Labour party's commitment to a comprehensive system of secondary education the rot had already set in. The minutes of the Direct Grant Joint Committee are littered with references to LEAs that declined to take up their quota of places so forcing the schools to either shop around for alternative LEA clients or to fill the places at their own cost (DGJC, *Minutes,* 8 February 1973). For some direct grant schools the regulations were proving exceedingly burdensome. Neither was it possible to always blame malevolent politicians as chief education officers found themselves pressured by more stringent budgets, had more places available in local authority controlled grammar schools, and faced the prospect of falling rolls. Moreover as many heads themselves recognized the peculiar distribution of direct grant schools (located disproportionately in various urban conurbations), and the fact that free places were not means tested, made it more difficult to defend the system as the political temperature rose. The bridge was not only narrow, it was decidedly rickety.

The publication of Circular 10/65, and the eventual inclusion of the direct grant schools in the terms of reference of the Public Schools Commission, intensified the search for a new form of association. It was necessary for the private sector to advocate reform rather than to cling to the past. The fact that twenty-five years earlier the Fleming Committee had proposed an Assisted Places Scheme as the means of bridging the divide between the private and maintained sector (in addition to a periodic refloating of the idea) made this an obvious alternative. In evidence to the Public Schools Commission the DGJC did not propose in explicit terms an Assisted Places Scheme but rather it said that: 'We have nothing but praise for the flexibility and generosity of concept in the direct grant regulations in force in England and Wales ... All the same, we believe the time is ripe for some redrafting, without alteration of the principles and general philosophy they embody. We should welcome discussion with the Commission on these lines before proposing a formal revision' (DGJC, December 1968, paragraph 29). Included in the Committee's suggested guidelines was the recognition of 'the need for a more realistic scale of fee remissions which would give parity of opportunity to all parents in a wider context' and the possibility of implementing proposals that would '... remove the anomaly by which reserved places are awarded without means test to parents who can well afford full fees' (*ibid.*).

Although the public pronouncements of the DGJC can best be described as coy their Committee minutes reveal a bolder spirit. In November 1967 Peter Mason, one of the leading forces behind the Assisted Places Scheme, argued that the inclusion of the direct grant schools in the PSC's terms of reference gave the DGJC '... valuable breathing space to work out satisfactory arrangements with government and to revise the terms and conditions of direct grant' (DGJC, *Minutes*, 3 November 1967). Later it is revealed that, in spite of the DGJC's open-ended formal submission to the PSC, it has been suggested in meetings that assisted places should replace free places although it was suspected that many would deprecate anything in the nature of a "means test" (DGJC, *Minutes*, 7 October 1969). As it turned out, all this manoeuvring was to no avail for Donnison came out against the continuation of direct grant status, a decision that was put on ice by the election of Mr Heath's government.

Although political circumstances had granted the direct grant schools a respite, it did not require much foresight to recognize that their days were numbered. A future Labour government was bound to act upon the recommendations of the Donnison Report in pursuit of its commitment to establish a universal system of comprehensive secondary schooling. Whereas the defenders of the direct grant schools would see this as the destruction of a valuable bridge between maintained and independent schooling, their opponents would see it as another stage in the long march towards comprehensive secondary schooling. In their imagery the direct grant schools were a barrier between the maintained and private sectors that had to be removed before the final assault could begin in earnest.

To forestall this possibility the leading lights in the DGJC realized that they had to make the best use of their respite. Early in Mrs Thatcher's term at the DES she was approached with a view to persuading her to back an Assisted Places Scheme (DGJC, *Minutes,* 17 July 1970). These early soundings were thwarted and were not renewed until the Heath government was well into its term of office, but again to no avail. Judging from the Committee minutes this perplexed the DGJC's leading lights as they recognized in Mrs Thatcher a good friend of the direct grant schools as evidenced by the Department's increase in their capitation grant during her secretaryship. The inclination was to see the rebuttal as the handiwork of departmental officials of whom there was deep suspicion. For example, a meeting between DGJC representatives and DES officials took place on 21 July 1970 and the DGJC notes on that meeting refer to 'the gloomy armour-plate' appearance of DES officials (DGJC, *Minutes,* undated). There is little concrete evidence to support these suspicions and, although the Department may have been irritated at the administrative untidiness of the direct grant system, it was well accustomed to dealing with the problems the schools posed. The failure to persuade Mrs Thatcher was a consequence of broader forces than Departmental obduracy. She had made primary schooling her top priority and her main brief was to direct attention at the experience of schooling rather than to encourage more institutional upheaval. Moreover, it is one thing to persuade a shadow minister and quite another to commit a minister to one's point of view when he or she is backed by the resources of a sceptical department. We have no evidence that the Assisted Places Scheme was at this time little more than a statement of general principles and as such it would have been difficult for a minister to have fitted it into an already crowded schedule.

In spite of its inability to make headway with Mrs Thatcher, the Assisted Places Scheme became the formal long-term policy objective of the DGJC. Document 158 of the DGJC (issued in May 1971) summarized 'the course of informal discussions which the Committee has had with the Secretary of State' and gave 'some information to schools about the courses of action open to them in the future'. On this latter point it reported 'the Catholic preference for the status quo' but it '. . . was the complete conviction shared by all other members of the Committee that a change envisaged by the Assisted Places Scheme was the best way of ensuring that the schools would continue to act in useful partnership with the state system of education. . . . The D.G. Joint Committee hopes that governing bodies, headmasters and headmistresses will, after discussion, agree that it is in the best interest of the schools to continue to foster a scheme on the lines proposed as the best long-term solution to their difficulties' (DGJC, May 1971, subsection 2).

Although other groups in the independent sector may have been supportive of the DGJC's clarion call, they were circumspect about making their views too public. For example, as late as January 1974 the Chairman of the Direct Grant Sub-committee of the Headmasters' Conference (which represented all direct grant schools in HMC) is reported as saying that he '. . . saw this (i.e. an Assisted Places Scheme) as a sensible basis for private discussion with Mrs Thatcher and even with moderate Labour MPs, but thought it would be a tactical mistake to admit publicly that we were dissatisfied with the D.G. regulations as they stood. The Committee agreed' (HMC (1974), *Bulletin,* No. 1, 31 January). The DGJC may have shared the same tactical sense but it is doubtful if discussions incorporating so many persons could have been kept secret. There were over 170 heads of direct grant schools who at the very least had to be kept informed of events and consulted as to their views. One suspects that the Direct Grant Sub-committee's circumspection reflects not so much a tactical sense as to how discussions should be conducted but some pique that it was not the leading force for change. That mantle had been assumed by the DGJC which was less constrained by the heads of the independent schools.

The Conservative party's October 1974 General Election manifesto contained a commitment to at least consider 'a complete system of assisted places so that every parent pays only according to his or her means' (Conservative Party, October 1974, p. 22). Apparently the inclusion of the clause was not a product of negotiations between the independent sector and the party. Furthermore, the Conservative party was thinking of incorporating an Assisted Places Scheme within prevailing direct grant regulations for the same manifesto also promised to strengthen the direct grant schools 'by reopening the direct grant list'. As the direct grant system was still intact such tentativeness is hardly surprising. It is evident that matters had to develop further before positive lines could be formulated.

The most decisive move was made by the subsequent Labour government. Once the regulations were abrogated, with the phasing out of direct grant commencing in September 1976, the situation had changed beyond redemption. It is much easier to innovate when there are no sacred cows to contend with, and a Labour government had done the independent sector the service of blowing up the bridge (or barrier) that the direct grant system represented. Without this vital step, even if an Assisted Places Scheme had been introduced, it probably would have taken a very different form. We will consider the subsequent chronological developments in the next two sections of the chapter but the bare outline of events is straightforward. Following the downfall of the Heath government, and more especially after the phasing out of direct grant commences, there is frequent contact between representatives of the independent sector and the Conservative party. This results in a formal commitment by the party to establish an Assisted Places Scheme which is incorporated in the 1979 General Election manifesto. Thanks to some detailed forward planning, Mrs Thatcher's first government moved swiftly to fulfil this pledge in the form of the 1980 Education (No. 2) Bill of which clauses 17 and 18 contain the essential principles of the scheme. The details were worked out in close consultation between representatives of the independent sector (the Independent Schools Joint Council assumed this responsibility), the government, and DES officials. These administrative particulars were subsequently submitted to Parliament as consequential regulations.

The Assisted Places Scheme is therefore a product of the independent sector's commitment to retain some form of association between itself and the maintained schools. The running was made by the direct grant schools because they constituted what was referred to as the bridge between the two sectors and because they were most threatened by developments in the educational policy of the Labour party. The potential for conflict between the independent and direct grant schools over the Assisted Places Scheme was considerable. In public they showed one another mutual respect but they represented different models of schooling and some independent heads had felt that the direct grant schools, with their built-in 'subsidies', represented unfair competition. Although the direct grant schools were in the vanguard of change, all the private sector institutions had discussed the scheme at both national and local level over many years. There was no sense in which the direct grant interests were stealing a march on their unsuspecting independent school colleagues. Furthermore, as enacted the Assisted Places Scheme did not constitute a straightforward reformulation of the old direct grant regulations for it incorporated the traditional independent schools as well as many ex-direct grammar schools that had opted for independent status. Although schools were officially discouraged from offering too few assisted places, the decision not to specify a precise quota meant that widely differing kinds of independent schools could be involved in the scheme. In other words the nature of the bridge between the independent and maintained sectors was changed: it was somewhat larger (over 220 schools offered assisted places in 1980 as compared to some 170 direct grant schools in September 1976) and composed of more varying elements. Moreover the lengthy consultation prior to implementation helped to allay, if not remove entirely, internal suspicion of the scheme.

In spite of the wide support within the independent sector for the Assisted Places Scheme it was not without its internal critics but they were motivated by deeper considerations than inter-school rivalries. They questioned the meaningfulness of an association that was dependent upon transferring a comparatively few, mainly academically gifted, pupils from the maintained schools into the independent sector. It may be a viable scheme but it would be very shallow. Furthermore, it would invoke the hostility of many who worked in maintained schools and was certain to be attacked politically. Indeed in all the negotiations leading up to the implementation of the Assisted Places Scheme neither the LEAs nor the teacher unions played anything but a minor role. Predictably the unions have attacked the scheme and equally predictably there had been a belated attempt to smooth ruffled feathers.

The internal tensions came to a head at the 1979 annual meeting of HMC which was held at Trinity College, Cambridge in September. The opposition to the scheme was led by the Headmaster of Westminster, Dr John Rae. The HMC Committee (Mr James Wodehouse, then the Headmaster of Rugby, was the current Chairman of HMC) had invited Stuart Sexton, political adviser to the Secretary of State, Mark Carlisle, to address a special session on the Assisted Places Scheme. David Baggley, Headmaster of Bolton School, put the following motion: 'That HMC is committed to the principle of assisted places and strongly believes that any such scheme should have two aims: (i) it should be so constructed that its prime purpose is to benefit children who have some form of need, especially that for an academic education; (ii) it should operate in such a way that it is clearly complementary to the provision in the maintained school system' (HMC, 1979, special session). The minutes do not reveal how the headmasters felt the scheme could be made 'complementary to the provision in the maintained school system'. Baggley's motion stressed 'academic need' rather than 'boarding need' so the subsequent manoeuvring of HMC on this point would seem to be a response to the hostile reaction to the Assisted Places Scheme.

The motion was approved overwhelmingly by 136 votes to fifteen with nineteen abstentions. But such a wide margin of approval could not disguise the tremors for it was unique for HMC to debate so fiercely (almost in the public eye) and certainly most unusual for a formal vote to be taken. The tension was understandable for who can doubt that the government's commitment to the Assisted Places Scheme would have ended there and then if the vote had gone the other way? As it was its promoters were greatly annoyed at Rae's stand and were quick to assure Mark Carlisle that Rae was a maverick.

John Rae has claimed that he failed to persuade his colleagues at Cambridge because he had not prepared himself with sufficient care for the meeting (interview, 20 August 1982). However, it is our conviction that the votes had been lined up long ago and the persuasiveness of speeches on either side could have only a marginal impact. HMC Committee had done its homework: over time the heads had been kept informed and they had discussed the issues at both divisional meetings and special conferences. They consistently recorded their approval. It is virtually impossible for individual initiatives to fight institutional forces, especially by last minute interventions. Although Rae has maintained his opposition, Westminster School has joined the Assisted Places Scheme and, pragmatist that he is, Rae continued as Head.

It is important not to overstress, with the benefit of hindsight, the almost inevitable success of policy proposals once the key institutional backing has been secured. Rae's opposition may have smacked of a futile personal gesture but it did raise the hackles of many of his colleagues and led the Secretary of State to question the extent of support for the Assisted Places Scheme amongst headmasters. Either Rae should have raised internal institutional opposition much earlier (in his Chairman's address to the 1977 annual meeting of HMC he actually stated: 'This scheme (i.e. the Assisted Places Scheme) is the Direct Grant Joint Committee's swift and constructive response to the ending of the direct grant'!) or have mounted his opposition through a more sympathetic external institutional base. But to have pursued the latter course would have risked being labelled as a traitor.

Prior proposals to link the maintained and private sectors of schooling, including some that had been supported by individual independent school heads, had invariably demanded that the schools make major concessions in terms of how far they opened their doors and whom they let in. For example, the First Report of the PSC proposed that 50 per cent of entrants should be assisted, boarding need should be an important criteria in awarding places, and the ability range should encompass children who were more likely to sit CSE rather than GCE examinations (Public Schools Commission, 1968a, pp. 2-3). Even the direct grant regulations required the schools to offer a minimum of 25 per cent free places, a constraint that proved increasingly burdensome as local authority support declined.

In comparison, the terms governing the Assisted Places Scheme are generous. James Cobban, as Chairman of the Assisted Places Steering Committee, (on this body see below) issued a Vade Mecum in November 1980 which sought to answer '. . . most of the questions that have been raised about the implementation of the Assisted Places Scheme' (p. 1). In this he makes the following points: 1. 'Selection is a matter for the head of each school'. 2. '. . . the head is fully entitled, in making the final selection, to take into account the denominational nature of the school'. 3. 'How flexible is the quota?' — 'The short answer is 'very' — provided that heads make every effort to fulfil their participation agreements'. 4. 'In general the financial control exercised by the Department of Education and Science will be much simpler, much less stringent, than that employed under the direct-grant system, no special forms will be issued. Normally the school's revenue accounts, presented in their customary form, will be sufficient; and the Department of Education and Science is likely to require to see them only where, for instance, justification is sought for a large increase of fee', and 5. 'Public subvention implies public accountability, but schools need not fear that they will find this a stumbling-block. The general intention is that the Department of Education and Science will take an interest in proposed increases of fee only if they seem significantly out of line with the general level of increases across the whole range of assisted places schools'. Cobban's review of the terms governing the operation of the assisted places scheme is taken from The Education (Assisted Places) Regulations 1980 which came into operation on 17 November 1980. Furthermore, the Assisted Places Scheme circumvents the local education authorities and following the recent decision of the Secretary of State to remove their veto on assisted places awarded to sixth-formers their exclusion is now complete.

If the Assisted Places Scheme had been a straight swop for the direct grant regulations then it would have been difficult to resist the temptation of interpreting it as a successful attempt by the direct grant schools to escape institutional constraints. As it is schools that had demonstrated their ability to survive in the marketplace were entering into arrangements that placed somewhat greater restrictions upon their freedom of action. It is evident however that the schools are in the driving seat for the flexibility as to the number of places they may offer enables them to cut their commitments to suit their interests. If a school has done its calculations carefully the main consequence of the scheme's termination would be anxious parents. In view of the difficulties that the direct grant schools experienced with their regulations, and the traditional opposition to major innovations, it is unlikely that the schools would have accepted more confining conditions or more radical change. The desire to reformulate an association akin to direct grant was strong but the instinct for self-preservation was undoubtedly stronger.

For all its practical advantages the Assisted Places Scheme lacks broad political respectability. The DGJC hoped that its initiative would receive wide political support but it had few ideas on how to achieve this and as the Labour party was committed to comprehensive secondary schooling the search for political consensus was little more than wishful thinking. Occasionally the architects of the Assisted Places Scheme have indulged themselves in the fantasy that public support can be built up to a point which would make it politically dangerous for a government to tamper with the scheme. They have promoted the idea that the scheme offers a chance for individuals to improve the quality of their schooling (which is most probably true) and is not designed to benefit independent schools (which inevitably it must do if good quality pupils are selected). As a theme with which to win over public sympathy it sounds decidedly limited and a Labour government, as demonstrated by the termination of the direct grant schools, has shown its capacity to ride roughshod over the feelings of an articulate segment of the schooling lobby.

The hostile political reception that the Assisted Places Scheme received took the independent sector unawares. HMC were concerned at the opposition of the Secondary Heads Association and by way of mitigation decided to identify '... with the concern which was being expressed in the state sector regarding proposed Government cuts in expenditure' (HMC (1979), *Bulletin* No. 5, October). Defensively it was claimed that the Assisted Places Scheme '... had acquired a different emphasis when introduced in the Conservative manifesto as an entirely scheme' (*Ibid.*). In the special session on the Assisted Places Scheme at its 1978 annual meeting, HMC had resolved that the scheme should operate in a manner that complemented educational provision in the maintained sector. To this end many independent school heads wanted boarding need as one of the criteria that would determine who was awarded places. The scheme, however, makes no provision for this and so as a sign of goodwill several schools have met boarding costs out of their own funds while the scheme covers tuition fees. No amount of tactical manoeuvring, regardless of how much genuine concern may accompany it, can disguise the fact that the Assisted Places Scheme directed state resources towards the independent sector at a time when the government was cutting funds to maintained schools and that the scheme takes talented pupils out of maintained schools and places them in independent schools on the assumption that their schooling will be improved. One powerful educational lobby — the organized teachers — will be hard to placate and without that political consensus is impossible.

The independent sector has therefore helped to replace direct grant with a form of association that is even more politically divisive. As such it is unlikely to survive a change of government and should that happen then the independent schools — assuming they still desire links with the maintained sector — will be forced to think again about the form of association. It is not the purpose of this chapter to speculate on such matters but it is self-evident that no bridge can be constructed on the basis of the state supporting the permanent one-way transfer of pupils from maintained to private schools unless it can be demonstrated to all the concerned parties that the maintained sector genuinely cannot cater for the needs of those pupils. To select most of those pupils primarily on the grounds of academic criteria is no way to achieve long-term agreement.

The Conservative Party Takes Over

In our opinion the future of the Assisted Places Scheme is dependent upon the maintenance of Conservative government. This raises the question of why the Conservative party was persuaded in the first place to support a scheme that has invoked considerable controversy and received few bouquets. It is tempting to see it as a product of the shifting ideological currents in the Conservative party, or to express the same idea more concisely as a manifestation of Thatcherism (Dale, 1983, pp. 233–55). Even if one accepts this line of argument how within the Conservative party are ideas translated into policy? Furthermore, what is the party's policy making process, who controls it and how? Even the concept of the Conservative party is nebulous for it could mean the agglomeration of the constituency parties, the parliamentary party or the permanent officers. The party exists in differing forms and one needs to know how they interrelate to produce policy. (For a discussion of these issues see chapter 7).

It has been widely and reasonably argued that in the twenty years following the passage of the 1944 Education Act political consensus underlay the development of the British educational system. That consensus was strained to the breaking point by the Labour party's commitment to a universal system of comprehensive secondary education. Initially, however, there was a concerted attempt by the Tory moderates to reach an accommodation on the issue. They realized that the 11+ examination was unpopular with most parents, that many local education authorities wanted to experiment with comprehensive schools, and that in certain parts of the country they made good economic sense. In spite of opposition at the grassroots of the party it is possible that the consensus could have been prolonged if the Tory moderates had been met half way by those controlling the Labour party's educational policy. After all it must be remembered that Mrs Thatcher, when Secretary of State for Education, rejected precious few of the secondary reorganization schemes submitted for her approval. The sticking point was the proposed scope of comprehensive schooling. The Conservative party believed that the matter should be left to the local authorities and that in any case there should be no attack upon either the direct grant or independent schools. In other words that comprehensive and selective schools could exist alongside one another. Although prepared to sanction different forms of comprehensive schooling, the Labour party was not prepared to concede that the two systems could co-exist and so the Tory moderates had little option but to part company.

The growing divisions between the Conservative and Labour parties on educational issues were illustrated by the Labour government's phasing out of direct grant schools and its 1976 Education Bill which gave the Secretary of State greater powers to enforce local authorities to produce proposals that reorganized their secondary schools along comprehensive lines. Both moves were bitterly opposed by all segments of the parliamentary Conservative party under the leadership of its shadow minister, Norman St John-Stevas. Party polarization had crystallized long before Mrs Thatcher formed her first government. Ironically during the 1974-79 period of opposition, when the Conservative party was preparing the general policy outlines for the first Thatcher government, ultimate formal control of the process lay with two well-known party wets, first Norman St John-Stevas and then Mark Carlisle.

The Conservative party, in the form of its shadow minister, committed the party to restoring the direct grant system, to reopening and extending the direct grant list, and to placing the system on a statutory basis so that it could not then be jeopardized by administrative action (that is of the sort that the Secretary of State, Reg Prentice, had employed to phase out the schools). Given the doubts within the independent sector about direct grant status, and the understandable wariness about being restored to a status which had been abolished once, it is unlikely that these proposals could have been implemented. At the same time the Conservative party, through one of its manifesto commitments, was pledged to test the feasibility of an Assisted Places Scheme. The time was ripe, therefore, for the concerned independent sector interests to make another push. The circumstances were more propitious than when they had approached Mrs Thatcher in 1970: the Conservative party was now in opposition and rethinking its policies, it was already tentatively committed to the Assisted Places Scheme, the Labour government was in the process of dismantling the direct grant system, and there was time to work out policy details and to line up the necessary support. Indeed the whole climate of opinion was changing within the Conservative party in a direction which favoured the independent sector given its dependence upon marketplace pressures and apparent responsiveness to consumer demands.

The consequence was a number of meetings between representatives of the independent sector (usually members of the DGJC) and the Conservative party. Although first Norman St John-Stevas and then Mark Carlisle were in charge of the Conservative party's negotiating team (although such a description suggests too much order and formality), most of the work was undertaken by their political adviser Mr Stuart Sexton. Sexton had a strong personal commitment to the scheme, was willing to undertake much of the detailed drafting and to engage in the protracted consultations. Although the eventual scheme cannot be said to be his personal product he undoubtedly left his mark. His role is best described as that of the intellectual broker, although ideas do not originate with him he has the vital function of transforming them into an acceptable political form. An alternative political adviser could have performed the same role but there is no guarantee that he or she would have been either as competent or as committed. The shake-up in the shadow cabinet just prior to the 1979 General Election provided an ideal opportunity for ditching the scheme because apparently Mark Carlisle was not strongly sympathetic but the continuity of political advisers in the shape of Stuart Sexton helped to keep matters on an even keel.

Besides requiring a broker who would translate the broad strokes of the Assisted Places Scheme into an acceptable political form, the independent sector also needed individuals who could serve as channels of communication between themselves and the Conservative party. Obviously to some extent Sexton also performed this function but he was by no means entirely acceptable to the private sector probably because he was too much of a political animal, not an intimate acquaintance of any of their own leading figures, and inevitably lacked the highest political standing within the Conservative party. His power may have been considerable but not his status. This was a delicate matter for the independent sector because, although it was realized that the Conservative party would give them most political support, there was no desire for too close a relationship. They had to deal with governments of differing political persuasions but in spite of these reservations the links had to be established if the Assisted Places Scheme was to be placed on the policy agenda of the political party that would probably constitute the next government. Too much discretion would simply result in failure.

Two individuals performed this key role of institutional linkage: Sir George Sinclair and Lord Belstead, both former Chairmen of the Independent Schools Joint Council (ISJC). Given this experience, both have been ideally placed to measure the pulse of the independent sector. Sir George Sinclair (Conservative Member of Parliament for Dorking 1964–79) was very actively involved in Parliament on educational issues and played a leading part in the protracted attack upon the Labour government's 1976 Education Bill. Lord Belstead has been a member of both the Heath and Thatcher governments and as such has the highest political connections. Both have been in a position therefore to advise on parliamentary tactics and to muster support in Commons and Lords for the cause of independent schooling.

The culmination of the interaction between the independent sector and the Conservative party was the formal commitment of the latter to put the Assisted Places Scheme on the policy agenda of the next government. Control of the decision-making agenda has been seen by political sociologists as one of the critical forms of power. What our analysis reveals is that the policy agenda is rarely so cut-and-dried that it is possible to say conclusively what is included and what is excluded. In terms of our case study at what stage can it be said that the Conservative party had incorporated the Assisted Places Scheme as party policy? The party's October 1974 General Election manifesto offered tentative support for an Assisted Places Scheme but the first reaction to the actual demise of direct grant was to promise its resuscitation. The crystallization of party thinking occurred after the Labour government's decision to phase out direct grant and was a consequence of that development of ideas that had taken place in meetings with the representatives of the independent schools.

The first — and Stuart Sexton has claimed, the most crucial — public manifestation of the new thinking was to be found in the Conservative party's painstaking opposition to the 1976 Education Bill. The object was to delay the passage of the Bill for as long as feasible and in the process embarrass the government, and in particular the Secretary of State, Fred Mulley, as much as possible. On both accounts the tactics appear to have worked and in the end the government was forced to apply the guillotine. Hansard's report of the various debates makes fascinating reading for the Conservative party also used its opposition to the bill to float several ideas that were to reappear when the party was back in office — for example: a parents' charter, vouchers and the Assisted Places Scheme. Sexton's claim that this constituted the critical stage in making the Assisted Places Scheme party policy is based on the fact that the parliamentary party had formally proposed it as a new clause (number 39) to the Bill. It was therefore publicly on the record as a scheme of which the parliamentary party approved. New clause 39, proposed significantly by Sir George Sinclair and Mr George Gardiner, was not called for debate so at that time the Commons neither discussed nor voted upon the matter but nonetheless the Conservative party had made its future intentions clearer.

Although there are close parallels between proposed new clause 39 to the 1976 Education Bill and clauses 17 and 18 of the 1980 Education (No. 2) Bill, the Assisted Places Scheme was still not party policy and it was not formally announced as such until late September 1977 when

Conservative Central Office issued a statement attributed to Norman St. John-Stevas (Conservative Central Office, 1977). By that time the shadow cabinet had given its official blessing. Interestingly the statement is couched in terms of the need to restore the direct grant schools but it would be a mistake to see this as another example of confused policy goals for the substantive content concerns the replacement of the old direct grant regulations by an Assisted Places Scheme. Presumably the references to the resurrection of direct grant were included to increase its public appeal. The direct grant schools represented tangible images — for example, centres of academic excellence and channels of social mobility for working-class pupils — with which the electorate could identify. The final proof that the Assisted Places Scheme was firmly embraced by the Conservative party was reaffirmed by the unequivocal 1979 manifesto pledge: 'The direct grant schools, abolished by Labour, gave wider opportunities for bright children from modest backgrounds. The direct grant principle will therefore be restored with an Assisted Places Scheme. Less well-off parents will be able to claim part or all of the fees at certain schools from a special government fund' (pp. 25-6).

What the analysis so far suggests, and we have yet to consider the transformation of party policy into government policy, is that the formation of the Conservative party's political agenda is a protracted and tentative process. In the very early 1970s Mrs Thatcher, when Secretary of State, had been urged to adopt an Assisted Places Scheme and *before* any of the lengthy negotiations of the mid-1970s the Conservative party had already made a formal commitment in the General Election manifesto of October 1974. One is reminded of the elaborate mating rituals of exotic birds in which contact can only be made after highly stylized courtship patterns. Numerous meetings, accompanied by the appropriate fluttering of the wings, convey the impression that progress is being made but it is never wise to assume that consummation has taken place. Even after Norman St. John-Stevas' September 1977 statement the Assisted Places Scheme had to survive a change in shadow Secretaries of State (Stuart Sexton's constancy was vital) and the sniping of the renegade Rae. Although it triumphed to become a manifesto proposal, this tells us nothing about the intensity of the commitment. The independent schools realized that they needed the Conservative party but there was always the suspicion that it was not an entirely trustworthy ally. If the political climate changed they feared desertion.

The listing of the Assisted Places Scheme on the policy agenda of the Conservative party was engineered by a very small number of individuals working from two institutional bases, that is the party itself and the private sector (first the DGJC and then the ISJC). In both cases these individuals could claim to be representing sentiments that were widely shared in their respective institutions. For example, the parliamentary Conservative party had proposed an amendment to the 1976 Education Bill supporting the principle of an Assisted Places Scheme, and there were repeated calls at the annual conference for the restoration of direct grant schools. Right across the independent sector there was dismay at the phasing out of direct grant and lengthy consultations had led to the general conclusion that the Assisted Places Scheme was the most viable alternative. It would be a perversion of the evidence to claim however that the Assisted Places Scheme had been nurtured at the grassroots and then taken up by the leading cadres. In neither institution could it be described as a popularly acclaimed policy. Rather the principles and policy details were worked out at the centre and then more widely dispersed for approval. It is difficult to avoid the impression that that approval was inevitable for no one was offering viable alternatives. In fact other policy avenues were purposefully squeezed out. A Mr Maynard-Potts, of the National Educational Association, much to the embarrassment of the DGJC, had developed his own version of an Assisted Places Scheme. The leading lights of the DGJC met him with a view to dissuading him from taking any further action (DGJC, *Minutes*, 15 February 1979). Furthermore, as Rae found out to his cost, to respond to a sentiment is more popular than failing to offer a positive alternative.

It is enlightening to list those segments of the Conservative party that played little or no part in the actual formulation of the policy. Central Office, the Conservative Research Department, the National Advisory Committee on Education, the parliamentary party — including its Education Committee, and the annual conference were all virtually excluded from the policy making process. The agenda was controlled by the shadow minister and his entourage subject, of course, to shadow Cabinet approval, the final stage of ratification in which the role of the party leader is pivotal. So a set of organized interests with 'privileged' access to the Conservative party (Lord Belstead is an old Etonian, and Sir George Sinclair was Chairman of Abingdon School's Board of Governors between 1971–79 — of which incidentally Sir James Cobban, for so long Chairman of the DGJC, is a former Headmaster) interacted with those few individuals who controlled the party's policy agenda. Working within the framework of broad institutional commitments, they produced a policy proposal that suited their mutual interests. The next step of selling the policy internally, both upwards and downwards, proved comparatively easy. But the ultimate step, of turning party policy into government policy, is always fraught with danger.

Coping with the Bureaucratic Dynamic

In our previous book we argued that the process of educational change in England and Wales was increasingly controlled by a bureaucratic dynamic located primarily in the central state apparatus, the DES. How was the DES to cope with a policy initiative which was backed by powerful political forces? Moreover, the party political conflict that surrounds private schooling has made it more difficult for the DES to pursue its customary consensual role. The best it can hope to do is to mitigate differences by trimming the excesses of both the major parties, but if governments should elect to follow bolder courses then it is hard to restrain them. The Department's problems were compounded in this case by the suspicions of the political dynamic: the private sector believed that the DES was unsympathetic to its cause and powerful elements within the Conservative party saw it as part of a leftish establishment which was responsible for most of the British educational system's ills. In spite of this friction the Department's actual track record in terms of private schooling was creditable. For example, Mrs Thatcher's government, after being made aware of the financial implications, decided not to restore those HMI inspections that led to independent schools being 'recognized as efficient'. Earlier, thanks partly to the advice of officials, direct grant was phased out in a manner that caused the schools the minimum of inconvenience — as DGJC acknowledged.

As is customary, the DES greeted the incoming Conservative ministers in 1979 with proposals for the implementation of their manifesto commitments. What the Department may have been surprised to find is that the ministerial team already had its own well-developed brief. The Assisted Places Scheme had been a long time in the making and the private sector had worked out in some detail what it wanted. During the gestation period Stuart Sexton was able to rework policy proposals (usually drafted initially by Peter Mason) and could depend upon the DGJC to provide the necessary facts and figures for supporting papers. So the private sector served as a resource base for the formulation of policy. This was unusual because ministers invariably take office with little more policy guidelines than the bare proposals contained in the election manifesto. Subsequently the Labour party has followed this lead in policy planning in the shape of its discussion document 'Private Schools'. One wonders how the DES views the erosion of its traditional responsibilities?

In the case of the Assisted Places Scheme the detailed preparation owes much to the personal commitment of individuals within the DGJC as well as Stuart Sexton but it would be naive to put all the hard work down to a fetish for careful planning. They feared that the scheme could be lost either by DES emasculation or by the incoming government according it a low priority. The aim was to avoid both pitfalls. At a general planning meeting held on 15 November 1977, at which representatives of both the Conservative party and schools were present, Sir George Sinclair apparently argued that the basis of legislation should be laid down as soon as possible for, should there be a General Election, those Bills with greatest background preparation would be the ones to be placed earliest on the programme for consideration in the next session (DGJC, *Minutes*, 15 November 1977). By the time of the election Sexton had prepared a draft outline of the legislation which apparently clashed with the DES proposals (Bennett, 1982). Initially Sexton was poorly placed to push his point of view because the Prime Minister was prevaricating as to whether she should continue with the system of personal political advisers that had been introduced by the Labour government. However, by June 1979 he was working out of the DES and in a better position to do battle. The legislative proposal that eventually prevailed conceded Sexton's main objection to the original DES draft that had limited the scheme to ex-direct grant schools. The Department's stance can probably be explained by the Conservative party's description of the scheme as a means of restoring the direct grant schools, rather than as a manifestation of any duplicity on its part.

The independent sector was intimately involved in the details of policy formation. As the scope of the Assisted Places Scheme was not to be restricted to the old direct grant schools negotiations were placed under the auspices of the ISJC which in customary fashion delegated responsibility to its Advisory Committee (ISJC-AC). The independent sector's involvement in the drafting of the government's legislation was approved by the Cabinet's Home Affairs Sub-Committee and the broad principles of the scheme emerged out of the interaction of political adviser, departmental officials and independent sector representatives. The Education Bill was published on 26 October 1979 and after the completion of its Second Reading on 5 November schools were invited to participate in the scheme and negotiations on details, as opposed to principles, commenced in earnest. Again the same parties were involved although the independent schools decided to delegate their authority to an Assisted Places Steering Committee, whose Chairman for its six meetings was the former Chairman of the DGJC, James (now Sir James) Cobban. Throughout the whole process the various parties had formed the Assisted Places Scheme Group and as one would expect the key coordinating role was occupied by a departmental official, Assistant Secretary Clive Saville, who had the formal responsibility for producing the legislation.

While meetings behind closed doors were hammering out the legislative details so more public meetings were serving complementary goals. It was necessary to demonstrate that the schools were behind the scheme and to involve them in the rallying of public support: thus followed the special session at HMC's annual meeting in late September 1979 at which the scheme was overwhelmingly endorsed in spite of John Rae's opposition. Later in June 1981 eighty-two heads of schools that intended to participate in the scheme met at King Edward's School, Birmingham. By then the scheme was almost operational and clearly the purpose was to straighten out any remaining uncertainties, to bolster the morale of the participants, and to ensure a smooth launching. Few of these heads would have participated directly in the policy-making process but they probably found it helpful to have their queries answered by the Department (Mr Morgan, Clive Saville's successor was present) and comforting to have their doubts eased by the presence of so many colleagues who had also taken the assisted places pledge.

Although the preparation for the necessary legislation was proceeding very smoothly in a technical sense, the scheme was running into rough political waters. In a memo to the Secretary of State Sexton (1979) clearly suspected a perfidious DES: 'It is infuriating to read so many inaccurate "authoritative" accounts of the Assisted Places Scheme. It is obvious that someone has leaked Clive Saville's letter to the ISJC outlining the scheme because Bruce Kemble and others print passages from it which I clearly recognize. However, someone is putting a pessimistic gloss on it at the same time'. And in order to counter this he requested that: 'At the appropriate time I would ask that I be allowed to write a short, concise, *accurate* summary of the Scheme, to be made public as a press release, and I would rather I write it and you checked it. Rather than the Press Office or anyone else in the DES' (*ibid.*). Leaks may have indeed occurred but they can scarcely be blamed for the scheme's political difficulties. The Labour party was obviously going to be hostile and many Conservatives must have had their doubts about a scheme which intended to channel state resources into private schools at the very time the government was cutting expenditure in the maintained sector. Moreover as the scheme implied that the maintained sector was incapable of educating many of its brightest pupils one had to be politically myopic not to recognize its probable effect on teacher morale in local authority schools. Party support, therefore, started to fray at the edges with those two former bastions of Tory educational thinking — Lords Butler and Boyle — siding with the Opposition. The government could count upon its usual press friends but that body of educational publications which is generally regarded as 'informed' was either sceptical or hostile.

It is possible that some of the hostility was beginning to affect the Secretary of State, remember he was not personally responsible for the scheme becoming party policy. In any case Stuart Sexton obviously felt that Mr Carlisle's resolve needed to be stiffened, so he fired off another hard-hitting memo:

> In addition to the arguments I have already deployed as to why we must continue with the AP Scheme in September 1981, might I point out that if the government does cancel the scheme, or postpone it indefinitely, no matter how much we might protest that our reasons were purely financial, it will be presented as us succumbing to the concerted attack from the Labour party over the past few months. In other words, if we are seen to crumble under such political attack on this one issue, we will be considered easy meat for yet more attacks on other policy and manifesto commitments. This really is a U-Turn we must not make. (Sexton, 1980)

The tone suggests that the argument was addressed to a man experiencing severe self-doubts.

Every time a policy proposal approaches realization this behind-the-scenes vacillation may occur. It may be a normal part of the decision-making process but in the end political logic prevails. Alternatively, parts of a government's policy agenda may be much weaker than others and it is possible that the Assisted Places Scheme was an especially vulnerable initiative. A wide range of factors can make a policy more or less fragile: the strength of party support, the extent to which concerned interests have been incorporated, the attempts that

have been made to ensure a favourable public reception, the competence of the ministerial team, and the professionalism of the departmental officials. We have no wish to evaluate the Assisted Places Scheme in
these terms — the result would undoubtedly be equivocal — but would
want to make the point that there is no foregone conclusion about what
happens to a government's decision-making agenda.

For all the internal prevarication the Assisted Places Scheme was
bound to be enacted once the government had decided to make it one of
its priorities. There was sufficient backing for it within the Conservative party and the government had a comfortable majority in the House
of Commons. Carlisle may have been a weak Secretary of State but the
other members of the ministerial team, Lady Young and Rhodes
Boyson, were powerful personalities and strong advocates of the
Assisted Places Scheme. The Prime Minister asked to be kept informed
of the scheme's progress. As a former Education Minister she naturally
had an interest in the matter, the more so as the scheme was consistent
with the values she had preached. *The Times* education correspondent
went so far as to describe the Prime Minister as '. . . the strongest
supporter of the new Assisted Places Scheme' (Geddes, 1979, p. 14).
Finally the organization of the government's parliamentary schedule
was in the hands of Norman St. John-Stevas who as Leader of the
House was ideally placed to ensure that an appropriate bill could be
accommodated. So it was the quality of party support as much as
anything else which guaranteed that the proposed legislation would
survive the political brickbats to become law.

But as governments can create, so they can destroy, for it was the
pressure of government policy which threatened to extinguish the
scheme before it had been put into effect. The DES, along with other
major spending departments, was required to cut its expenditure. The
Assisted Places Scheme was an ideal target: no places had been
awarded, to cut it would be a sop to those Conservatives who disliked
subsidizing the private sector, no major interest group would object,
and there were qualms within the private sector that some schools
could become unduly reliant on assisted place pupils. In fact the
controversy over the financing of the scheme had been highly embarrassing to the government. It had been claimed that because on average
it cost no more to educate a pupil in the independent than the
maintained sector the scheme would be self-financing. It requires more
than the removal of a few pupils from widely scattered schools to
reduce a local education authority's costs. Fears were expressed that to
become bogged down in an argument about cost comparisons would

result in the political argument being lost (Macfarlane, 1980). It was widely discussed in the press that the scheme was to cost £55m each year before it was made clear that this would be the cost of the scheme only when it was fully operational. In its initial year the scheme was costed at £6m and was to support approximately 12,000 places. Subsequently the Department complied with the Treasury's request for expenditure cuts by halving this initial resource allocation to £3m.

The alternative to trimming the scheme was to postpone its launching. This possibility was considered within the Department but there was always the danger that the economic climate would never be judged conducive to a full launch. Furthermore, it was felt that the scheme needed to prove itself before the next General Election, in the belief that the more firmly it was part of the educational picture the more difficult it would be to eradicate it. But it had been a close run thing and it does demonstrate the precariousness of small projects when placed on the alter of government priorities. Although spending departments may have been quite adroit at avoiding the Treasury axe, some concessions have been unavoidable. The fact that the scheme survived at all is testament to the quality of its political support.

Evaluating Policy and the Policy Making Process

The Assisted Places Scheme originated from the widely shared belief that private and maintained schooling should be part of one educational system. Independent schooling may gain certain tangible benefits from a close association with the maintained sector, as indeed the pay-offs may flow in the other direction, but its ultimate purpose is to further the proposition that the differing forms of schooling perform complementary roles within the framework of one educational system. The Conservative party was prepared to make the Assisted Places Scheme party policy because it was consistent with a traditional party view that the two sectors should be associated, that certain comprehensive schools could not provide the appropriate environments for their brightest pupils, and that parental choice should be extended. The form of association created by the Assisted Places Scheme was conducive to the interests of independent schools, i.e. as enabling them to select limited numbers of pupils in return for marginal institutional controls. Although certain elements of the Tory party (anti-Thatcher backbenchers and the eminence grise of its former educational establishment) may have found this disconcerting, there would be few viable alternatives if the bridge was to be reconstructed in this form. It is comparatively easy to snipe from the Lords and the backbenches.

Thus the policy-making process was set in motion which in turn intensified the prevailing ideological conflict (although the themes of parental choice, academic standards, selection, equality of opportunity etc., were all very well worn) and concentrated attention upon the policy agenda of the Conservative party. In time the party formally committed a future Conservative government to implement an Assisted Places Scheme. The purpose of our analysis has been to illustrate the precariousness of the concept of policy agenda, and formal commitments tell us nothing about their intensity. On the very verge of its implementation the Assisted Places Scheme was almost the victim of more important government priorities. In spite of all the vacillation, however, the first pupils were in receipt of their scholarships by September 1981. The scheme had been conceived within the private sector, translated into an acceptable political form by Stuart Sexton, nurtured by its elevated protagonists, and finally placed on the statute book thanks to the quality of its political support.

Although the good intentions of the DES were questioned by some both within the independent sector and the Conservative party, everything about the Department's involvement in the Assisted Places Scheme suggests that it acted with the utmost propriety. The statement of general principles found in clauses 17 and 18 of the 1980 Education (No. 2) Bill may have presented few drafting problems but the Department was deeply immersed in painstaking negotiations involving the minutiae of the scheme. As if in recognition of its gratitude Clive Saville was invited to attend the dinner that marked the formal winding up of the DGJC. In the circumstances the Department's behaviour was entirely predictable. The pitfalls of the Assisted Places Scheme were self-evident, although the ferocity of the reaction may have surprised ministers, but the government was in the last analysis prepared to incur the political costs. What the Department had to do was to make a technically competent job of the necessary legislation. No doubt it will make an equally competent job should legislation be needed to rescind the Assisted Places Scheme.

The above analysis does not contradict our claim that the process of educational change is increasingly controlled by centralized state apparatuses. The bureaucratic and political dynamics were not in conflict over the Assisted Places Scheme. It was important to segments of the government and whereas most officials in the DES may have doubted its wisdom it was too insignificant to provoke a major battle. To the political left the sum of money involved may have great symbolic significance but in terms of the overall size of the educational budget it is paltry. If the scheme was a manifestation of a new ideological consensus within the Tory party then it would have a greater claim to fame but in fact its roots pre-date Mrs Thatcher's present dominance. Tories of most hues opposed the abolition of direct grant, accept the limitations of comprehensive secondary education, and seek some form of association between maintained and private schooling — invariably one in which the latter is used to compensate for the alleged shortcomings of the former.

For the Assisted Places Scheme to have a pronounced influence upon the character of the British educational system then either its indirect vibrations must be strong or it has to be a harbinger of things to come. As it stands it is a small innovation that is unlikely to survive a government of a different colour. The indirect effect depends upon the reaction of parents, especially those who at present use the maintained schools but could afford private schooling. Will the Assisted Places Scheme, with its clear message that certain comprehensive schools cannot cater for bright children, tip the scales in favour of independent schooling? Presumably many parents who are in a position to choose are experienced at making such calculations and will judge in terms of their own circumstances rather than general images.

As only a few years have passed since the passage of the 1980 Education (No. 2) Bill it would be foolhardy to predict with any degree of confidence the precise course of educational change in Britain. If, however, the Assisted Places Scheme represents an attempt to force change by increasing consumer choice then it is a high watermark rather than a harbinger of things to come. Costs and administrative problems, no doubt strongly emphasized by departmental officials, have constrained innovations with vouchers, open enrolment, and student loans. In the critical fields of curriculum reform, more flexible certification, the restructuring of higher education, or the very broad area of relating schooling more closely to the needs of industry the government is heavily dependent upon the traditional technique of institutional bargaining. Although it may rely increasingly upon the Manpower Services Commission with its new techniques of control rather than the DES. If one bureaucratic structure is incapable of performing the job then others will be created that can. The trick is to make sure that the state apparatus, in harmony with the government's will, can dominate the bargaining process. There is some irony about the fact that one of the key figures in furthering this process is Sir Keith Joseph who is considered by many to be the chief Thatcherite guru.

9   Conclusions and Prospects

Introduction

In 1964 the political position of the private schools was dangerously exposed. Their pupil numbers were falling, their internal organization was weak and fragmented, the prevailing climate of opinion was swinging against elitist education and the Labour party was about to begin its programme of comprehensive education which was bound at some point to lead to an attack on independent education. As agents for the reproduction of the ruling class, private schools were looking less than convincing. Even their natural ally, the Conservative party, seemed a little a short of ideological backbone when it came to an unequivocal defence of the educational status quo. Two decades later, their fortunes have undergone a renaissance: their pupil numbers constitute an increasing proportion of the total school population, their organization is unified and efficient, in 1983–84 the government sponsored Assisted Places Scheme subsidized 13,000 of their pupils and public opinion is encouraged to see them as leaders in the educational marketplace. Even their natural enemy, the Labour party, is quiescent. Having developed a policy for the abolition of the independent schools the Labour party has yet to solve the more difficult problem of how best to sell such a policy to an unsympathetic electorate.

The transition of the private schools over a period of twenty years from a position of weakness to one of strength was achieved through the exercise of all three types of educational power: ideological; agenda-setting; and decision-making. Using these three types of power, the independent sector organized itself to influence educational policy-making on both specific and general issues. Specifically, it obtained categorical assurances of protection from the Conservative party plus financial support in the form of the AP Scheme. More generally, and in the long run more importantly, it helped to generate a new ideological consensus in education which views independent schools as valuable and worthwhile as opposed to ideologically suspect as was the case in the 1960s. A consensus which emphasizes the importance and interrelationship of quality, standards and parental choice in education affords a natural protective cloak to the private schools. It gives them the status of models which show how consumer preference in the education market can produce beneficial educational results. By supporting this ideological initiative, private schools have thus helped to define what are, and what are not, acceptable items for the political agenda. As key agents in the process of class reproduction, private schools perform a function which, according to our definition (see pp. 16–23), make them an important part of the network of institutions which constitute the educational state. What we have witnessed over the past decade, therefore, is the regeneration of what was previously a declining section of the educational state with inevitable repercussions for other parts of the state. For it has to be remembered that the separate institutions of the educational state are functionally interdependent through their linked contributions to the reproduction of the technical and social relations of production. When Oxbridge, for example, modified its traditional entrance requirements better to accommodate GCE 'A' levels, independent schools were obliged to follow suit and gear their teaching much more explicitly to this form of accreditation — with highly successful results. And if, in the future, Oxbridge decides that BTEC qualifications should be included in the entry system, private schools will have to take the lead there as well if they are to retain their dominant position in the high status areas of higher education. It is because the various institutions of the educational state are by definition functionally interdependent that the detailed examination of one field of educational change should be placed in the broader context of the educational state as a whole. In this final chapter we therefore begin by assessing the significance of recent developments in the larger arena of educational change building on our concern with the bureaucratization of educational power in *Education, Politics and the State* and our refinement of that concern in Chapter 2 of this book. Secondly, we examine the likely party political input to this arena in the light of changes in their policy-making machinery, their ideological commitments and their use of intellectuals. Thirdly, we conclude by considering what this all means for the independent sector.

Continuities and Conflicts

In *Education, Politics and the State* we traced the way in which the bureaucratic dynamic of the DES had produced a drive by the Department to gain exclusive control of educational policy-making and to develop the means for the more efficient management of the education system. This impetus could be detected in its actions on finance, the curriculum, examinations and teacher training and in its sponsorship of an ideology of education which, through its advocacy of educa-responsiveness to the economy which, through its advocacy of education's responsiveness to the economy and the world of work, provides a convenient justification for the DES's managerial inspirations. According to this view, the party political input to educational policy making is not, in the long term, likely to be very significant. As the 1979 DES *Annual Report* put it: 'There is underlying the whole education programme a continuity of purpose which reflects the abiding and deep-seated problems affecting our education system' (p. ix). Likewise Stuart Maclure, in his review in 1983 of Sir James Hamilton's seven years as Permanent Under-Secretary of State, observed: 'Every new minister means a new set of pet projects to look at — loans, vouchers, assisted places . . . The long-term policy of DES goes underground, to re-emerge when ministers have been taken patiently through the old arguments' (p. 2).

While we do not deny that the Department's bureaucratic dynamic is still a powerful force shaping the direction of educational change, nonetheless this view has to be revized on two counts: first, the MSC has shown itself to be a highly adroit competitor capable of taking over DES's ideas and administrative territory; second, the impact on the policy agenda of the New Right's educational campaign should not be underestimated. An aggregate of 'pet projects' could in fact represent a substantial policy shift, particularly when they are sponsored by Sir Keith Joseph, the man who initiated the review of Conservative party philosophy a decade ago. As a result of the MSC's skilful exploitation of the economic ideology of education to expand its empire and the Right's influence on the climate of educational opinion the balance of educational power has shifted. But precisely how much it has shifted is open to dispute and we will return to the issue later in the chapter. The immediate task is to identify the continuities in the operation of the DES.

If the Department is to determine the major directions of educational change it has, directly or indirectly, to control the curriculum in schools. In our last book we showed the development of the Department's thinking on how this could be achieved and maintained that:

> There can be no question of the continuity of theme and ambition from the Yellow Book of 1976 through the DES documents for the Great Debate conferences, the Green Paper *Education in Schools* (1977), the Circular 14/77 recommended by the Green Paper and the report *Local Authority Arrangements for the Curriculum* (1979) in response to the Circular to, most recently, the consultative proposals *A Framework for the School Curriculum* (1980) and the White Paper *The School Curriculum* (1981). (pp. 231–2)

At the time by no means everyone agreed that this continuity existed or, if it did, that it amounted to much. In its leader comment on *The School Curriculum, The Times Educational Supplement* (1981) described the document as 'trite', 'a harmless tract' and as representing the 'liquidation of commitments to a core curriculum and a defined framework' (p. 3). How wrong can you be? Commenting on the same document two years later, Sir James Hamilton, who as Permanent Secretary was closely concerned with the document, felt that the government had shown too much 'delicacy' about making its presence felt in the classroom and had 'erred on the side of safety' (Wood, 1983a, p. 3).

While there can be no doubt that the DES is committed to greater central control of the school curriculum, the question is how does it get it when it has to rely on the LEAs to implement its ideas? *The School Curriculum* requested LEAs to review their policies for the school curriculum, to plan future developments accordingly and to report back in 1983. Yet in 1983 the DES is obliged to issue Circular 8/83 requesting a progress report from LEAs: obviously there is some slippage here. How can the DES exercise effective control in a decentralized education system when, unlike the MSC, it does not have a direct financial sanction it can bring to bear?

In 1981, when writing *Education, Politics and the State,* it seemed possible that the new system of local authority financing based on the calculation of Grant Related Expenditures (GREs) for each local authority could develop into a control mechanism to be used by the DES over the LEAs (p. 230). Given that the educational GRE 'for a particular authority is a formula-based assessment of how much it would cost that authority to provide a typical standard of service' (DES, 1980, p. 65) and given that anything more than a 10 per cent overspend incurs a penalty, it seemed a reasonable possibility that LEAs could be obliged to toe the DES line. So far this has not happened. For one thing it is the Department of the Environment, not the DES, which controls the allocation of the GREs. Professor Stewart (1984) has argued that 'The Department of the Environment has become as significant a central government department for the education service as the Department of Education and Science, for it is the announcements of the Secretary of State for the Environment on local government finance that increasingly influence the capacity of education authorities to pursue their own policies' (p. 2). At the same time, the Department of the Environment is limiting the use of the rates to raise extra money for education through the introduction of rate-capping. So although local authority choice on the amount it can spend on education is being restricted both through the GRE system and by rate-capping this does not mean that the DES has more control over how the local education budget is spent. But nor, necessarily, does the Department of the Environment. Although local authorities may have a smaller education budget than they would wish, they can still decide how they will spend it.

Of itself, financial control cannot lead to curriculum control unless the allocation of finance is linked to specific educational targets. For the foreseeable future, the functional division between the DES and the Department of the Environment will severely limit the exercise of influence, backed by financial sanctions, over the primary and secondary school curriculum. (Following the 1983 Education Grants and Awards Act, the Secretary of State for Education and Science now has a fund of about £50m which he can allocate directly to particular schemes and innovations, but this is too small an amount — 0.5 per cent of the total education budget — to have a general impact.) But in other areas of LEA provision, local autonomy is less secure. In 1984 the White Paper *Training for Jobs* announced the transfer of £65m in 1985/86 and £110m in 1986/87 from the LEA rate support grant to the MSC. The purpose of the transfer was to give the MSC an extended capacity to purchase work-related, non-advanced further education (NAFE). There can be no doubt that the MSC will use this financial control to push the curriculum in particular directions. Shortly after the transfer was announced *The Times Educational Supplement* (TES) reported that local authorities faced 'a demand from the Manpower Services Commission for a share of control over the whole of non-advanced work-related further education — not just the quarter which the government plans to fund through the Commission' (Jackson, 20 July,

(1984) p. 1). The MSC shares none of the 'delicacy' of the DES in these matters. (We will discuss the issue of the MSC–DES conflict later in the chapter.)

If the DES had to rely on financial controls to realize its centralizing ambitions in primary and secondary education its prospects would be dim indeed. Fortunately, or otherwise, it does not. In 1984, tired of hiding its actual and potential influence under a bushel for so long, the DES came clean in the Green Paper *Parental Influence at School: A New Framework for School Government in England and Wales.* In a key passage it stated:

> The Secretary of State influences the nature and pattern of what pupils in these schools are taught through the exercise of many of his functions, including the power to approve proposals for the pattern and character of maintained schools; the power to make regulations in respect of schools and teachers; the duty to secure an adequate supply of teachers and adequate arrangements for their training; the duty to cause inspections to be made of schools; limited powers to make grants for specific purposes; and the power to cause LEAs and governing bodies to remedy a default in respect of a statutory duty and to prevent them from exercising a function unreasonably. By virtue of his office he also influences policy on school examinations and the school examinations system and practice. In exercising these functions, which reflect his duty to promote the education of the people, the Secretary of State cannot but have a view of the school curriculum from a national standpoint, and policies for the curriculum based on that view; and he answers to Parliament for both. (p. 12)

— thus recognizing the importance of indirect as well as direct controls over the curriculum. It is significant that over the past five years most of the functions outlined in this quotation have been expanded in a consistent effort to create a web of Department controls and thereby an embryonic system of indirect management. In part the progress made is, as we discuss below, the product of the convenient overlap between bureaucratic and political party ambition but in part also it is the result of a route planning exercise undertaken by the DES when it produced the notorious Yellow Book in 1976.

One of the important milestones mentioned by the Yellow Book was the removal of the Schools Council for Curriculum and Examinations. Set up in 1963 to oversee the development of innovations in the curriculum and examinations following an abortive attempt by the Ministry of Education to establish its own Curriculum Study Group, the Schools Council was dominated by the teacher unions and a constant obstacle to DES attempts to extend its influence over the curriculum (see Salter and Tapper, 1981, Chapter 6). It therefore had to go. In *Education, Politics and the State* we predicted that 'the Department will shortly absorb the Council in order to be able to control the future direction of the curriculum' (Tapper and Salter, 1978, p. 231). This it duly did. In April 1982 the Department announced that the Schools Council would be replaced by two bodies: the Secondary Examinations Council (SEC) and the School Curriculum Development Committee (SCDC). The organization and composition of the two bodies stands in sharp contrast to that of the old Schools Council. The SEC is financed by the Department and its members are personally appointed by the Secretary of State. The SCDC is funded jointly by the DES and the LEAs and the responsibility for the appointment of its members divided between the two. It is a clear sign of the rapidly waning power of the teacher unions that none of those which submitted nominations were appointed to the SCDC when its composition was announced in November 1983 (Wood, 1983c, p. 8). (The NUT refused to put forward nominees for the SCDC as part of its opposition to the new Committee, justifying its boycott by attacking the government's increasing desire to centralize control of the school curriculum and to limit the role of the classroom teacher (Wood, 1983b, p. 6).)

The well-worn, and valid, maxim that 'he who controls examinations controls the curriculum' means that the SEC is potentially by far the most powerful of the two bodies. The way that knowledge is organized and taught in secondary schools is in large part governed by external systems of accreditation. Traditionally, the power of accreditation has rested with the examination boards: self-financing bodies which value their independence and which are a natural barrier to DES aspirations in the accreditation field. It is now the responsibility of the SEC 'to coordinate and seek to improve the school examination system and other forms of school-based assessment in England and Wales, and it is the source of advice to the government on these areas of policy' (DES, 1983a, p. 9). If the SEC is to coordinate the examination system effectively then it is inevitable that the exam boards will have to relinquish some of their independence and some of their powers. How willing, and how likely, are they to do this?

In our last book, when the Schools Council was still with us and the SEC and the SCDC just twinkles in the Department's eye, we speculated that 'the DES may use the reorganization of the CSE and GCE boards required for the new 16+ examination to make some inroads on exam board autonomy' (p. 231). In fact it has done rather more than that and used the 16+ examination issue as a vehicle for rapidly concretizing the powers of the SEC and establishing firm precedents for the SEC's future relationship with the exam boards. In this context, it is interesting to note the long history of the merger of CSE and GCE 'O' levels, beginning with the Schools Council's feasibility studies between 1971 and 1976, the Waddell Committee's recommendation in 1978 of a single system, the ensuing protracted discussions about who should run it, the request by Mark Carlisle in 1980 that exam boards should draw up national criteria, the DES discussion document (1982) *Examinations at 16+* and, last but not least, the allocation to the SEC by Sir Keith Joseph in 1982 of its first task: 'to advise the Secretary of State on draft national criteria for syllabuses and assessment procedures on which a single system of examinations at 16+ might be based' (DES, 1982a, p. 11). The convenience of the 16+ issue to the development of a national examination body financed and appointed by the DES cannot be underestimated. Equally, the long history of the issue reflects the Department's lack of interest in it while there was no mechanism which the DES could use to control the outcome. With the arrival of the SEC came the political incentive for the Department to get things moving.

The result is a new examination to be introduced in 1986, the GCSE, run by five examining groups of existing CSE and GCE boards approved by the Secretary of State. Syllabus approval and the mainte-nance of standards across the groups will be in the hands of the SEC. There can be no doubt that this is a significant advance for the Department in its battle for greater control of the curriculum. As for the exam boards, having already committed themselves to a joint examination prior to the setting up of the SEC, they were then obliged to accept the overarching authority of the new body as the only means of making further progress.

Running parallel to the DES's success with the SEC has been a noticeable shift in the operative style of Her Majesty's Inspectorate (HMI). While the SEC provides the Department with the opportunity to influence the parameters of the curriculum via the secondary examination system, the changing role of the Inspectorate provides the opportunity for the DES to define and monitor what happens within those parameters. When HMI was reviewed in 1982 as part of Lord Rayner's series of efficiency studies its role was defined thus:

(a) to assess standards and trends throughout the education system and to advise central government on the state of the system nationally on the basis of its independent professional judgment. This is its first and overriding duty; and at the same time (b) to contribute to the maintenance and improvement of standards in the system by the identification and dissemination of good practice; by bringing to notice weaknesses which require attention; and by advice to those with a direct responsibility for the operation of the service. (DES, 1982b, p. 91)

This statement publicly makes clear HMI's role as a servant of DES policy-making needs. Eric Bolton, who succeeded Sheila Browne as Senior Chief Inspector in 1983, has also noted HMI's changing role: 'We are quite clearly under increasing pressure to use more of our time in relation to policy and policy interests and developing policy than we have ever had to do in the Inspectorate's history'. This, he remarks, inevitably produces some 'fractious' and 'troublesome' effects as a shift occurs from 'years ago when nobody bothered what HMI said' to a situation where 'suddenly everybody wants to know what HMI thinks' (Gold, 1984, p. 11).

In fact, the shift was not as sudden as all that. In *Education, Politics and the State* we argued that an ambitious bureaucracy such as the DES requires both a suitable supply of information on which to base its policy-making and the ability to sponsor particular educational values with which to shape the policy-making agenda. HMI was the natural vehicle to fulfil both these requirements. Effectively this meant that HMI would become, to use a Gramscian concept, the organic intellectuals of the DES (pp. 212–15). When we wrote the last book the move of the Inspectorate towards the new role had already begun. Since then the process has accelerated. Each step by the DES to create new lines of educational management has implications for the Inspectorate in terms of either the information it collects, the values it propagates, or both. In the last few years, much greater emphasis has been placed on the monitoring function of HMI. This has been aided by the decision of the Secretary of State that from January 1983 all HMI reports should be published, including reports of visits to schools made before that date: thus in 1983 alone over 220 reports were published by HMI on individual schools and groups of schools as well as the state of play in particular subjects. The effect of this large and publicly visible flow of information was two-fold. Firstly, it extended HMI's influence at the level of the individual institution and local authority concerned particu-

larly following the ruling that they should report what changes had
been made within three months of publication (Gold, 1984, p. 11).
Secondly, it meant that HMI is under pressure to build up a central
bank of criteria in order that its judgments could be seen to be consistent. The significance of this pressure should not be underestimated:
it derives from the changing relationship between the Inspectorate and
the Department.

As HMI becomes more and more an agent of the DES's managerial ambition so its modus operandi will be influenced by the Department's bureaucratic dynamic. This is likely to be revealed in an
increasing tendency by HMI to develop criteria about educational
standards which can be used to assist DES in extending its control over
the curriculum. Unless the Department is in a position to pronounce
authoritatively and in specific terms on what *should* be happening in
schools and other educational institutions it will never be able to
activate anything other than indirect lines of control. And as the
organic intellectuals of the Department, it is the HMIs' job to help it
achieve such extension of its control even if this means jettisoning the
Inspectorate's traditional independence and traditional commitment to
a broad and humanistic conception of education and moving towards a
prescriptive, rather than an advisory, style of operation.

English from 5 to 16, the first in a new HMI series called Curriculum
Matters, exemplifies the Inspectorate's new style. In an inserted
preface, the document describes itself as the first in a series dealing with
curriculum aims and objectives which 'can serve as a basis for policy at
national and local level' and which forms part of the Government's
policies for raising standards in schools outlined at the North of
England Conference, January 1984 (see p. 229). It is remarkable for the
specificity of the listening, speaking, reading and writing targets listed
for different age groups and for the prescriptive manner in which they
are couched. What is not remarkable, given the emerging role of the
Inspectorate, is the way in which *English from 5 to 16,* and its successors
in other subjects, will provide explicit and public criteria for monitoring what happens in primary and secondary schools. The Curriculum
Matters series is obviously intended to dovetail with whatever initiatives the DES takes following the local authority responses to Circular
8/83. It would, however, be a mistake to suppose that the transition
through which HMI is now passing is an easy one. For example,
Curriculum 11 to 16, Towards a Statement of Entitlement, published only a
year before *English from 5 to 16,* presents the completely different idea of
measuring the balance of curricular provision against a check list of

eight areas of experience 'as necessary elements which, together, would offer pupils a preparation for their personal as well as for their working and leisure life' (p. v). Though subject areas form part of the approach adopted in this report it is very much in a subordinate role to the pupil-centred 'areas of experience'. Such a broadly-based approach with its attendant difficulties and uncertainties of measurement of curricular balance is unlikely to find favour with the new model Inspectorate because it is an approach which does not readily fit DES monitoring needs.

The changing role of HMI is also apparent in the support it has given to DES intervention in higher education. In the public sector of higher education, as we predicted in *Education, Politics and the State* (p. 228) the Department has succeeded in its long struggle to prise control away from the local authorities with the setting up in February 1982 of the National Advisory Body (NAB) for Local Authority Higher Education. The purpose of the NAB is:

> to advise the Secretary of State on the academic provision to be made in institutions in selected fields and, in respect of those fields, on the appropriate use of his powers with regard to the apportionment of the advanced further education pool and to the approval of advanced courses. (DES, 1981, p. 24)

It was of critical importance that in the advanced FE area the NAB gained control of both the financial and the curriculum lines of management since, as we noted earlier in the case of the DES-Department of Environment relationship, separation of the two prevents effective management by the centre of education at the local level. Once established, the NAB did not lose, or was not allowed to lose, any time in undertaking a wide-ranging review of maintained higher education and in December 1983 produced a plan for the restructuring of colleges and polytechnics in 1984/85 which was readily accepted by Sir Keith Joseph. HMI's contribution to this major planning exercise was the provision of detailed costings and staff: student ratios for every subject in the public sector, a study of 100 degree courses in public sector higher education and one-off studies of particular subject areas or institutions. By swiftly supplying the information appropriate to the emerging functions of the NAB, the Inspectorate carefully nurtured the progress of the new body through its initial difficult phase. In addition, it no doubt helped to ensure that the NAB developed along lines consistent with DES interest.

Four years before the NAB was created its existence and rationale were foreshadowed in the Oakes Report (1978) on the management of higher education in the maintained sector. The fact that it took four years of institutional conflict to progress from the model to the reality is an indication of the pace at which the DES is obliged to move. One of the reasons why it is so easy to identify the continuities in the operation of the Department's bureaucratic dynamic is that watching its management of educational change is like watching a film in slow motion, with replays. Its weak lines of control mean that all change has to be seen to be negotiated (even if the results of the negotiations are pre-ordained). Nowhere is this more apparent than in the Department's relationship with the university sector of higher education. Here the pace is funereal. In *Education and the Political Order* we traced the rise of the economic ideology of higher education from the 1950s onwards, its conflict with the traditional university ideal and its implications for the role of the University Grants Committee (UGC) (Chapter 7). With its emphasis on socially 'relevant' knowledge (particularly science and technology), student responsiveness to employment opportunities, and institutional responsiveness to economic (particularly industrial) needs, the economic ideology of education provided the DES with the justification for arguing that universities should be subject to central planning as a means of increasing their organizational efficiency. Greater cost-effectiveness in the management of the university sector, it was argued, would enhance education's contribution to economic growth.

Yet although by the late 1970s the ideological battle had been largely won by the DES, the problem remained of how the ideological advantage could be translated into political gain. The equivocations of the UGC, caught between the pressure for more intervention from the DES and the power of the myth of university autonomy, delayed things marvellously. The UGC could recognize, as it did for example in a quinquennial report in 1968, that 'The sheer number of universities, their decreasing homogeneity and the correspondingly increasing variety of their offerings, together with national considerations... demand some central appraisal if uneconomic duplication is to be avoided and a reasonable degree of differentiation of function is to be achieved' (p. 179). Yet if one examines its annual reports for a management strategy which could ensure that duplication does not occur and differentiation of function does, it will not be found. The evolution of the UGC into what Lord Wolfenden, Chairman of the UGC from 1963 to 1968, has rather prematurely called a 'strategic planning agency' (Wolfenden, 1976, p. 5) appeared likely to take a very long time. Meanwhile, the bureaucratic pressure within DES for a rationalization of the organization of the whole of higher education was mounting: in 1980 Higher and Further Education Branch 1 (HFE 1), which was responsible for non-university higher and further education, was merged with HFE 3, which handles university policy, to form a new 'super-branch', FHE 1. The clear intention of the DES was to develop the means for managing higher education as a single entity and removing the binary divide.

But getting the university sector to accept *any* detailed manage-ment, let alone transbinary management, had up to this point been a tortuous task. Then in 1980 a catalyst for change was introduced in the form of the education cuts. Between 1980/81 and 1982/83 the university sector's income from the state was reduced by not less than 13 per cent (UGC, 1983, p. 39). Suddenly the UGC was in the business of the allocation of scarce resources whilst lacking the administrative machin-ery to carry out the task. Suddenly it faced elementary management issues: what should be its allocation criteria? How should these criteria be developed? Given certain criteria, what information was necessary to enable decisions to be made using these criteria? The history of the UGC since 1980 is the history of an organization struggling to deal with these kinds of management issues and, equally important, strug-gling to legitimize its inevitable intervention in university affairs.

Having forced the UGC to take on a more active management stance, the DES has subsequently adopted the strategy of prodding the Committee every so often to keep it moving. Furthermore, it has prodded the Committee in particular directions. While the UGC was still off balance, Sir Keith Joseph wrote to it in July 1982 requesting the development of a strategy for higher education in the 1990s. The following year a further letter from the Secretary of State spelt out what was wanted in the familiar terminology of the economic ideology of education: more efficient use of resources, a shift towards technolo-gical, scientific and engineering courses and to other vocationally rele-vant forms of study (UGC, 1984a, p. 41). The letter also echoed a recurring theme in UGC reports since 1982: the importance of coopera-tion across the binary divide. Sir Keith continued, 'I am sure that it is essential that the Committee and the NAB cooperate in the parallel exercises on which they are embarked' (*Ibid.*, p. 42) — which they duly did. As *A Strategy for Higher Education into the 1990s* (1984), the report of the UGC's exercise, was still being produced the Jarratt and Sizer enquiries were being launched into different aspects of the efficiency of university management (Crequer, 1984). These will no doubt feed into the UGC's own review of the distribution of resources to universities begun in November 1984 with its concern to develop 'a range of inter-university comparative costs and performance indicators' (UGC, 1984a). And so the momentum for change is maintained. Nowhere is this more obvious than in the research field where a procession of reports from the UGC, the Advisory Board for the Research Councils (ABRC) and the Advisory Committee for Applied Research and Development (ACARD) have examined the funding and organization of university research and ways in which research resources can be more selectively allocated (see ABRC, 1983a and 1983b; ABRC/ ACARD, 1983; ABRC/ACARD/DES, 1982). Having carefully fostered a number of new political options in the management of the university sector the Department is now in the position to take advantage of the ensuing uncertainty and offer a definite view of higher education's future in the forthcoming (1985) Green Paper.

The continuities in the intention and effect of the Department's bureaucratic dynamic are important because they establish many of the parameters of educational change. They provide much of the context within which another part of the educational state, the private schools, must operate. But on their own they do not provide a complete understanding. The rise of a competing state bureaucracy, the Manpower Services Commission, has created new possibilities and new parameters. In making predictions, it is no longer sufficient to extrapolate from existing trends in DES activities and relate the MSC to those activities. Our analysis of the MSC's bureaucratic dynamic in Chapter 2 showed that its organization is sufficiently adaptable to allow it to contemplate much more radical forms of educational change than the DES can take on board. Furthermore, also unlike the DES, the MSC has the power to implement changes much more directly and swiftly. An example has been the use made by the MSC of its newly acquired control of a *quarter* of the (work-related) NAFE programme funds. The Commission immediately used it as a lever to try and obtain more control by making the allocation of funds conditional on local authorities submitting their plans for the *whole* of work-related NAFE, not just a quarter. This style of operation contrasts vividly with that of the DES which is unaccustomed to using direct purchasing power as a political weapon.

The rapid expansion of the MSC is a product of its ability to respond much more readily to economic pressures for educational change. High unemployment, particularly youth unemployment, and a rapidly changing industrial base are continually creating a demand for new forms of knowledge and knowledge accreditation. The institution which organizes and controls the supply of knowledge to meet this new demand will command a key position in the reproduction of class relations and thus considerable educational power. So far the Commission is ahead, but the real battle for control of what is effectively a new knowledge market is only just beginning.

If an institution is to maximize its political gain from the emergence of a new knowledge area, it is essential that it gains control of the accreditation process. For it is the qualification obtained at the end of a period of study which largely determines the organization of the knowledge within it. As an ambitious institution, the MSC has no desire to foot the bill for educational experience without controlling the nature of the experience. But to begin with, the Commission was obliged to accept the power of the existing accrediting bodies, in particular the City and Guilds of London Institute (CGLI), the Royal Society of Arts (RSA), the Business Education Council (BEC) and the Technician Education Council (TEC). (The latter two subsequently merged to form BTEC). They provided the qualifications for courses funded by the MSC and many of the courses sponsored through the Training Opportunities Scheme (TOPS) still use this arrangement. But increasingly, the MSC has sought to extend its influence in the field of accreditation. In its self-appointed drive to modernize occupational training it has cast itself in the role of 'accreditation broker' whereby it helps to improve links between existing qualifications and organizes systems of credit transfer. Using its influence over the industrial training boards it has encouraged the assessment of standards of competence as a means of introducing uniformity across a range of training qualifications.

Nonetheless, although there is scope in the vocational training field for the MSC to move towards its vision of becoming the 'national training authority', in the short-term the growth area, and hence the conflict area, will be pre-vocational education. In 1983/84 354,000 school-leavers entered the MSC's year-long Youth Training Scheme (YTS) launched in April 1983. This constituted 60 per cent of that year's school-leavers and so took the Commission some considerable way towards its target announced in its *New Training Initiative* (1981) that all young people under 18 should have the opportunity either to continue in full-time education or to enter a period of training and planned work experience. Having embarked on this massive educational experiment the MSC has to decide how to accredit the YTS experience and how this will be linked to other qualifications. In the

White Paper *Training for Jobs* (1984), drafted using MSC advice, the government announced that in the assessment of YTS, standards will 'correspond closely with those required for the successful completion of pre-vocational and vocational courses in schools and further education'. It continued:

> To this end we will seek to define standards of performance and to develop a system of certification which can be applied to both and which will link with other training standards and qualifications. In this the Manpower Services Commission will have a leading role. (Secretaries of State for Employment, Education and Science, Scotland and Wales, 1984, p. 10)

There can be no doubt that the MSC is making an ambitious bid for the power of accreditation in the pre-vocational field. Nor is it likely to limit itself to post-compulsory education. The establishment by the MSC of fourteen pilot projects under the Technical and Vocational Education Initiative (TVEI) in September 1983 aims to stimulate the provision of technical and vocational education for 14 to 18 year olds in secondary schools. At present TVEI, like YTS, can lead to existing national qualifications. But the MSC is unlikely to leave the matter there. What it will probably do is to use the financial muscle of both YTS and TVEI to open up new accreditation territory by developing its own forms of assessment and linking these to the claim that it can rationalize the whole pre-vocational field.

The skirmishing over who will control accreditation in this area was very much evidenced in the run up to the publication in May 1984 of the consultative document *The Certificate in Pre-vocational Education* (CPVE), a one-year course for the 17+ group. Both the CGLI and BTEC were prominent in these arguments, not least because they already run their own pre-vocational courses (which are used by the YTS) and therefore stand to lose both influence and money (both are self-financing) if they lose the accreditation initiative. (Not surprisingly, it was the CGLI and BTEC which after much argument with the DES, established the Joint Board for Pre-Vocational Education which drew up the CPVE document.) So far the DES has come a poor second in the political in-fighting and the future conflict may well be mainly between the CGLI and BTEC, on the one hand, and the MSC on the other.

Unlike the DES, the MSC is not a bureaucracy with an incremental approach to the acquisition of educational power. Its structure and history militate against a gradualist approach. It is opportunistic in its style and has the flexible organization necessary to support its opportunism. It does not have institutional game plans assiduously developed over many years for extending its control but reactive strategies backed by financial clout. Unlike the DES, the MSC's bureaucratic dynamic does not have the patience to feign a belief in the consensus approach to educational change. Likewise its statements of commitment to the economic ideology of education are unequivocal. That this ideology has permeated the upper reaches of government is clear from the style of the MSC-influenced *Training for Jobs* White Paper where statements such as: 'training is not an end itself. It is a means to doing a good job of work for an employer or on one's own account. Training must therefore be firmly work-oriented and lead to jobs' (p. 4) are laid out like self-evident truths. No nonsense about education and personal development here.

It is ironic that the FE sections of the DES, which were the first to sponsor the economic ideology of education back in the 1950s (Tapper and Salter, 1978, pp. 148-54), should be the part of the DES most likely to suffer from a successful exploitation of the ideology by a rival bureaucracy. For while primary, secondary and higher education are still well within the Department's sphere of influence, further education is dangerously exposed. The whole dynamic of the MSC's operative style lends itself to the claim that it can make education economically relevant within a given period of time. It already has a considerable stake in further education, the sector traditionally closest to the world of work, and this will expand. The ability of the DES to resist the MSC's colonization of FE is highly suspect. When MSC made its bid for work-related NAFE the DES strenuously opposed it and, after lengthy negotiations, reduced the proportion to 25 per cent of courses (Passmore, 1984, p. 11). However, the chances are that this is only a holding operation.

The Party Political Input

The continuities in the operation of the Department's bureaucratic dynamic and the burgeoning conflict with the Manpower Services Commission determine major parameters to the process of educational change. The general trends of these continuities and conflicts would exist regardless of the political party in power. However, with the rise of the New Right in the early 1970s and the consequent tensions in the educational consensus between the Conservative and Labour parties a constant was removed from the policy making equation. In future, the bureaucratic dynamics of the DES and MSC would be obliged to interact with the party political dynamic in the formulation of the details of policy. That this interaction did not prevent both bureaucracies from continuing to expand their power has already been demonstrated in the previous section. What we will discuss now is how far the form of that expansion has been guided by the ideological and policy commitments of the Right in general and the Conservative party in particular which were dealt with in Chapter 7.

The principal aim of the Right's educational ideology is the improvement of the quality of the educational experience. Obviously the Right has a particular understanding of what 'quality in education' consists of in terms of knowledge content, teaching methods and modes of assessment (see pp. 175–7). If this quality is to be achieved, the ideology insists, then education has to be subject to a system of accountability which, as Rhodes Boyson (1975) observed, could be 'either a nationally-enforced curriculum or parental choice or a combination of both' (p. 141). With the emphasis within the thinking of the Right on the importance of the social market, it was natural that parental choice should receive most attention to begin with as the appropriate mechanism for ensuring educational quality. The Conservatives' 'Parents Charter' (see pp. 179–80) embodied this idea and was subsequently translated into legislative form in the 1980 Education Act.

The Act provided parents with a statutory right to express a preference for the school of their choice and an appeals system for dissatisfied parents; obliged local authorities to make available full information about their schools, including the results of public examinations and admission criteria, in order that parents could make an informed choice; gave parents the right to choose a school outside the area of the home local education authority; put parents and teachers on the governing bodies of maintained schools; and, of course, introduced the Assisted Places Scheme. A more radical suggestion to bring market mechanisms to bear in education was through the use of educational vouchers. Despite the intellectual attractiveness of the idea to Sir Keith Joseph, it eventually faded from sight.

Once the initial impetus of the Conservative party's ideological and policy commitments had found expression in the 1980 Act and its predecessor the 1979 Act (which removed the compulsion from LEAs to go comprehensive) new ways had to be found to pursue the objective of raising educational standards. At this point the convenient overlap between the Right's concern with how what goes on in the classroom can be made accountable to an external authority and the continuities in the DES's managerial ambitions becomes self-evident. If anything, the Conservatives' concern with educational quality and content has pushed the Department into looking at more detailed methods of managing education than it had previously considered.

The happy marriage of the Conservative party's educational ideology and the Department's centralizing instincts gave an added fillip to the DES's continuing search for mechanisms of control. Equally importantly, it unequivocally legitimized that search. The hard work of the right-wing educationists to change the dominant climate of educational opinion has resulted in an hegemony which accepts that there should be central monitoring of standards, be this in primary, secondary, further or higher education. And of course the DES is only too pleased to help. At the same time, the limits placed on educational expenditure have given a nice cutting edge to the Right's educational doctrine and, carefully honed by the Department's managerial instincts, have produced a concern for effectiveness and efficiency in education. When combined with the reality of limited resources, the idea of accountability is enlarged to include the issue of how best to get value for money in education. Such an issue dovetails neatly with the Department's natural bureaucratic concern with rational planning and administrative controls.

The overlap between the Right's ideological objectives and the continuities in the DES's managerial ambitions is apparent not only in the policies which have emerged but also in the way in which they have been presented. The policies on the secondary school curriculum, the NAB, the UGC and teacher training all show a commitment to the raising of standards through the development of systems of accountability and the efficient management of resources. At the 1984 North of England Conference in Sheffield, Sir Keith Joseph made a speech which represents both an ideological watershed and a key manifestation of the overlap of political and bureaucratic interest. In it, he was able to translate broad ideological goals about standards and efficiency into specific administrative strategies and present them as both reasonable and convincing. As an authoritative statement of intent which organizes and crystallizes existing preoccupations it is on a par with Callaghan's Ruskin speech at Oxford in 1976 and was clearly intended to have a similar directive effect on the educational community.

Sometimes the ideological impetus carries policy-making into unexplored realms which the Department, left to its own devices, would not have considered. For example, the logic of raising educational standards requires that an improvement in standards is capable of being measured. Yet, as Sir Keith Joseph pointed out in his Sheffield speech 'When we try to judge standards, and to improve them, we cannot say precisely what we mean by them' (TES, 1984, p. 4). Thus the SEC is given the task of developing absolute, grade-related standards for the new GCSE exam and, conveniently for the centralizers, further checks are placed on the independence of the exam boards. Similarly, it is not at all clear that the Department would have pursued the monitoring of teacher training in the detail that it has without firm ideological support from the Secretary of State. In its introduction, the White Paper *Teaching Quality* justifies more central intervention in teacher training with the emphatic statement 'In the schools the teacher force ... is the major single determinant of the quality of education' (DES, 1983b, p. 1). The document then goes on to detail appropriate criteria for the approval of initial training courses as well as advice to LEAs on how they could manage the teaching force to achieve higher quality. Thirteen months later Circular 3/84 announced the setting up of the Council for the Accreditation of Teacher Education (CATE) with the initial task of reviewing existing courses and their modification in the light of criteria laid down in an annex to the Circular.

Suspicion of the teaching profession is a recurring theme in the educational ideology of the Right and thus any curb on the profession's independence, be it through increased parental influence or greater DES management control, is welcomed. Not all are convinced that the subversive effect of left-wing teachers has yet been adequately dealt with. Indeed, Professor Cox, one of the editors of the *Black Papers*, argues in a CPC publication (1981) that the 'alternative hegemony' is still very much with us and may get worse:

> At present the worst excesses of the new consciousness, the new hegemony, are held in check by the need to prepare for external exams. In future, for example, left-wing activists among teachers will be able to set projects on working class revolt in the nineteenth century, and so subtly manipulate their pupils' minds. (p. 17)

Even if not all right-wing intellectuals are as pessimistic as Professor Cox there is nonetheless a feeling of the need to maintain the ideological momentum. 'For too long' write Cox and Marks (1982) of the Centre for Policy Studies (CPS) 'educational "experts" of the left have had the initiative; we are committed to challenging their ideas and turning what is seen as politically unthinkable today into the everyday common sense wisdom of tomorrow' (p. 5). Neither the CPS nor the National Council for Educational Standards (NCES) are content to rest on their laurels and both continue to publish books promoting the Right's educational values. Other institutions on the New Right network help sustain the flow of ideas. Recent examples include *The Omega Education Report* from the Adam Smith Institute and an article by Professor Patrick Minford (occasional consultant to Mrs Thatcher) in *Economic Affairs,* the house journal of the Institute of Economic Affairs, both advocating the complete privatization of education (Adam Smith Institute, 1983; Minford, 1984). Their importance, and that of publications like them, is not that they are likely to be translated literally into policy, which obviously they are not, but that they help to reinforce a dominant climate of opinion in education.

Private Schools and the New Consensus

The significance of change in a society's dominant ideology is usually underestimated at the time that it occurs because even the most detached observer cannot escape his ideological context. If he could, the concept of hegemony would have no meaning. Reflecting on this problem in relation to one decade of Thatcherism, Alfred Sherman (first Director of the CPS) remarked that it is necessary 'to slough off the aura of inevitability automatically conferred by retrospect, in order to savour the whole sequence's intrinsic implausibility' (1985 p. 9). (Mrs Thatcher, he maintains, has succeeded in 'modifying the political culture substantially' (*Ibid.*).) Most people do not, or cannot, slough off the accumulated values of a decade of change. And therein lies the power of a dominant ideology: once ensconced, the inertia of its acquired inevitability makes it very difficult to shift.

In education, the private schools have helped foster an ideology which, with its emphasis on parental choice, the market mechanism and standards has given them a place in the mainstream. Through coordinated institutional action and diligent, if discreet, support for the New Right in education, the independent sector first shored up its defences and then went on the attack. Effectively, over the past two decades we have witnessed the regeneration and adaptation of a set of institutions which play a key role in the reproduction of class relations. As part of the educational state, private schools have exercized ideological, agenda-setting and decision making power through their impact on the policy-making process in their search for protection, stability and influence.

It has not been an untroubled progress to calmer waters. The fragmentation and low morale which characterized the independent sector in the 1960s were not easily overcome. Institutions traditionally suspicious of each other for religious and status reasons did not happily trot into the same fold. Political organization and harmony was not (and is not) a natural feature of schools normally engaged in cut-throat competition with each other. That they achieved a political working relationship is a tribute to the perceived severity of the threat in the 1960s from an unsympathetic public opinion and a hostile Labour party. The setting up of the Independent Schools Information Service (ISIS) and the Independent Schools Joint Council (ISJC) was an essential platform for the exercise of educational power in defence of their interests.

In terms of ideological influence, ISIS has provided the private schools with professional public relations support capable of disseminating both sophisticated and more popular justifications of private education through a network of journalistic contacts. For the schools themselves it has supplied a focus and a continuing reassurance of identity and values. At the same time, the informal network of contacts between independent sector intellectuals and the Right has lent its weight to the challenge to the progressive educational consensus of the 1960s. By bringing the private sector into the ideological mainstream, or, more accurately, by taking the ideological mainstream to the private sector, these activities have made it much more difficult for an attack on private schools to be put on, and to be kept on, the political agenda.

Back in the 1950s, the Labour party had the problem of reconciling the principle of parental choice with the class evil of independent schooling (see pp. 111–7). Now, like a bad dream, the problem recurs; only now it is bigger. The evaporation of the progressive consensus in education and the rehabilitation of such ideological marginals as Rhodes Boyson has put Labour party intellectuals into a quandary. How can they 'sell' a policy which aims to eradicate private education, and hence the ability of parents to choose it, in an ideological atmosphere which eulogizes not only parental choice but also the values of competition and standards which independent schools epitomize? Mr. Giles Radice, Labour's education spokesman, is, for one, sensitive to the new climate of opinion and its implications for party policy. He chose his speech to a NCES conference as the appropriate forum to announce the party's 'Achievement Charter', a programme to raise standards in comprehensive schools (Lister, 1985, p. 4). 'The Labour party' he said 'has always been a party of high educational standards not just for the few but for the many' (*Ibid.*).

But if the Labour party is to avoid reacting to the new consensus in education in a purely passive and imitative manner, it has to reassess the role of its intellectuals in order that the Party's ideological messages can be promoted much more effectively than they are at present. As we showed in Chapter 7, the Conservatives recognized this issue fifteen years ago and have been very successful in developing the appropriate intellectual roles. That the Labour party has also, rather belatedly, recognized the issue was apparent at the annual conference following defeat at the 1983 General Election. A full scale debate took place around motions concerned with the party's ability, or lack of it, to communicate its policies to the electorate effectively. Tony Clark (appropriately enough, Union of Communication Workers), for example, argued that it is not sufficient simply to get policies across to the party activists: 'Simply to cobble together conference motions does not produce a coherent and comprehensive policy for people to understand. We need public support in pursuing these policies; we cannot do it with some of the gobbledegook that this party indulges in on occasions' (Labour Party, 1983, p. 38). and Michael Haynes (Oldham Central and Royton CLP) pointed out that 'Although policies are fundamental, you may have the most wonderful goods in the world but if you do not have the proper salesmen you will fail' (*Ibid.*, p. 47). Similar comments permeated the debate and calls were made for organizational review, campaigning strategies, and the use of marketing and professional media techniques.

Following the 1983 election defeat and the rather rude awakening to the realities of modern political marketing, changes have been made in the machinery of Labour's policy formation and presentation. Firstly, joint policy committees have been set up between the party organization and the Parliamentary Labour Party (PLP) to get the PLP involved in the details of policy making and to reduce the customary frictions between party and PLP. Secondly, in late 1983 the Campaign Strategy Committee met for the first time with a membership composed of representatives from the shadow Cabinet, NEC and unions. Its brief is to develop a campaigning strategy for both local and general elections. Robin Cook, appointed in 1985 to coordinate the work of the Committee, recognizes that Labour has a long way to go to match the Conservatives' expertise in this field: 'They are steadily improving on that magnificent [electoral] machine. Unless we improve faster than they are doing we are going to be left even further behind' (*The Guardian,* 1985, p. 11).

The Labour Party's new, or resurgent, interest in the translation of policy into electoral appeal is reflected in the activities of its education Policy Committee. Public opinion polls produced by MORI specifically for the Labour party are used to monitor salient educational issues and help guide the Committee's response. The 'Achievement Charter', for example, was a response to the ' standards' issue and poll data showing that the public believed that the Conservatives were more likely to raise standards. In the case of private schools, the increased use of polls has a direct bearing on the critical issue of how party policy can best be presented to the electorate. Surveys have shown that while the public is against the ending of fee-paying education it is in favour of the removal of state subsidies to private schools (Clough, 1985). But although these findings reveal public support for part of Labour's private schools policy, as an issue it is scarcely an election winner and is unlikely to enjoy much prominence in Labour's campaigning on education. It is also a difficult issue to package. Labour's unaccustomed sensitivity to the details of the election market means that one of the criteria for deciding whether or not to give a high profile to a particular policy is the ease with which it can be made into a saleable product. Private schools do not rate very highly on this criterion. Gone are the days when a policy would be seen as presentable if it was supported by a 100 page document with impeccable statistical tables. The rational and frequently tedious intellectual style of Labour's policy presentation is giving way to the more popular style of the 'Achievement Charter'.

Given the Right's dominance of the new educational consensus and Labour's sensitivity to the electoral market, the private schools policy will remain very much to the rear in any educational campaign by the Labour party. However, this does not automatically mean that the party will not implement some of the policy if it is returned to office. Internal ideological forces may overcome electoral considerations for a time and, in any case, there appears to be public support for the removal of state subsidies to the independent schools. If this were to happen the private schools would have to consider what educational power they could use to oppose Labour's challenge. As Chapter 4 has shown, the legal hegemony from which some of the state subsidies to the private sector derive is complex and difficult to challenge directly. This is of itself a residual power on which the private schools could rely in the last resort. However, before this stage is reached they would mobilize their very considerable decision making power through the ISJC, its sub-committees and their network of political contacts in the Conservative party. This would be particularly important if the Labour party decided to implement Neil Kinnock's pledge to 'tear out' the

Assisted Places Scheme (APS) with a 'short, sharp Bill' (see pp. 122–3) given that such a measure would be administratively straightforward. In the past, the private schools have demonstrated through their use of the three types of educational power that in terms of both internal and external relationships they can engineer educational change to their advantage. If the Labour Party gained office they would be obliged to mobilize these three types of power to resist change. And given their experience, they could make the political cost to Labour of forcing through anti-independent school measures very high.

Alternatively, if the Conservatives remain in office there will be little incentive for the private sector to engage in anything other than routine hegemony maintenance to ensure that the values which support them remain prominent. Now that the AP Scheme is in place there is no point in the private schools using their power in relation to either the political agenda or decision-making to influence the Conservative party further. The use of such power would merely bring an unwelcome political visibility at a time when the maintained sector is suffering from government cuts.

An intriguing grey area is the SDP-Liberal Party Alliance. The SDP attitude is that, on the one hand, 'In a free society it is not possible to stop people founding private schools and charging fees for them' but, on the other, 'there should clearly be no element of public support for these institutions' (Social Democratic Party, 1981). There appears to be sufficient ambivalence here to warrant a concerted effort by the independent sector to establish selective links with the SDP. Such links would be of particular relevance in the situation where the Labour party was elected as the single largest party but lacked an overall majority and therefore required other party support. In this event, policy compromises would have to be reached which the private sector might be able to influence in advance.

The relationship between the private schools and the other institutions of the educational state is unlikely to present any problems for their function as key agents in the process of class reproduction. They remain largely isolated from the immediate effects of the bureaucratic dynamic which is propelling both DES and MSC in the direction of greater control over the management of the maintained sector in education. However, one implication of this dynamic for change which they cannot afford to neglect, and indeed must anticipate, is the organization and accreditation of high status knowledge. Progress into the dominant occupations in British society is increasingly dependent on obtaining the appropriate formal qualifications for entry. Cultural and social skills, which the private schools also provide, remain important but alone are not enough. If the independent schools are to retain their leading position as the educators of the future elite, they must therefore ensure that they command the market in the provision of high status qualifications.

While at the present time the 'A' Level system is secure and the new GCSE preserves the subject-based approach to the curriculum, the CPVE, TVEI and YTS assessment procedures do not share that approach and their development has radical implications for the way in which the curriculum is organized and taught. So long as the status of these new developments is low or uncertain as at present, the private schools do not need to concern themselves with them. However, should a shift occur, for example should TVEI become high status as a result of the DES's insistence on the importance of science and technology (part of the economic ideology of education), then the independent sector would have to respond. Similarly, an example quoted earlier, should the universities respond to the same pressure and change their entry requirements to include BTEC qualifications, this would automatically enhance the status of these qualifications and the private schools would have to adjust accordingly. Given the scale of the other adjustments made by the independent schools over the past two decades, this would present them with few problems. Indeed, their ability to manage both internal and, where necessary, external educational change to suit their own interests casts an interesting light on the more fragmented efforts by other institutions of the educational state, notably those of the DES.

APPENDIX: Methodological Reflections

Gathering the material for this book took us about three years. During that period the development of theory and method became inextricably intertwined and generated a number of methodological issues. The way in which we dealt with these issues will hopefully be of use to others working in this field, or at least, will show them the mistakes to avoid.

Our concern was to study in depth a single example of educational change in a way which would allow us both to refine our existing theory and enlarge it to include the contribution made by political parties. The chosen area was independent schooling because of its centrality to the reproduction of class relations and its clear divisiveness as a party issue. Having made that decision we were then faced with the first question of method: how to determine the data to be collected?

It would have been nice, if a little boring, if other studies of the relationship between education and politics had already blazed a methodological path for us to follow. A scan of related work reassured us that no such path existed. In part this is because others have not seen the relationship between theory and method as problematic. On the one hand, theorists such as Apple (1982), Dale *et al.* (1976) and Sarup (1982) treat empirical evidence with some nonchalance drawing on historical examples when the theoretical discussion warrants it. On the other, the much narrower focus on LEA decision-making by authors such as Batley *et al.* (1970), Jennings (1977), Saran (1973) and Urwin (1965) use detailed information from committee minutes and interviews. In between (in terms of method) can be found Parkinson (1970) with his culling of government reports, circulars, Hansard, Labour party annual conference reports and pamphlets on education. By far the most comprehensive methodological approach is that adopted by Kogan in his *Educational Policy-Making* (1975) where he employs a battery of methods including interviews with the leaders of most of the main educational interest groups, former DES officials and educational journalists, scans of educational journals and the confidential minutes of the Association of Education Committees, Association of Municipal Corporations and County Councils' Association. But despite the range of methods used no one asks why one method rather than another? Most in fact, do not even describe what information was collected and how it was collected leaving it to the reader to infer this for himself. To be fair, Kogan does raise a logically subsequent issue when, after describing his method, he asks 'How usable are conclusions based on data such as these?' but then, whimsically, avoids giving an answer (p. 20).

Even if the issue had been discussed in other studies, the nature of our theory would itself have provided us with quite distinctive problems. Firstly it is interdisciplinary. It draws on and combines theoretical elements from the Marxist and non-Marxist approaches to the sociology of knowledge, educational sociology and political science. As a consequence, its focus ranges from the minutiae of decision-making through middle range inter-institutional relationships to the macro-level of class reproductive pressures, ideological conflict and hegemony. The different levels of analysis would frequently require different types of evidence. Secondly, the theory was not, and is not, static. It evolved in the course of doing the research and writing the book so that the need to acquire fresh data from new sources only became apparent as the work progressed. An obvious example of this is Chapter 4 where we explore the complex nature of the legal hegemony protecting the independent schools. This aspect of hegemony was not fully apparent to us when we began the work.

The general method is that of the case study. We take a single issue, independent schooling, and study it in depth in order to illuminate and progress our theory of educational change. The data sources were as follows.

Primary Sources

1   Committee minutes and papers of the Direct Grant Joint Committee, the Independent Schools Joint Council and its sub-committees, the Headmasters' Conference, and Independent Schools Information Service.
2   Internal papers and memorandum of the Labour Party's Education

Study Group and the Education and Science Sub-Committee of the Home Policy Committee (1955–82).
3 Personal papers of Stuart Sexton, political adviser successively to Norman St John-Stevas, Mark Carlisle and Sir Keith Joseph.

Secondary Sources

1 Education debates in Hansard (1960–82); Select Committee on Education and Science (1960–82); DES publications and circulars.
2 Conservative and Labour party annual conference reports, election manifestos and publications on education policy (1960–82); Conservative Campaign Guides (1964–83); Conservative Political Centre and Conservative Research Department publications (1960–82).
3 Centre for Policy Studies publications; Institute of Economic Affairs publications, individual protagonists and opponents of independent schooling (for example the Black Papers); scans of educational journals.
4 Court cases.

Statistical Sources

Independent Schools Information Service; re-examination of existing data on independent schools (for example Public Schools Commission, Halsey *et al.* (1980) *Origins and Destinations*).

Interviews

Semi-structured interviews guided by a check-list of items to be covered were conducted with members of the key committees in the independent sector, politicians, DES officials and officers of the Conservative and Labour parties.

We began with the independent sector itself. We already had some access established as a result of interviews with public school headmasters conducted for the chapter 'Redefining the ideology of public school education' in *Education, Politics and the State*. If the study was to develop at all this access, and the goodwill associated with it, had to be carefully nurtured and expanded. Without the cooperation of independent school headmasters and officials we would have had to rely on the normal social science practice of looking at the sector through the wrong end of a telescope. There was undoubtedly a certain reticence in the private sector towards social scientists. One headmaster we interviewed described social scientists as 'only slightly less undesirable than journalists'. Another, unsure as to whether he should allow us to see the files of a particular committee, asked 'How do I know you are not snakes in the grass?' Indeed. While there is no easy answer to this kind of question there are ways of negotiating an arrangement for the handling of sensitive information.

Firstly, we could point to how we had dealt with this issue in previous publications: there was a track record which the interviewee could consult. Secondly, nearly all the interviews with people in the independent sector resulted from the recommendation of a previous interviewee. An earlier judgment of our worth had therefore been made by someone whom the interviewee usually respected. The more interviews we conducted and access we gained, the more secure became our credibility as it became clear that we were 'known' to opinion leaders in the independent school network. It was not, however, an unshakeable position. While we were working in this field one rather clumsy approach from another, unrelated, social scientist to one of our major contacts very nearly caused the closing of access to all social scientists, including ourselves. Thus maintaining the goodwill of our network over time was very important.

In discussing the arrangements for the release and use of, say, committee papers we distinguished between matters of fact and matters of interpretation. It was made clear to the individual providing the information that he might well disagree with our subsequent interpretation of it. While we were quite willing to submit drafts of our work for correction on matters of fact we would not necessarily accept a respondent's views on matters of interpretation — though we encouraged such comments as an aid to our own understanding. For the most part this arrangement worked perfectly well and, in addition to the access itself, supplied us with frequent 'insider' insights into the politics of the independent schools. Compromises nonetheless had to be made. In one case the access was only partial (more recent information being regarded as too sensitive) and in another we signed a legal document to the effect that the publication of information from that particular source would require the express permission of a particular official (which, as it happened, was given without any problem).

Broadly speaking, we applied the same principles on gaining access developed in the independent sector to subsequent approaches to the Conservative and Labour parties and to the DES. However, each of these three groups constituted separate networks and none was as coherent as the independent school network, some of whose members had worked together for several decades.

There are dangers with this approach both in terms of how the researcher 'weights' the information gathered (either directly from the interviewee himself or indirectly from the access provided) and in terms of the subtle and not so subtle pressures to interpret the data in a particular way. On the first point, the use of 'reputation' to identify the key influentials to be interviewed and consulted aroused much argument in the United States following Hunter's systematic use of this method in his *Community Power Structure* (Hunter, 1953). Polsby in particular criticized it for merely producing a map of those reputed to be influential as opposed to those who were *actually* influential (Polsby, 1963). In order to break 'closed-circuit' problems of the reputational approach it is important to build in cross-checks using independent sources of information such as committee minutes and newspaper reports wherever possible. In his classic study of community influence *Who Governs?* Dahl argues that 'One way to compensate for the unsatisfactory character of all existing operational measures of influence is to be eclectic' (1961 p. 330). Cross-checks were also important in this study because there was a tendency on the part of many of those interviewed to exaggerate their own contribution and influence, and 'to read history backwards' in a way favourable to themselves. In one instance, the contents of an individual's personal files seemed to contradict part of the information he had given verbally.

The pressures to interpret the data in particular ways came from the comments made by interviewees on draft chapters and from our own perception of the effect of what we wrote on the rapport we had established. The first was the easiest to handle because it was explicit and because we had directly discussed the issue of scholastic autonomy when the contact was first made. But to an extent it could be pre-empted by conscious or unconscious self-editing on our own part. Conscious self-editing occurred only in that we avoided personalizing events. Unconscious self-editing as a result of being seduced into agreeing with a particular interpretation is more difficult to deal with. However, given the lack of consensus among the range of people to whom we talked (independent sector heads and officials, Conservative and Labour MPs and officials, DES officials) and the range of comments we received from them on draft chapters it is unlikely such unconscious editing occurred. As a further check, academic colleagues were asked to comment on draft chapters bearing this possibility in mind and no consistent bias was remarked on.

The analysis of the primary source material gathered through the network of contacts became easier as the research progressed. The criteria for selecting a small amount of information from a range of material became clearer as our familiarity with the basic actors, events and institutions increased and the theoretical task assumed a sharper focus. On the theory side, the intra-and inter-institutional levels of analysis required the identification of flows of influence which, sooner or later, revealed themselves in committee decisions, conference resolutions and government action. The criteria for selecting material which would help us understand this policy-making process could therefore be related to a definite endpoint. The task was complex and frequently laborious but it had known parameters. Where the situation was much less clear was in the selection of material which either lay outside the institutions of independent sector, parties and government or lay inside these institutions but related to a higher level of analysis.

One problem which particularly exercised us in this respect was what method to use in collecting information on the contribution of ideology and hegemony to this area of policy making. While both *Education and the Political Order* (Chapter 7) and *Education, Politics and the State* (Chapters 8 and 9) contain analyses of ideological development these relate mainly to the official manifestation of ideological currents and therefore largely employ official publications as their empirical base. In this book we were concerned with two different aspects of ideology. One was the extent to which the development of a new policy which challenged independent schools was inhibited by a legal hegemony which protected them and the other was how to trace the emergence of an ideology which supported them. The first meant a foray into a discipline which was new to us, the law, using ideas, terminology and sources with which we were unfamiliar. Helpful advice and direction from legal colleagues and a focus on the single issue of charitable status enabled us to trace and interpret the relevant court cases and judgments without too much difficulty. Less obvious was what method should be used to collect information on the rise of the so-called 'new right' ideology and its impact on Conservative educational policy. Within the Party itself the task was relatively straightforward and entailed sifting the publications of the Conservative MPs such as Rhodes Boyson who were known proponents of the

New Right. Sources of the new ideology outside the party were more of a problem. A very general profile of the ideology was built up by interviewing its most frequently mentioned protagonists and reading their publications. These sources then gave rise to a list of institutions such as the Centre for Policy Studies, the Institute of Economic Affairs and the Adam Smith Institute which supported the new ideology and whose publications impinged in various ways on the thinking of the Conservative party. Having culled the material produced by these institutions it was then possible to make links between the ideas they were propounding and Conservative policy on education in general and private schools in particular.

In discussing the differences between elite and survey interviewing Dexter comments that 'It is not usually possible to determine by any mechanical method who should be interviewed. The population cannot be satisfactorily randomized or stratified in advance; and different interviewees make quite different and unequal contributions to the study' (1970 p. 39). The method therefore has to be adaptive. In this study this remark was true not only of the interviews and the access which they provided but of the other parts of the method as well. The dialogue between theory and method meant that as the theory evolved new demands for information were created. Tracing the lines of influence on policy formation became doubly complex when the theory suggested that new sources of influence should be explored. It was an interesting learning experience, we hope the result is an equally interesting book.

Bibliography

ABRC (1983a) *A Study of Commissioned Research*, Mason Report, London, HMSO.

ABRC (1983b) *The Support Given by Research Councils for In-House and University Research*, Morris Report, London, HMSO.

ABRC/ACARD (1983) *Improving Links Between Higher Education and Industry*, Wood Report, Cmnd. 8957, London, HMSO.

ABRC/ACARD/DES (1982) *Report of a Joint Working Party on the Support of Scientific Research*, Merrison Report, Cmnd. 8567, London, HMSO.

ADAM SMITH INSTITUTE (1983) *The Omega Report*.

AHIER, J. and FLUDE, M. (Eds) (1983) *Contemporary Education Policy*, London, Croom Helm.

ALTHUSSER, L. (1972) 'Ideology and ideological state apparatuses', in COSIN, B. (Ed.) *Education, Structure and Society*, Harmondsworth, Penguin Books.

ANDERSON, P. (1964) 'The origins of the present crisis', *New Left Review*, 23, pp. 26–53.

APPLE, M. (Ed.) (1982) *Cultural and Economic Reproduction in Education*, London, Routledge and Kegan Paul.

APTER, D.E. (1964) *Ideology and Discontent*, Edinburgh, Free Press of Glencoe.

ARCHER, M.S. (1979) *The Social Origins of Educational Systems*, London, Sage.

ARCHER, M.S. (1982) 'Introduction: Theorizing about the expansion of educational systems', in ARCHER, M.S. (Ed.) *The Sociology of Educational Expansion*, Beverley Hills, Calif., Sage.

ASSOCIATION OF GOVERNING BODIES OF PUBLIC SCHOOLS (1969) *Evidence Prepared by the Direct Grant Joint Committee for the Public Schools Commission*.

ASSOCIATION OF GOVERNING BODIES OF PUBLIC SCHOOLS (1971) *Future Policy for Public Schools*.

ASSOCIATION OF GOVERNING BODIES OF PUBLIC SCHOOLS/HEADMASTERS' CONFERENCE (1968) *Public Schools Commission*.

BACHRACH, P. and BARATZ, M.S. (1962) 'The two faces of power', *American Political Science Review*, 56, pp. 947–52.

BACHRACH, P. and BARATZ, M.S. (1963) 'Decisions and non-decisions: An analytical framework', *American Political Science Review*, 57, pp. 641–51.

BACHRACH, P. and BARATZ, M.S. (1970) *Power and Poverty: Theory and Practice,* New York, Oxford University Press.

BAMFORD, T. (1967) *The Rise of the Public Schools,* London, Nelson.

BARKER, R. (1972) *Education and Politics, 1900–51,* Oxford, Oxford University Press.

BARKER, R. (1978) 'Freedom to grow: "A" level business studies', *Conference,* 15, No. 2, pp. 21–5.

BATLEY, R. *et al.* (1970) *Going Comprehensive,* London, Routledge and Kegan Paul.

BEER, S. (1965) *Modern British Politics,* London, Faber.

BENN, C. (1980) *Letters to Bert Clough,* March and May.

BENNETT, N. (1982) 'An examination and analysis of the development of the assisted places scheme', paper presented in partial fulfillment of the requirements for the MA in Education, University of Sussex.

BERNBAUM, G. (Ed.) (1979) *Schooling in Decline,* London, Macmillan.

BLAKE, LORD R. and PATTEN, J. (Eds) (1976) *The Conservative Opportunity,* London, Macmillan.

BLONDEL, J. (1978) *Political Parties: A Genuine Case for Discontent,* London, Wildwood House.

BOARD OF EDUCATION (1944) *The Public Schools and the General Educational System,* The Fleming Committee, London, HMSO.

BOISSEVAIN, J.F. (1974) *Friends of Friends: Networks, Manipulators and Coalitions,* London, Blackwell.

BOSANQUET, N. (1982) *After the New Right,* London, Heinemann.

BOTTOMORE, T. (1965) *Classes in Modern Society,* London, Allen and Unwin.

BOWLES, S. and GINTIS, H. (1976) *Schooling in Capitalist America: Educational Reform and the Contradictions of Economic Life,* London, Routledge and Kegan Paul.

BOYD, D. (1973) *Elites and Their Education,* Slough, NFER.

BOYSON, R. (Ed.) (1970) *Right Turn,* London, Churchill Press.

BOYSON, R. (1975) *The Crisis in Education,* London, The Woburn Press.

BRIDGEMAN, T. and FOX, I. (1978) 'Why people choose private schools', *New Society,* 44, pp. 702–5.

BURCH, M. (1980) 'Approaches to leadership in opposition: Edward Heath and Margaret Thatcher', in LAYTON-HENRY, Z. (Ed.) *Conservative Party Policy,* London, Macmillan.

BUTLER, R.A. (1971) *The Art of the Possible,* London, Hamish Hamilton.

BUTT, R. (1975) 'Politics and education' in COX, C.B. and BOYSON, R. (Eds.) *The Fight for Education: Black Paper 1975,* London, J.M. Dent and Sons.

CASTLE, B. (1973) 'Mandarin power', *Sunday Times,* 10 June, p. 17.

CAWSON, A. (1982) *Corporatism and Welfare: Social Policy and State Intervention in Britain,* London, Heinemann Educational.

CENTRE FOR CONTEMPORARY CUTURAL STUDIES (1981) *Unpopular Education,* London, Hutchinson.

CENTRE FOR POLICY STUDIES (1977) *Stepping Stones.*

CHARITY COMMISSION (1966) *Report.*

CLOUGH, B. (1984) 'Educational policy making in the Labour party', seminar paper, *Politics, Education & Society Group,* Kings College, London, 25

January.

CLOUGH, B. (1985) *Interview,* 31 January.

COATES, D. (1975) *The Labour Party and the Struggle for Socialism,* Cambridge, Cambridge University Press.

COATES, D. (1980) *Labour in Power? A Study of the Labour Government 1974–79,* London, Longmans.

COBBAN, J. (1980) 'The assisted places scheme: Question and answer', paper prepared to answer 'most of the questions that have been raised about the implementation of the assisted places scheme'.

COLEMAN, J.S. *et al.* (1957) 'The diffusion of innovation among physicians', *Sociometry,* 20, pp. 253–70.

COMMITTEE ON THE LAW AND PRATICE RELATING TO CHARITABLE TRUSTS (1952) *Report,* Nathan Committee, London, HMSO.

CONGDON, T. (1978) *Monetarism: An Essay in Definition,* London, Centre for Policy Studies.

CONSERVATIVE CENTRAL OFFICE (1977) *Restoring Direct Grant Schools.*

CONSERVATIVE INDEPENDENT SCHOOLS COMMITTEE (n.d.) *Independent Schools: Speakers Notes.*

CONSERVATIVE PARTY (1965) *Annual Conference.*

CONSERVATIVE PARTY (1970) *Annual Conference.*

CONSERVATIVE PARTY (1974) *Manifesto.*

CONSERVATIVE PARTY (1979) *Manifesto.*

CONSERVATIVE RESEARCH DEPARTMENT (1975) 'Education', *Notes on Current Politics,* No. 6.

COURT CASE: ATTORNEY GENERAL V. LONSDALE (1827) 1. Sim. 109, reprinted in *English Reports,* Volume 57, p. 519.

COURT CASE: INCOME TAX SPECIAL PURPOSES COURTS V. PEMSEL [1891] A.C. pp. 531–92.

COURT CASE: MORICE V. BISHOP OF DURHAM (1805) 10 Ves. 532, reprinted in *English Reports,* Volume 32, p. 951.

COURT CASE: OPPENHEIM V. TOBACCO SECURITIES TRUST CO. LTD. [1951] A.C. pp. 297–319.

COURT CASE: THE ABBEY, MALVERN WELLS, LTD. V. MINISTRY OF LOCAL GOVERNMENT AND PLANNING (1951) 2 All E.R. pp. 154–61.

COWLING, M. (Ed.) (1978) *Conservative Essays,* London, Cassell.

COX, C.B. (1981) *Education: The Next Decade,* London, Conservative Political Centre.

COX, C.B. and BOYSON, R. (Eds) (1977) *Black Paper 1977,* London, Temple Smith.

COX, C.B. and DYSON, A.E. (Eds) (1971) *The Black Papers on Education,* London, Davis Poynter.

COX, C.B. and MARKS, J. (Eds) (1982) *The Right to Learn,* London, Centre for Policy Studies.

CREQUER, N. (1984) 'Putting the system under the microscope', *Times Higher Education Supplement,* 4 January, p. 11.

CROSLAND, C.A.R. (1956) *The Future of Socialism,* London, Jonathan Cape.

CROSSMAN, R.H.S. (1975) *The Diaries of a Cabinet Minister, Volume 1: Minister of Housing 1964–66,* London, Hamish Hamilton.

CROUCH, C. (Ed.) (1979) *State and Economy in Contemporary Capitalism,* London, Croom Helm.

CROUCH, C. (1982) 'The peculiar relationship: The party and the unions', in KAVANAGH, D. (Ed.) *The Politics of the Labour Party,* London, Allen and Unwin.

CROWTHER HUNT, LORD (1976a) 'Long term planning takes second place' *Times Higher Education Supplement,* 7 May, p. 7.

CROWTHER HUNT, LORD (1976b) 'The inadequacies of departmental planning in action', *Time Higher Education Supplement,* 14 May, p. 13.

DAHL, R. (1961) *Who Governs?,* New Haven, Conn, Yale University Press.

DALE, R. *et al.* (Eds) (1976) *Schooling and Capitalism,* London, Routledge and Kegan Paul.

DALE, R. (1981) *Society, Education and the State,* Milton Keynes, Open University.

DALE, R. (1983) 'Thatcherism and education' in AHIER, J. and FLUDE, M. (Eds) *Contemporary Education Policy,* London, Croom Helm.

DANCY, J. (1963) *The Public Schools and the Future,* London, Faber and Faber.

DEPARTMENT OF EDUCATION AND SCIENCE (1972) *Teacher Education and Training,* James Committee, London, HMSO.

DEPARTMENT OF EDUCATION AND SCIENCE (1975) *A Language For Life,* Bullock Committee, London, HMSO.

DEPARTMENT OF EDUCATION AND SCIENCE (1978) *Report of the Working Group on the Management of Higher Education in the Maintained Sector,* Oakes Report, Cmnd. 7130, London, HMSO.

DEPARTMENT OF EDUCATION AND SCIENCE (1980) *Annual Report 1980,* London, HMSO.

DEPARTMENT OF EDUCATION AND SCIENCE (1981) *Annual Report 1981,* London, HMSO.

DEPARTMENT OF EDUCATION AND SCIENCE (1982a) *Annual Report 1982,* London, HMSO.

DEPARTMENT OF EDUCATION AND SCIENCE (1982b) *Study of H.M. Inspectorate in England and Wales,* London, HMSO.

DEPARTMENT OF EDUCATION AND SCIENCE (1983a) *Annual Report 1983,* London, HMSO.

DEPARTMENT OF EDUCATION AND SCIENCE (1983b) *Teaching Quality,* Cmnd 8836, London, HMSO.

DEPARTMENT OF EDUCATION AND SCIENCE (1984) *Parental Influence at School: A New Framework for School Government in England and Wales,* Cmnd 9242, London, HMSO.

DEUTSCH, K.W. *et al.* (1971) *France, Germany and the Western Alliance: A Study of Elite Attitudes on European Integration and World Politics,* New York, Scribners.

DEVLIN, T. (1983) 'Independent but indebted', *Times Educational Supplement,* 26 August, p. 4.

DEXTER, L.A. (1970) *Elite and Specialized Interviewing,* Evanston, Northwestern University Press.

DIRECT GRANT JOINT COMMITTEE (1966–80) *Minutes.*

DIRECT GRANT JOINT COMMITTEE (1971) *Document 158.*

DRUCKER, H.M. (1979) *Doctrine and Ethos in the Labour Party*, London, Allen and Unwin.

ECCLESHALL, R. (1977) 'English conservatism as ideology', *Political Studies*, 25, pp. 62–83.

EXPENDITURE COMMITTEE (Education, Arts & Home Office Sub-Committee), (1975) *Charity Commissioners and their Accountability*, London, HMSO.

FERNS, H.S. (1969) *Towards an Independent University*, Occasional Paper No. 25, Institute of Economic Affairs.

FOWLER, G. (1979) 'The politics of education', in BERNBAUM, G. (Ed.) *Schooling in Decline*, London, Macmillan.

FOWLER, G. (1981) 'The changing nature of educational politics in the 1970s', in BROADFOOT, P. *et al.* (Eds) *Politics and Educational Change*, London, Croom Helm.

FOX, I. (1984) 'The demand for a public school education: A crisis of confidence in comprehensive schooling?', in WALFORD, G. (Ed.) *British Public Schools: Policy and Practice*, Lewes, Falmer Press.

FOX, I. (1985) *Private Schools and Public Issues*, London, Macmillan.

GALE, G. (1978) 'The popular communication of a Conservative message', in COWLING, M. (Ed.) *Conservative Essays*, London, Cassell.

GAMBLE, A. (1974) *The Conservative Nation*, London, Routledge and Kegan Paul.

GAMBLE, A. (1979) 'The decline of the Conservative party', *Marxism Today*, 23, No. 11, November, pp. 6–11.

GAMBLE, A. (1981) *Britain in Decline: Economic Policy and Political Strategy*, London, Macmillan.

GEDDES, D. (1979) 'Who is backing the assisted places scheme?', *The Times*, 30 November, p. 14.

GELLA, A. (1976) *The Intelligentsia and the Intellectuals*, London, Sage.

GIDDENS, A. (1974) 'Elites in the British class structure', in STANSWORTH, P. and GIDDENS, A. (Eds) *Elites and Power in British Society*, Cambridge, Cambridge University Press.

GLADSTONE, F. (1982) *Charity, Law and Social Justice*, London, Bedford Square.

GLENNERSTER, H. and PRYKE, R. (1973) 'The contribution of the public schools and Oxbridge: 1 "Born to Rule"', in URRY, J. and WAKEFORD, J. (Eds) *Power in Britain*, London, Heinemann.

GOLD, K. (1984) 'Watching and listening', *Times Higher Education Supplement*, 8 October, p. 11.

GOULDNER, A.W. (1979) *The Future of Intellectuals and the Rise of the New Class*, London, Macmillan.

GRAMSCI, A. (1957) *The Modern Prince and Other Writings*, London, Lawrence and Wishart.

GRANOVETTER, M.S. (1973) 'The strength of weak ties', *American Journal of Sociology*, 78, pp. 1360–80.

GRANOVETTER, M.S. (1974) *Getting a Job: A Study of Contacts and Careers*, Cambridge, Mass., Harvard University Press.

GRAY, J. *et al.* (1983) *Reconstructions of Secondary Education: Theory, Myth and Practice Since the War*, London, Routledge and Kegan Paul.

THE GUARDIAN (1985) 'Rough rider on the campaign trail', 26 January, p. 11.

HALL, S. (1979) 'The great moving right crisis', *Marxism Today,* January, pp. 14–20.

HALL, S. *et al.* (1978) *Policing the Crisis,* London, Macmillan.

HALL, S. and JACQUES, M. (1983) *The Politics of Thatcherism,* London, Lawrence and Wishart.

HALSBURY (1974) *Laws of England,* Volume 5, London, Butterworth.

HALSEY, A.H. *et al.* (1980) *Origins and Destinations,* Oxford, Clarendon Press.

HALSEY, A.H. *et al.* (1984) 'The political arithmetic of public schools' in WALFORD, G. (Ed.) *British Public Schools: Policy and Practice,* Lewes, Falmer Press.

HANSARD (1964/65–1983/84).

HARRIS, LORD (1980) *The Challenge of a Radical Reactionary,* London, Centre for Policy Studies.

HARRIS, R. and SELSDON, A. (1977) *Not From Benevolence: 20 Years of Economic Dissent,* London, Institute of Economic Affairs.

HARRISON, M. (1960) *Trade Unions and the Labour Party Since 1945,* London, Allen and Unwin.

HATFIELD, M. (1978) *The House the Left Built: Inside Labour Policy Making 1970–75,* London, Victor Gollancz.

HEADMASTERS' CONFERENCE (1963–82) *Bulletin.*

HEADMASTERS' CONFERENCE (1979) *Annual Meeting.*

HEARNSHAW, F.J.C. (1933) *Conservatism in England,* London, Harrap.

HER MAJESTY'S INSPECTORATE (1983) *Curriculum 11 to 16, Towards a Statement of Entitlement,* London, HMSO.

HER MAJESTY'S INSPECTORATE (1984) *English from 5 to 16: Curriculum Matters I,* London, HMSO.

HOARE, Q. and NOWELL SMITH, C. (Eds) (1971) *Antonio Gramsci, Selections from the Prison Notebooks,* London, Lawrence and Wishart.

HOBSBAWM, E.J. (1978) 'The new dissent: Intellectuals, society and the left', *New Society,* 46, pp. 443–5.

HODGKINSON, H. (1966) 'The smaller public school and its place in Britain', *Conference,* 3, 2, pp. 11–15.

HODGSON, G. (1984) 'Now is the time for all right-thinking men ...', *Sunday Times Colour Supplement,* 4 March, pp. 44–52.

HONEY, J. F. DE S. (1977) *Tom Brown's Universe,* London, Millington.

HOWELL, D. (1980) *The Conservative Tradition in the 1980s,* London, Centre for Policy Studies.

HUDSON, M. (1976) 'The political secretary', *Political Quarterly,* 47, pp. 297–306.

HUNTER, F. (1953) *Community Power Structure,* Chapel Hill, University of North Carolina Press.

INDEPENDENT SCHOOLS CAREERS ORGANIZATION (1983) *Prospectus 1983/84.*

INDEPENDENT SCHOOLS INFORMATION SERVICE (1973) *Newsletter No. 3,* September.

INDEPENDENT SCHOOLS INFORMATION SERVICE (1982) *Newsletter No. 33,* autumn

INDEPENDENT SCHOOLS INFORMATION SERVICE (1983a) *Newsletter No. 34,* spring

INDEPENDENT SCHOOLS INFORMATION SERVICE (1983b) *Newsletter No. 35,* summer.

INDEPENDENT SCHOOLS INFORMATION SERVICE (1983c) *Independent Schools and Charitable Status: Why They Deserve to Retain It.*
INDEPENDENT SCHOOLS INFORMATION SERVICE (1983c) *Annual Census.*
INDEPENDENT SCHOOLS INFORMATION SERVICE (1984) *Annual Census.*
JACKSON, M. (1984) 'MSC seeks more power over colleges', *Times Educational Supplement,* 20 July, p. 1
JAMES, LORD (1967) 'The maintenance of academic standards', address to the annual meeting of HMC.
JENKINS, R. (1971) 'The reality of political power', *The Sunday Times,* 17 January, pp. 25–6.
JENNINGS, R.E. (1977) *Education and Politics: Policy-Making in Local Education Authorities,* London, Batsford.
JOSEPH, SIR KEITH (1976) *Stranded in the Middle Ground,* London, Centre for Policy Studies.
KALTON, G. (1966) *The Public Schools: A Factual Survey,* London, Longmans.
KATZ, F.E. (1958) 'Occupational contact networks', *Social Forces,* 37, pp. 252–8.
KAVANAGH, D. (1982) 'Representation in the Labour party', in KAVANAGH, D. (Ed.) *The Politics of the Labour Party,* London, Allen and Unwin.
KOGAN, D. and KOGAN, M. (1982) *The Battle for the Labour Party,* London, Fontana.
KOGAN, M. (1971) *The Politics of Education,* Harmondsworth, Penguin Books.
KOGAN, M. (1975) *Educational Policy-Making,* London, Allen and Unwin.
KOGAN, M. (1978) *The Politics of Educational Change,* London, Fontana.
KOGAN M. (1983) 'The central-local government relationship: A comparison between the education and health services', *Local Government Studies,* 9, 1, pp. 65–85.
KOGAN, M. (1984) 'Over the top', *The Times Educational Supplement,* 5 June, p. 4
LABOUR PARTY (1958) *Learning to Live.*
LABOUR PARTY (1960–1984) *Annual Conference.*
LABOUR PARTY (1960–1984) *Manifesto.*
LABOUR PARTY (1980) *Private Schools: A Discussion Document.*
LABOUR PARTY (n.d) *Internal Memorandum.*
LAYTON-HENRY, Z. (Ed.) (1980) *Conservative Party Politics,* London, Macmillan.
LESTER A. and PANNICK, D. (1982) *Independent Schools and the European Convention on Human Rights: A Joint Opinion,* London, ISIS.
LINDSAY, D.D. (1968) 'The Newsom Commission', *Conference,* 5, 3, pp. 3–8.
LISTER,, D. (1983) 'Composing a theme with no variations', *The Times Educational Supplement,* 5 April, p. 6.
LISTER, D. (1985) 'Labour's charter to raise standards at all-in schools', *The Times,* 7 January, p. 4.
LODGE, P. and BLACKSTONE, T. (1982) *Educational Policy and Educational Inequality,* London, Martin Robertson.
LUKES, S. (1974) *Power: A Radical Critique,* London, Macmillan.
MCCONNELL, J.D.R. (1967) *Eton — How it Works,* London, Faber and Faber.
MACFARLANE, N. (1980) *DES Memorandum,* 2 May.
MCKENZIE, R. (1963) *British Poltical Parties,* London, Heinemann.

McKenzie, R. (1976) 'Some recent developments in British political parties with special reference to the Labour party', paper presented to the Political Studies Association Conference.

McKenzie, R. (1982) 'Power in the Labour party: The issue of intra party democracy', in Kavanagh, D. (Ed.) *The Politics of the Labour Party*, London, Allen and Unwin.

MacLure, S. (1983) 'Unrepentant centralist', *The Times Educational Supplement*, 29 April, p. 2.

Mandel, E. (1975) *Late Capitalism*, London, New Left Books.

Mangan, J.A. (1981) *Athleticism in the Victorian and Edwardian Public School: The Emergence and Consolidation of an Educational Ideology*, Cambridge, Cambridge University Press.

Mannheim, K. (1954) *Ideology and Utopia*, London, Routledge and Kegan Paul.

Manpower Services Commission (1974–84) *Annual Reports*.

Manzer, R.A. (1970) *Teachers and Politics*, Manchester, Manchester University Press.

Markall, G. and Gregory, D. (1982) 'Who cares? The MSC intervention: Full of Easter promise', in Rees, T.L. and Atkinson, P. *Youth Unemployment and State Intervention*, London, Routledge and Kegan Paul.

Marsden, P.V. and Lin, N. (Eds) (1982) *Social Structure Network Analysis*, London, Sage Publications.

Maude, A. (1963) 'Party paleontology', *Spectator*, 15 March, pp. 319–21.

Maude, A. (1967) *The Consuming Society*, Conservative Political Centre.

Meisel, J.H. (1958) *The Myth of the Ruling Class: Gaetano Mosca and the 'Elite'*, Ann Arbor, Mich, University of Michigan Press.

Miliband, R. (1961) *Parliamentary Socialism: A Study in the Politics of Labour*, London, Allen and Unwin.

Miliband, R. (1969) *The State in Capitalist Society*, London, Weidenfeld and Nicolson.

Minford, P. (1984) 'State expenditure: A study in waste' *Economic Affairs*, 4, 3.

Murray, P. (1980) *Margaret Thatcher*, London, Allen and Unwin.

Nairn, T. (1964) 'The nature of the Labour party 1 and 2', *New Left Review*, 27, pp. 38–65, and 28, pp. 33–62.

National Council for Educational Standards (1972) *Conference 1972: The Basic Unity of Education*, London, Critical Quarterly Society.

National Council of Social Services (1976) *Charity Law and Voluntary Organizations*, The Goodman Committee, London, Bedford Square Press.

Nightingale, B. (1973) *Charities*, London, Allen Lane.

Norton, P. and Aughey (1981) *Conservatives and Conservatism*, London, Temple Smith.

O'Keeffe, D.J. (1979) 'Capitalism and correspondence: A critique of Marxist analyses of education', *Higher Education Review*, 12, pp. 40–52.

Panitch, L. (1971) 'Ideology and integration in the case of the British Labour party', *Political Studies*, 19, 2, pp. 184–200.

Panitch, L. (1976) *Social Democracy and Industrial Militancy: the Labour Party, the Trade Unions and Incomes Policy, 1945–74*, Cambridge, Cambridge University Press.

PARETO, V. (1968) *The Rise and Fall of Elites*, New Jersey, The Bedminster Press.

PARKINSON, M. (1970) *The Labour Party and the Organization of Secondary Education*, London, Routledge and Kegan Paul.

PASSMORE, B. (1981) 'Born again conservatives', *The Times*, 13 February, p. 6.

PASSMORE, B. (1984) 'The power struggle behind the scenes', *The Times Educational Supplement*, 4 February, p. 11.

PATTEN, C. (1980) 'Policy making in opposition', in LAYTON-HENRY, Z. (Ed.) *Conservative Party Politics*, London, Macmillan.

PEACOCK, A. and WISEMAN, J. (1964) *Education for Democracy*, Hobart Paper No. 25, Institute of Economic Affairs.

PEELE, G. (1976) 'The Conservative dilemma', in BLAKE, LORD and PATTEN, J. (Eds) *The Conservative Opportunity*, London, Macmillan.

PIMLOTT, B. (1977) *Labour and the Left in the 1930s*, Cambridge, Cambridge University Press.

PLASKOW, M. (Ed.) (1985) *Life and Death of the Schools Council*, Lewes, Falmer Press.

POLSBY, N. (1963) *Community Power and Political Theory*, New Haven, Conn, Yale University Press.

POULANTZAS, N. (1973) *Political Power and Social Classes*, London, New Left Books.

POULANTZAS, N. (1975) *Classes in Contemporary Capitalism*, London, New Left Books.

POWELL, E. and WOOD, J. (Eds) (1969) *Freedom & Reality*, London, Batsford.

PREST, A.R. (1966) *Financing University Education*, Occasional Paper No. 12, London, Institute of Economic Affairs.

PRINGLE, R. (1977) *The Growth Merchants — Economic Consequences of Wishful Thinking*. London, Centre for Policy Studies.

PUBLIC SCHOOLS COMMISSION (1968a) *First Report, Volume I*, London, HMSO.

PUBLIC SCHOOLS COMMISSION (1968b) *First Report, Volume II*, London, HMSO.

PUBLIC SCHOOLS COMMISSION (1970a) *Second Report, Volume I*, London, HMSO.

PUBLIC SCHOOLS COMMISSION (1970b) *Second Report, Volume II*, London, HMSO.

PUTMAN, R.D. (1973) *The Beliefs of Politicians: Ideology, Conflict and Democracy in Britain and Italy*, New Haven, Conn, Yale University Press.

RAE, J. (1981) *The Public School Revolution*, London, Faber and Faber.

RAE, J. (1982) *Interview*, 20 August.

RAMSDEN, J. (1980) *The Making of Conservative Party Policy*, London, Longmans Group.

RD/RE Indexing system used by the Labour Party for its Research Department series, containing committee papers and internal memorandum.

REES, A. (1966) 'Information networks in labor markets', *American Economic Review*, pp. 559–566.

REGAN, P. (1977) *Local Government and Education*, London, Allen and Unwin.

RICHMOND, P. (1975) *The Conservative Party's National Policy on Education, 1944–71*, thesis submitted for the MEd, University of Durham.

ROSE, R. (1974) *The Problem of Party Government*, London, Macmillan.

St John-Stevas, N. (1974) *A Tory Education Policy*, Monthly Report No. 98, Conservative Political Centre.

Salter, B. and Tapper, T. (1981) *Education, Politics and the State: The Theory and Practice of Educational Change*, London, Grant McIntyre.

Saran, R. (1973) *Policy-Making in Secondary Education*, Oxford, Clarendon Press.

Sarup, M. (1982) *Education, State and Crisis*, London, Routledge and Kegan Paul.

Saville, J. (1973) 'The ideology of Labourism', in Benewick, R. *et al.* (Eds) *Knowledge and Belief in Politics*, London, Allen and Unwin.

Schattschneider, E.E. (1960) *The Semi-Sovereign People: A Realists' View of Democracy in America*, New York, Holt, Rinehart and Winston.

Scruton, R. (1982) *Salisbury Review*.

Scruton, R. (1983) 'Voting out the people's trust', *The Times*, 19 July, p. 12.

Secretaries of State for Employment, Education and Science, Scotland and Wales (1984) *Training for Jobs*, Cmnd 9135, London, HMSO.

Sedgwick, P. (1970) 'Varieties of socialist thought', in Crick, B. and Robson, W.A. (Eds) *Protest and Discontent*, Harmondsworth, Penguin Books.

Seldon, A. (1981) 'The essence of the IEA', in Seldon, A. (Ed.) *The Emerging Consensus?*, London, Institute of Economic Affairs.

Sexton, S. (1979) *Memorandum to the Secretary of State*, 7 August.

Sexton, S. (1980) *Memorandum to the Secretary of State*, 29 January.

Shanks, M. (1960) 'Labour philosophy and the current position', *Political Quarterly*, 31, pp. 241–54.

Sherman, A. (1985) 'The hunger for change shaping a second Thatcher decade', *The Guardian*, 11 February, p. 9.

Shils, E. (1972) *The Intellectuals and the Powers*, Chicago, University of Chicago Press.

Social Democratic Party (1981) *Annual Conference*, Education Discussion Paper.

Spring, J.H. (1972) *Education and the Rise of the Corporate State*, London, Beacon Press.

Stewart, J. (1983) *Local Government, the Conditions of Local Choice*, London, Allen and Unwin.

Stewart, J. (1984) 'Whose policy is it anyway?' *The Times Educational Supplement*, 9 September, p. 2.

Stothard, P. (1983) 'Who thinks for Mrs Thatcher?', *The Times*, 31 January, p. 10.

Tapper, T. and Salter, B. (1978) *Education and the Political Order*, London, Macmillan.

Tapper, T. and Salter, B. (1984) 'Images of independent schooling : Exploring the perceptions of parents and politicians', in Walford, G. (Ed.) *British Public Schools: Policy and Practice*, Lewes, Falmer Press.

Taylor-Gooby, P. (1981) 'The new right and social policy', *Critical Social Policy*, 1, pp. 18–31.

The Times Educational Supplement (1981) 'Cautious DES prefers platitude to prescription', *The Times Educational Supplement*, 17 March, p. 3.

The Times Educational Supplement (1984) 'View from the top', *The Times Educational Supplement*, 13 January, pp. 4–5.

TUC-LABOUR PARTY LIAISON COMMITTEE (1981) *Private Schools.*

TURK, H. (1970) 'Interorganizational networks in urban society: Initial perspectives and comparative research', *American Sociological Review*, 35, pp. 1–19.

UNIVERSITY GRANTS COMMITTEE (1968) *University Development, 1962–67*, London, HMSO.

UNIVERSITY GRANTS COMMITTEE (1983) *Annual Survey 1981–82*, Cmnd. 8965, London, HMSO.

UNIVERSITY GRANTS COMMITTEE (1984a) *Annual Survey 1982–83*, Cmnd. 9234, London, HMSO.

UNIVERSITY GRANTS COMMITTEE (1984b) *A Strategy for Higher Education into the 1990s*, London, HMSO.

UNIVERSITY GRANTS COMMITTEE (1984) *Planning for the Late 1980s*, Circular letter, 17 November.

URWIN, K. (1965) 'Formulating a policy for secondary education in Croydon', in DONNISON, D.V. and CHAPMAN, V. (Eds) *Social Policy and Administration*, London, Allen and Unwin.

VAIZEY, J. (1983) *In Breach of Promise*, London, Weidenfeld and Nicolson.

VAN OSS, O. (1969) 'A speech made at the annual general meeting of the Headmasters' Conference', *Conference*, 6, 3, pp. 3–8.

WALFORD, G. (1983) 'Girls in boys' public schools: A prelude to further research', *British Journal of the Sociology of Education*, 1.

WALFORD, G. (Ed.) (1984) *British Public Schools: Policy and Practice*, Lewes, Falmer Press.

WALKER, M. (1983) 'The unthinkable men behind Mrs Thatcher', *The Guardian*, 1 March, p. 17.

WALKER, P. (1972) *The Cabinet*, London, Jonathan Cape.

WAPSHOTT, N. and BROCK, G. (1983) *Thatcher*, London, MacDonald.

WEAVER, T. (1979) *The DES: Central Control of Education*, Milton Keynes, Open University.

WHITE, R.J. (Ed.) (1950) *The Conservative Tradition*, London, Kaye.

WHITELEY, P. (1984) *The Labour Party in Crisis*, London, Methuen.

WILSON, H. (1976) *The Governance of Britain*, London, Weidenfeld and Nicolson.

WOLFENDEN, Lord (1976) 'The UGC: A personal view', *The Times Higher Educational Supplement*, 2 April, p. 5.

WOOD, N. (1983a) 'DES should have greater curriculum control', *The Times Educational Supplement*, 1 July, p. 3.

WOOD, N. (1983b) 'Curriculum body complete', *The Times Educational Supplement*, 4 November, p. 6.

WOOD, N. (1983c) 'Teachers' unions angered by curriculum snub', *The Times Educational Supplement*, 25 November, p. 8.

WOODS, J. (1981) 'How it all began: Personal recollections', in SELDON, A. (Ed.) *The Emerging Consensus?*, London, Institute of Economic Affairs.

Name Index

Subject Index

Assisted Places Scheme (APS), 10, 51, 53, 55, 119, 122–123, 125, 132, 150, 183–209. *See also* Conservative Party, Labour Party.

The Battle for the Labour Party, 105
Battle Lines for Education, 179
Black Papers, 172–175, 176, 177, 178, 179. *See also* The Right
British Political Parties, 160, 164
Bullock Committee, 147
Butskellism, 156, 160, 180

Campaign for Labour Party Democracy (CLPD), 105
Capitalism,
  Schooling and 5, 21–22
Centre for Policy Studies (CPS), 166, 168, 243
Charities Act (1960), 77
Charity Commission, 71, 84–89
Charity Commissioners and their Accountability, 73
Charity Law and Voluntary Organisations, 81–82
Circular 10/65, 129–132
Class Reproduction, 8, 41–70
Community Power Structure, 241
Conservative Independent Schools Committee (CISC), 149
Conservative Party, 10, 131–132
  Assisted Places Scheme and 195–202

educational ideology of 146–148, 175–180, 227–231
Heath and policy making 162–165
"Parents Charter" 148, 179–180, 228
policy making 160–166, 201–202, 207–209
political advisers and 164–165, 198–199. *See also* Intellectuals
Conservative Philosophy Group (CPG), 171
Curriculum 11 to 16, Towards a Statement of Entitlement, 220

Department of Education and Science (DES), 22–25, 229–230
  Assisted Places Scheme and 202–207
  bureaucratic dynamic of 24–25, 108, 208–209
  curriculum control 213–218
  higher education control 221–224
  MSC and 3–4
  power of 2–3
Direct Grant Joint Committee (DGJC), 129–131, 136–137, 141–143, 186–189
Direct Grant Schools, 50–51, 118–119, 185–186, 200, 201

Education
  functions of 19–22
Education Act 1976, 130

259